OCT 1 2 2001

35 $\frac{00}{}$

D0146634

GABRIEL GARCÍA MÁRQUEZ

Critical Companions to Popular Contemporary Writers
Second Series

Julia Alvarez *by Silvio Sirias*

Rudolfo A. Anaya *by Margarite Fernandez Olmos*

Maya Angelou *by Mary Jane Lupton*

Ray Bradbury *by Robin Anne Reid*

Louise Erdrich *by Lorena L. Stookey*

Ernest J. Gaines *by Karen Carmean*

John Irving *by Josie P. Campbell*

Garrison Keillor *by Marcia Songer*

Jamaica Kincaid *by Lizabeth Paravisini-Gebert*

Barbara Kingsolver *by Mary Jean DeMarr*

Maxine Hong Kingston *by E. D. Huntley*

Terry McMillan *by Paulette Richards*

Larry McMurtry *by John M. Reilly*

Toni Morrison *by Missy Dehn Kubitschek*

Chaim Potok *by Sanford Sternlicht*

Amy Tan *by E. D. Huntley*

Anne Tyler *by Paul Bail*

Leon Uris *by Kathleen Shine Cain*

Gloria Naylor *by Charles E. Wilson, Jr.*

GABRIEL GARCÍA MÁRQUEZ

A Critical Companion

Rubén Pelayo

CRITICAL COMPANIONS TO POPULAR CONTEMPORARY WRITERS
Kathleen Gregory Klein, Series Editor

Greenwood Press
Westport, Connecticut • London

Library of Congress Cataloging-in-Publication Data

Pelayo, Rubén, 1954–
    Gabriel García Márquez : a critical companion / Rubén Pelayo.
      p. cm.—(Critical companions to popular contemporary writers, ISSN 1082–4979)
    Includes bibliographical references and index.
    ISBN 0–313–31260–5 (alk. paper)
    1. García Márquez, Gabriel, 1928–   —Criticism and interpretation. I. Title.
II. Series
  PQ8180.17.A73Z665   2001
  863'.64—dc21   2001023337

British Library Cataloguing in Publication Data is available.

Library of Congress Catalog Card Number: 2001023337
ISBN: 0–313–31260–5
ISSN: 1082–4979

First published in 2001

Greenwood Press, 88 Post Road West, Westport, CT 06881
An imprint of Greenwood Publishing Group, Inc.
www.greenwood.com

Printed in the United States of America

The paper used in this book complies with the
Permanent Paper Standard issued by the National
Information Standards Organization (Z39.48–1984).

10 9 8 7 6 5 4 3 2 1

I dedicate this book both to
Gerald A. Lamb, my adoptive father,
and to the memory of my mother.

Contents

Series Foreword

The authors who appear in the series Critical Companions to Popular Contemporary Writers are all best-selling writers. They do not simply have one successful novel, but a string of them. Fans, critics, and specialist readers eagerly anticipate their next book. For some, high cash advances and breakthrough sales figures are automatic; movie deals often follow. Some writers become household names, recognized by almost everyone.

But their novels are read one by one. Each reader chooses to start and, more importantly, to finish a book because of what she or he finds there. The real test of a novel is in the satisfaction its readers experience. This series acknowledges the extraordinary involvement of readers and writers in creating a best-seller.

The authors included in this series were chosen by an Advisory Board composed of high school English teachers and high school and public librarians. They ranked a list of best-selling writers according to their popularity among different groups of readers. For the first series, writers in the top-ranked group who had received no book-length, academic, literary analysis (or none in at least the past ten years) were chosen. Because of this selection method, Critical Companions to Popular Contemporary Writers meets a need that is being addressed nowhere else. The success of these volumes as reported by reviewers, librarians, and teachers led to an expansion of the series mandate to include some writers with wide critical attention—Toni Morrison, John Irving, and Maya Angelou, for example—to extend the usefulness of the series.

The volumes in the series are written by scholars with particular expertise in analyzing popular fiction. These specialists add an academic focus to the popular success that these writers already enjoy.

The series is designed to appeal to a wide range of readers. The general reading public will find explanations for the appeal of these well-known writers. Fans will find biographical and fictional questions answered. Students will find literary analysis, discussions of fictional genres, carefully organized introductions to new ways of reading the novels, and bibliographies for additional research. Whether browsing through the book for pleasure or using it for an assignment, readers will find that the most recent novels of the authors are included.

Each volume begins with a biographical chapter drawing on published information, autobiographies or memoirs, prior interviews, and, in some cases, interviews given especially for this series. A chapter on literary history and genres describes how the author's work fits into a larger literary context. The following chapters analyze the writer's most important, most popular, and most recent novels in detail. Each chapter focuses on one or more novels. This approach, suggested by the Advisory Board as the most useful to student research, allows for an in-depth analysis of the writer's fiction. Close and careful readings with numerous examples show readers exactly how the novels work. These chapters are organized around three central elements: plot development (how the story line moves forward), character development (what the reader knows of the important figures), and theme (the significant ideas of the novel). Chapters may also include sections on generic conventions (how the novel is similar to or different from others in its same category of science fiction, fantasy, thriller, etc.), narrative point of view (who tells the story and how), symbols and literary language, and historical or social context. Each chapter ends with an "alternative reading" of the novel. The volume concludes with a primary and secondary bibliography, including reviews.

The alternative readings are a unique feature of this series. By demonstrating a particular way of reading each novel, they provide a clear example of how a specific perspective can reveal important aspects of the book. In the alternative reading sections, one contemporary literary theory—way of reading, such as feminist criticism, Marxism, new historicism, deconstruction, or Jungian psychological critique—is defined in brief, easily comprehensible language. That definition is then applied to the novel to highlight specific features that might go unnoticed or be understood differently in a more general reading. Each volume defines two or three specific theories, making them part of the reader's understanding of how diverse meanings may be constructed from a single novel.

Taken collectively, the volumes in the Critical Companions to Popular Contemporary Writers series provide a wide-ranging investigation of the complexities of current best-selling fiction. By treating these novels seriously as both literary works and publishing successes, the series demonstrates the potential of popular literature in contemporary culture.

Kathleen Gregory Klein
Southern Connecticut State University

Acknowledgments

I am forever grateful to Richard P. Finn and Sr. María Inés Aparicio, O.L.G., for their enthusiasm, comments, suggestions, and corrections throughout the production of the manuscript. I am also thankful to Penny Snow and Lynn Araujo Malloy.

1

The Life of Gabriel García Márquez

The genius, popularity, and charisma of Gabriel García Márquez make him peerless among Spanish American writers of the second half of the twentieth century. The name Gabriel García Márquez is as synonymous with *One Hundred Years of Solitude* as is the name of Spanish novelist, playwright, and poet Miguel de Cervantes Saavedra (1547–1616) with *Don Quixote*. Grouping the names of García Márquez and Cervantes is not as arbitrary as it may seem. In fact, most literary oriented people around the world have come to associate the name of each of these authors, directly or indirectly, with one particular work out of the many that they wrote. Though Gabriel García Márquez, to date, is an active and prolific writer, he continues to be primarily associated with his 1967 novel *One Hundred Years of Solitude*.

The life of García Márquez is filled with literary prizes, homages, honorary degrees, and friendship with world figures in literature, politics, and the Church. Among the list of friends most frequently mentioned by scholars are Cuban Prime Minister Fidel Castro, Mexican writer Carlos Fuentes, British novelist Graham Greene, French President François Miterrand, Chilean poet Pablo Neruda, Panamanian nationalist General Omar Torrijos, and the Colombian priest Camilo Torres. Camilo Torres, a friend from García Márquez's years in college, became a priest; baptized García Márquez's first son, Gonzalo; and in the 1960s became a popular figure for turning priesthood into a form of rebellion (Liberation Theology). He was killed by the Colombian armed forces in 1966. Gabriel

García Márquez, now in his seventies, enjoys wealth and fame. Fame, he says, is great—but after all the fanfare associated with being famous is over, he adds humorously, the only real benefit is not having to stand in line (Lemus 272).

In August 1995, invited by the American author William Styron to a dinner party at Styron's summer home in Martha's Vineyard, Massachusetts, García Márquez met U.S. President Bill Clinton. At the dinner party, where Mexican novelist, short-story writer, playwright, and critic Carlos Fuentes was also a guest, García Márquez reminded President Clinton that during his first campaign for the presidency, Clinton had said that his favorite book was *One Hundred Years of Solitude*, perhaps in an effort to win the Hispanic vote. Clinton replied that his comment regarding *One Hundred Years of Solitude* was a sincere one and recited the opening sentence: "Many years later, as he faced the firing squad, Colonel Aureliano Buendía was to remember that distant afternoon when his father took him to discover ice." The dinner started at eight and ended around midnight. García Márquez wrote an article about it for the Argentine newspaper *Clarín Digital* (available through the Internet). But aside from being a friend of important people, who exactly is this man, whose works have been translated into all leading languages and who, in October 1982, was awarded the Nobel Prize in literature?

Gabriel García Márquez was born on March 6, 1928, in Aracataca, Colombia. "Aracataca is a small town in the foothills of a spur of the Andes, near the Atlantic coast. The town has a small railroad station, a river with clear water and large white boulders, a street of Turks, and a few African Colombians" (Janes 1991, 4). However, Colombia is larger "than Texas, Oklahoma, Arkansas, and Louisiana taken together" (McNerney 3). The town of Aracataca, where García Márquez was born, is hardly visible on most maps. However, it is now a common name for scholars and students of Spanish American letters. Aracataca is the geographical reference García Márquez uses to create the imaginary *Macondo*. Known the world over as Gabriel García Márquez but to his family and friends as *Gabo* or *Gabito*, García Márquez was baptized Gabriel José. He was the firstborn of twelve children, of whom seven were boys. He was named after his father, Gabriel Eligio García.

Gabriel Eligio García, of whom the author very seldom speaks, came to the small town of Aracataca looking for a better life as a telegraph operator after having dropped out of medical school at the University of Cartagena, Colombia. It was in Aracataca that Gabriel Eligio García met Luisa Santiaga Márquez Iguarán, the only child of Colonel Nicolás Márquez Iguarán and Tranquilina Iguarán Cotes. Although the town's telegraph operator eventually married the young, beautiful, and aristocratic Luisa Santiaga Márquez Iguarán, her parents were against it. The Márquez Iguarán family was among the most prominent families of the town's aristocracy and did not want a poor outsider to marry their daughter (Vargas Llosa 14). As a condition to consenting to the young lovers' marriage, the bride's parents demanded that the newlyweds move away from the town. Consequently, the young couple moved to Ríohacha in 1927. (Ríohacha is a coastal town in the Guajira peninsula, facing the Caribbean.) These biographical details appear in such García Márquez's works as *One Hundred Years of Solitude* and *Love in the Time of Cholera*.

García Márquez's maternal grandparents, Colonel Nicolás Márquez Iguarán and his wife, Tranquilina, came to Aracataca in the early 1900s. Aracataca, at that time, was little more than a village of a few families, where the colonel was greatly respected as a retired military man with liberal ideals. Colonel Nicolás Márquez Iguarán came to Aracataca after fighting in a war known to historians as La guerra de los mil días or the War of a Thousand Days (1899–1902), which had left Colombia bankrupt. García Márquez's grandfather fought under the orders of the liberal general Rafael Uribe Uribe. Understanding the background of García Márquez's maternal grandparents and the War of a Thousand Days is important in appreciating the plot of most of García Márquez's works. In fact, most of his writings were both inspired by, and modeled after, his maternal grandparents, his parents, and the stories they told him when he was growing up. Either because his mother's parents did not want the young couple to live in the town of Aracataca or because it did not offer the upward mobility necessary for the young couple to prosper, García Márquez spent the first eight years of his life in the house and care of his maternal grandparents. Doña Tranquilina, his grandmother, seems to have been an example of the materfamilias (female head of the household); she was a matriarch, empress of the house, industrious and forceful, prolific, with great common sense, incorruptible in adversity, and iron-willed. She was the organizer of the life of a large family, for which she served as the head and the unifying force. She was one of García Márquez's literary pillars and also the model for a series of female characters that appear in his books (Vargas Llosa 24). Of his maternal grandparents, García Márquez pointed out that "they were descendants of Galicians, great yarn spinners remotely related to the Celts" (McNerney 7).

Nine months after García Márquez was born, another incident of major proportions took place in Colombia, which was to appear, in fictional form, in *One Hundred Years of Solitude*: "On 6 December, in the Ciénaga train station, striking banana workers are fired on by troops from Antio-quia. Casualty estimates range from 9 to 3,000 dead" (Janes 1991, ix). This incident, as conveyed through oral tradition (a story or incident passed on by word of mouth) and, later, by way of publications was to stay in the author's mind forever. In addition to its mention in *One Hundred Years of Solitude*, it also appears, as a reference, in *Love in the Time of Cholera* (1985).

In 1940, when García Márquez was twelve, he obtained a scholarship to study at the Colegio Nacional (national secondary school) at Zapa-quirá near Bogotá, the capital of Colombia. In 1946 he finished high school and entered the national university in Bogotá to study law. In 1947 he published his first short story, later translated as "The Third Resignation," in a liberal daily newspaper in Bogotá called *El Espectador* (The Spectator). A year later he began work as a journalist for the same newspaper. García Márquez's first publications were all short stories, which appeared from 1947 to 1952 in the newspapers *El Espectador* of Bogotá and *El Heraldo* (The Herald) of Barranquilla. During those years he published a total of fifteen short stories.

"The Third Resignation," as might be expected by most readers of García Márquez, deals with the theme of death. George McMurray, among many others, has emphasized that this and the other tales of these years were influenced by readings of the Czech-born German writer Franz Kafka. The other short stories McMurray mentions were translated as "The Other Side of Death," "Eva Is Inside Her Cat," and "Someone Has Been Disarranging These Roses." McMurray also noted the influence of other authors in several of Márquez's other short stories, such as the influence of the American novelist and short story writer William Faulk-ner in "Nabo, the Black Man Who Made the Angels Wait" and the in-fluence of another American novelist and short story writer, Ernest Hemingway, in "The Woman Who Arrived at Six O'Clock" (McMurray 1977, 6). These suggested influences in Gabriel García Márquez's short stories, as well as in his novels, will be discussed further in Chapter 2.

By 1978, all the short stories except "Nabo, the Black Man Who Made the Angels Wait" were published under the title *Innocent Eréndira and Other Stories*. In 1984, "Nabo, the Black Man Who Made the Angels Wait" and twenty-five other stories were published in one volume, *Collected Stories*, in the chronological order in which they appeared in Spanish (see Chapter 5).

During García Márquez's second year as a law student, Colombia was going through a period of civil unrest. On April 9, 1948, Jorge Eliécer Gaitán, a populist left-wing politician and presidential candidate, was assassinated. (Populism is a political philosophy opposing the concentration of power in the hands of corporations, the government, and the rich.) The murder of Jorge Eliécer Gaitán unleashed what journalists and historians have called the Bogotazo, a "bloody uprising that raged for several days in the capital city" (McMurray 1977, 6).

The assassination of Jorge Eliécer Gaitán is also remembered as the beginning of a savage, undeclared civil war between conservatives and liberals better known as La violencia (the Violence). In response, hundreds of people rushed onto the streets of Bogotá and the rest of the country to fight the people of the Conservative Party, who had killed their leader. Ironically, it was the elitist members of the Liberal Party, in conjunction with elitist Conservative members, who had actually killed Eliécer Gaitán. While the Bogotazo is supposed to have lasted for three days of constant gunfire, the period known as La violencia lasted well into the 1960s (roughly from 1948 to 1964), thus amounting to an unofficial civil war. This violent period of sixteen years in Colombian history, which pitted liberals against conservatives, took as many as 300,000 lives. The hatred of those years is clearly reflected in the main theme of García Márquez's *In Evil Hour* and plays an important role in his *No One Writes to the Colonel*.

In 1948, due to the unrest taking place in Bogotá, García Márquez, now twenty, moved to Cartagena, the coastal city where *Love in the Time of Cholera* takes place. When García Márquez was a youth of twenty, wrote Anderson, pictures showed him as skinny and badly dressed. He wanted to be a journalist and to write novels; he also wanted to do something to bring about a more just society. He continued to study law but spent most of his time writing for the local newspaper. By 1950, he gave up his aspirations of becoming a lawyer and left the city of Cartagena for Barranquilla. The newspaper *El Heraldo* gave him a column, for which he wrote under the pseudonym of Septimus (Latin for "seventh"). The young García Márquez took the pseudonym, points out Regina Janes, from a book by Virginia Woolf, *Mrs. Dalloway* (Janes 1991, 3). The newspaper column was known as "La Jirafa" (The Giraffe). Perhaps it was here, in the port city of Barranquilla on the Magdalena River, that García Márquez decided to become a writer. Now aged twenty-two, having left legal studies and formally writing a newspaper column, he joined an informal group of young, aspiring writers that revolved around Ramón Vinyes, an older Catalan refugee from the Spanish Civil War (1936–1939), whom García Márquez depicted as a fictional character, an old Catalan who owns a bookstore, in *One Hundred Years of Solitude*. Among the group's members, most scholars mention Alvaro Cepeda Samudio, Germán Vargas, and Alfonso Fuenmayor, whom García Márquez depicted as secondary characters in *No One Writes to the Colonel* and as a mere reference in *One Hundred Years of Solitude*. Among the authors that the young group read, in translation, were Irish novelist James Joyce; American writers John Dos Passos, Ernest Hemingway, William Faulkner, and Edgar Allan Poe; British author Virginia Woolf; French novelist Marcel Proust; and French poet and adventurer Arthur Rimbaud. Although this group of non–Latin American writers is nearly always mentioned when describing what the group read, rarely is there any mention of the Latin American writers that also served García Márquez as models (see Chapter 2).

García Márquez continued to write for *El Heraldo* for four years and then, in 1954, returned to Bogotá. This time his work as a newspaper writer was not as a columnist, but as a reporter for *El Espectador*.

In 1955, a year after his return to Bogotá, García Márquez published short stories, including "One Day After Saturday" and "Monologue of Isabel Watching It Rain in Macondo," along with his first novella, *Leaf Storm* (see Chapter 3).

It was while García Márquez was working as a reporter of news and sports and writer of political commentaries that *El Espectador* sent him to Europe. He worked in Geneva, Switzerland, and Rome, Italy, as a foreign correspondent. In Rome he studied cinematography for several months but soon found himself unemployed: the dictator of Colombia, Gustavo Rojas Pinilla, closed down *El Espectador* due to its liberal orientation. García Márquez's short stay in Rome did allow him to write his second novel, *In Evil Hour*, which was not published until years later. One of the reasons for postponing its publication until 1966 may have been the references to Rojas Pinilla's dictatorship. *In Evil Hour*, which serves as a sort of prelude to *One Hundred Years of Solitude*, portrays the political tension and oppression in a rural town, whose inhabitants aspire to peace and justice but get neither. Triggered by mysteriously distributed lampoons, the townspeople end up killing each other.

After his stay in Rome, García Márquez moved to Paris in 1956. In Europe, he learned that he was indeed a Latin American writer. He realized, then, that he belonged to this group geographically, culturally, and emotionally. Besides being Colombian, he was Latin American; he could identify with the Latin American people he met in Paris, whether Argentines, Mexicans, Guatemalans, Bolivians, or Brazilians, yet not with the Europeans (Lemus 271).

In Paris, although broke and unemployed, he managed to survive. He cashed in his return ticket and was helped by the generosity of an understanding landlady, who waited patiently for the rent on the cheap hotel room where he stayed. Paris, nevertheless, inspired him to write *No One Writes to the Colonel*, which was published in 1958.

The previous year, in the company of Plinio Apuleyo Mendoza, a friend from his college days, García Márquez traveled to what was then the Soviet Union and to other Eastern European nations. The following year, now aged thirty, he found himself once again working as a journalist. This time he was writing for two Venezuelan newspapers: *Venezuela gráfica* (Venezuelan Graphics) and *Elite*, both in the country's capital city, Caracas. In that same year (1958), there was "a major political event, which inspired one of his subsequent works, the downfall of the Venezuelan dictator, Marcos Pérez Jiménez" (McMurray 1977, 7). This event provided the seed for his work *The Autumn of the Patriarch* (1975). Among the many important events in the life of García Márquez, two occurred in 1958. One was his marriage to Mercedes Barcha, the striking daughter of an Egyptian emigrant; the other was the publication of *No One Writes to the Colonel* in Spanish.

No One Writes to the Colonel presents the reader with a simple story line: an impoverished, seventy-five-year-old colonel waits for his veteran's pension. In the meantime, the police kill his son, the town falls under martial law, and the pension never arrives. The colonel nonetheless has faith that his pension will come, but his wife, who is more realistic, does not. The tension, violence, and oppression of the fiction reflect the Colombia under the dictatorship of those times. As if explaining why García Márquez could not identify with Europeans, in *No One Writes to the Colonel* the narrator states: "To the Europeans, South America is a man with a mustache, a guitar, and a gun. . . . They don't understand the problem" (138).

In the next year, 1959, García Márquez's first son, Rodrigo, was born in Bogotá. (Rodrigo is now a movie director and lives in Los Angeles, California.) The same year, the Cuban *guerrilla* (an irregular military force; from the Spanish *guerra*, meaning "war") under Fidel Castro marched triumphantly into Havana, Cuba. Fidel Castro defeated the regime of General Fulgencio Batista. Batista (1901–1973) was twice president of Cuba, from 1940 to 1944 and 1952 to 1959. The overthrow of Fulgencio Batista brought changes in the minds of most Hispanic intellectuals, students of higher education, and the like. Gabriel García Márquez was no exception. He joined the Castro regime and became director of the "Castro government's news agency, *Prensa Latina* [Latin Press], first in Bogotá, then in Havana, and finally in New York. He resigned from this position in 1961" (McMurray 1977, 7). However, according to a long article published in *The New Yorker* magazine in 1999, although García Márquez ran *Prensa Latina* in Bogotá, the head was actually Jorge Ricardo Masetti, a young Argentine journalist who was the protégé of the now-legendary Ernesto Guevara, better known as Che Guevara (Anderson 66). After his resignation from *Prensa Latina*, García Márquez traveled to Mexico City by bus, by way of the American Southeast. As many scholars have noted, he wanted to see the American South, which had inspired the writings of William Faulkner; and so he, his wife, Mercedes, and his two-year-old son, Rodrigo, traveled through Mississippi to New Orleans and then to Mexico City, where they settled.

In 1962, now living in Mexico City, García Márquez and Mercedes had a second son, Gonzalo. (Gonzalo, currently a graphic designer, still lives in Mexico City.) In that same year García Márquez published two books: *Big Mama's Funeral*, a collection of short stories, and the short novel *In Evil Hour*, for which Colombia awarded him the Esso Literary Prize. Most of the short stories discussed in Chapter 5 of this book come from the collection *Big Mama's Funeral*.

Life in Mexico City suited García Márquez, who wrote prolifically there. While working for the Walter Thompson advertising agency, he wrote a screenplay with the noted Mexican novelist Carlos Fuentes. The screenplay, based on a short story by Mexican writer Juan Rulfo, was called *The Golden Cock* (El gallo de oro). Gabriel García Márquez's passion for cinematography influenced much of his writings and encouraged others to adapt some of his works for the big screen. Several of his works, both short stories and novels, have been presented as films and on television. The following list is available in videocassette format: *Maria My Dearest*, in Spanish, Mexico, 1979; *Eréndira*, in Spanish with subtitles, Mexico, 1983; *Chronicle of a Death Foretold*, in Spanish with subtitles, 1987; *A Very Old Man with Enormous Wings*, in Spanish with subtitles, Cuba, 1988. A year later, in 1989, *A Very Old Man with Enormous Wings* became the title work of a collection of six short stories by García Márquez advertised in the United States as a "boxed set." The collection included the following stories in videocassette format: *Letters from the Park, Miracle in Rome, The Summer of Miss Forbes, I'm the One You're Looking For*, and *The Fable of the Beautiful Pigeon Fancier*. All six were filmed in Spanish, with English subtitles.

García Márquez has three other major screen plays: *Dangerous Game*, in Spanish, Mexico, 1966; *A Time to Die*, in Spanish, Mexico, 1985; and *Oedipus Mayor*, in Spanish, cowritten with Stella Malagón, Colombia, 1996. The most recent screenplay is *No One Writes to the Colonel*, in Spanish, Mexico, 1999. *No One Writes to the Colonel* was shown at the 1999 Cannes Film Festival.

According to several scholars, 1964 was a year of seclusion and of writer's block. García Márquez overcame his writer's block in January 1965 while driving to the Mexican tourist port of Acapulco. A novel that had been somehow appearing as if in segments—with the invention of Macondo and the character of Colonel Buendía, the use of a cyclical form of time and the repetitiveness of events, the image of identical twins, and other elements—seemed to come together, like pieces of a puzzle that suddenly fit perfectly. Gabriel García Márquez has said that he turned back, right there and then, and returned to his home studio to write. He did not want to miss the opportunity to put into writing this novel, which had been in gestation since he was in his early twenties. Back in Mexico City, in his house on the street of La Loma (The Hill), in the opulent neighborhood of *San Angel* (Saint Angel), he closed the doors of his studio—known to the García Márquez family and friends as "La Cueva de la Mafia" (the Mafia's cave)—for nearly a year and a half. As always, the superstitious García Márquez wrote with a yellow rose, for luck, on top of his desk. During those eighteen months, he worked for eight to ten hours each day.

In June 1967 his masterpiece, *One Hundred Years of Solitude*, was published in Buenos Aires, Argentina. The book became an immediate bestseller: "not since *Madame Bovary* [by French novelist Gustave Flaubert] has a work been received with the simultaneous popular success and critical acclaim that greeted *One Hundred Years of Solitude*" (Janes 1991, 13). *One Hundred Years of Solitude*, in the original Spanish, was a great success, and

> the first edition sold out in a few days, as well as the second, and the third, and the ones thereafter. In three and a half years, the book sold almost half a million copies; and his previous four books were reprinted in large numbers in the Spanish speaking world. (Vargas Llosa 78)

The popularity of this book soon reached the interest of publishing houses the world over. Some of the first translations were also winners of honors: in 1969 in Italy, the book won the Premio Chianchiano (Chianchiano award); the same year in France, it won the Prix du meilleur livre étranger (Award for Best Foreign Book); in 1970 in the United States, it was selected as one of the best twelve books of the year by *Time* magazine. As of 1997 *One Hundred Years of Solitude* has now been translated into more than thirty languages and has sold close to 30 million copies.

In 1967, for both personal and professional reasons, García Márquez moved to Barcelona, a port city on the Mediterranean in northeastern Spain. In 1970 the Colombian government offered him a consul post in Barcelona but he declined the offer. Although García Márquez never finished college, in 1971 Columbia University in New York City awarded him an honorary doctorate of letters. In 1972 he published a book of short stories, some of which were intended for children. The book holds the longest title of all his books: *The Incredible and Sad Tale of Innocent Eréndira and Her Heartless Grandmother*. In that same year, he also received, for his works to date, the literary Rómulo Gallegos Prize in Venezuela.

In 1974 García Márquez founded a left-wing magazine, *Alternativa* (Alternative), which ran through 1980. After eight years in Barcelona, Spain, he returned to Mexico. In 1975 he published a novel, *The Autumn of the Patriarch*. The novel depicts a place in the Caribbean, never identified, where the protagonist is a general and a dictator. American critic Raymond Williams found it difficult to read. The plot, Williams wrote, is not developed in a consistent fashion; the anecdotes do not appear in chronological order, and, moreover, they sometimes include such gross anachronisms as the presence of Christopher Columbus and U.S. Marines in the same scene. Nonetheless, he considers it a major book for both García Márquez and the field of the contemporary Latin American novel (Williams 1989, 149, 147). The plot, although difficult to follow, traces the fight for absolute power and the exploitation that the Spanish Americas have gone through, from Christopher Columbus to the present (1975 in the novel). The basis for this novel is the Venezuelan government of Marcos Pérez Jiménez during the period when García Márquez worked as a journalist there. In Latin America there is a literary tradition called *novela de la dictadura* (dictatorship novel). *The Autumn of the Patriarch* serves to enrich this tradition.

Whether because, as García Márquez announced in 1975, he would not write any more fiction for as long as right-wing (conservative and reactionary) General Augusto Pinochet ruled Chile, or because he was so involved in the politics of the Third World, the second half of the 1970s came and went without any new published works. García Márquez's political ideas have a left-wing or socialist orientation (individuals on the left wing pursue liberal or egalitarian political goals). They became most obvious right after the assassination of Chilean President Salvador Allende in 1973. The right-wing dictatorial regime of Augusto

Pinochet, which followed the assassination, continued in power through the 1980s. Gabriel García Márquez, however, broke his vow to publish no fiction during Augusto Pinochet's regime by publishing, in 1981, *Chronicle of a Death Foretold*. In the same year, García Márquez attended the inauguration of Socialist president François Miterrand in France, where he was awarded the Legion of Honor medal for his work as a writer and activist.

Chronicle of a Death Foretold presents the reader with a text that explores why an entire town allows a senseless murder to occur in the name of hypocritical honor codes (Alvarez-Borland 219). The action of the novel revolves around a matter of honor. Twin brothers, Pedro and Pablo, announce at the town's main plaza that they are going to kill Santiago Nasar. No one in the town does anything to stop the killing (hence, the death is foretold). The reason for the killing is to restore the family's honor—Santiago Nasar is supposed to have taken their sister's virginity. The story (made into a film in 1987) is based on an actual murder that occurred in Colombia in 1951 (Penuel 188).

Fifteen years after the great global success of *One Hundred Years of Solitude*, García Márquez won the greatest recognition that can be bestowed on a writer. In 1982, in the city and port of Stockholm, Sweden, the Nobel Foundation awarded him the Nobel Prize in literature. The speech that he delivered, as his readers may imagine, was on "The Solitude of Latin America"; in fact, that was also the speech's title. Winning the Nobel Prize brought him fame and fortune, but his political orientation did not change. His work as a left-wing political activist is well known, and his newspaper columns, as well as his essays, short stories, and novels, often reflect his political interest in fighting for egalitarian goals.

In 1983 García Márquez started a Colombian newspaper, *El Otro* (The Other), for which he interviewed M-19 (a Colombian guerrilla movement) leader Jaime Bateman in an attempt to establish a dialogue between the guerrillas and the Colombian government. The guerrilla movement in Colombia has grown, and to date, the dialogue with the Colombian government has not made a difference in bringing peace.

In 1985 García Márquez appeared with Fidel Castro in Managua, Nicaragua, at the inauguration of president Daniel Ortega (McMurray 1977, 8). The same year, in Barcelona, Spain, he published a novel in the form of a nontraditional love story, *Love in the Times of Cholera*. It is nontraditional because the lovers find love in their "golden years"—in their seventies, when death is all around them (see Chapter 8).

Although Gabriel García Márquez is better known as a novelist and short story writer, his work as a journalist has been documented in several volumes throughout the years. In 1981, García Márquez's journalistic work was published in book form in Barcelona, Spain, under the title *Obra periodística: Volume 1, Textos costeños* (Newspaper articles: Volume 1, Coastal texts). Volumes 2 and 3 were published the following year and share the title *Entre cachacos* (Among cachacos). To Colombians, the word *cachaco* functions to describe someone both elegant and courteous. More often than not, however, the word carries a pejorative meaning; coastal peoples of Colombia believe that *cachacos*, a term used to refer to those from the interior, are often not trustworthy. A fourth volume of journalism was published in 1983 under the title *De Europa y América (1955–1960)* (Of Europe and America, 1955–1960). Although, perhaps with false modesty, García Márquez calls himself primarily a journalist, critics seldom study his journalistic work.

One of García Márquez's most popular recent journalistic accounts is *The Adventure of Miguel Littín Underground in Chile*, first published in Madrid, Spain, in 1986. The book, which depicts the dictatorship of Augusto Pinochet in Chile, "went through three editions within a few months, helped, perhaps, by the burning of some 15,000 copies by supporters of Pinochet in Santiago [Chile's capital city] who felt threatened by such exposure" (McNerney 12).

By the end of the 1980s (1989, to be exact), García Márquez had published another novel about decay and death: *The General in His Labyrinth*. This time, as the author wrote in the acknowledgments, the idea was not his own. His friend, Colombian writer Alvaro Mutis, started the project and passed it on to García Márquez. To write this novel, which focuses on the last fourteen days of the life of the great South American liberator Simón Bolívar (1783–1830), García Márquez used historians, political figures, a linguist, a geographer, and an astronomer, among others, as consultants. His writing style, nevertheless, makes the historical events and the long list of biographical names and geographical places almost as accessible as his fictional works. One sees Simón Bolívar as a man with strengths and weaknesses, not a mythic historical hero.

In the 1990s, worldwide audiences enjoyed more of García Márquez's mastery of magic realism with the publication in 1992 of *Doce cuentos peregrinos (Strange Pilgrims)*. The book, as the title suggests in Spanish, contains twelve (*"doce"*) short stories, some of which, explains García Márquez in the prologue, were previously published. In *Strange Pilgrims*, "Márquez not only tells stories, he weaves spells" according to the *New York Daily News*; "García Márquez remains one of the most entertaining writers in the world, as well as one of the best," stated the *Washington Post*.

The success of *Strange Pilgrims* was followed by *Of Love and Other Demons* in 1994. *Of Love and Other Demons* is a complex novel of forbidden love between a priest and a twelve-year-old girl; the background of the novel is the city of Cartagena. This is where Gabriel García Márquez commissioned the Colombian architect Rogelio Salmona to build his house, which became known as "La Casa del Escritor" (The House of the Writer).

Theater is one of the genres that Gabriel García Márquez has explored the least. However, in 1994, he published his first play in book form, *Diatribe of Love against a Sitting Man*. The play was originally written and staged in 1987, first in Havana, Cuba, and later in Buenos Aires, Argentina. Graciela, an older woman, is the only character. She carries on a long monologue in front of her husband, who is played by a mannequin. The mannequin is seated in a chair throughout the whole play, with a newspaper in his hands, as if reading and ignoring what she says. The role of Graciela is strongly critical of the upper class in a Colombian coastal town. Graciela's experience, defying a patriarchal world, reflects a feminist approach.

In 1996 García Márquez published *News of a Kidnapping*. Combining the testimonial orientation of journalism and the author's own narrative style (humor included), the story depicts the huge wave of violence and kidnappings that Colombia continues to face. The book reports the news of ten kidnappings masterminded by drug kingpin Pablo Escobar of the Medellín drug cartel. It follows the government's response under President César Gaviria's term in office (1990–1994) and examines the psychology of the people involved: those kidnapped, their families and friends, and the nation at large. The book, explains García Márquez in the acknowledgments, took nearly three years to write and closely follows the account of the abduction of Maruja Pachón and her husband, Alberto. In an interview for *El Tiempo*, a Colombian newspaper in Bogotá, García Márquez told journalist Roberto Pombo that reality indeed surpasses fiction. *News of a Kidnapping* reads like fiction, but it is all news, reported as a journalist would report it. "Throughout the book I use not one single fact that is not truthful and documented, and the language that I use has not one single metaphor so as to keep the austerity of language in journalism" (Pombo 457).

In September 1999, American author Jon Lee Anderson published (in *The New Yorker*) a most revealing account of Gabriel García Márquez. Anderson had the opportunity to meet with the Colombian author and his wife, Mercedes, for several months at García Márquez's house in Bogotá. Anderson, who visited Aracataca, the town that inspired the creation of Macondo in *One Hundred Years of Solitude*, focused on recent events in Colombia and the role that García Márquez has played as a mediator of peace. Anderson comments on the social and historical aspects that helped to shape the background of García Márquez's writing and remarks on some of García Márquez's books. His account recounts the facts of Gabriel García Márquez's life, as commonly known to scholars and documented in this chapter, and it also examines García Márquez's friendship with Fidel Castro.

According to Anderson, in 1999 García Márquez traveled in a midsize sedan with bullet-proof windows and a bomb-proof chassis, followed by secret-service agents. He describes the Colombian author as a short, deep-chested man with a careful, almost regal bearing. His curly hair is gray, and he has a white mustache and bushy eyebrows. García Márquez seems to be what Colombians call a *mamagallista* (a joker). The humor a reader often finds in García Márquez's writings is mirrored in the author's own life. For instance, minutes before receiving the prestigious Nobel Prize in literature, he jokingly posed for a photo in which he is shoeless and dressed in thermal underwear. His hand is resting on the arm of Colombian media director Alvaro Castaño Castillo, who is impeccably dressed in formal attire.

Sadly, at the time of this writing, García Márquez suffers from lymphatic cancer, for which he is receiving treatment. "He's essentially a Social Democrat, with a little Communist hidden in his heart" (Anderson 66). García Márquez's relationship with Fidel Castro continues to be questioned by his other friends. Plinio Apuleyo Mendoza, one of García Márquez's life-long friends, compares Fidel Castro to Soviet leader Joseph Stalin and was quoted as saying that when Castro dies, "we will hear about all the atrocities that happened during his [Fidel Castro's] rule. And I don't think it will help Gabo to have been such a friend of his" (Anderson 68). Several times García Márquez has been offered senior ministerial positions and ambassadorships in Colombia, but he has always refused (Anderson 70). As of this writing, this grandfather of four was working on three novels and two volumes of memoirs.

2

Literary Contexts

Gabriel García Márquez belongs in any list of great names in literature. He is probably the best-known Latin American writer of the twentieth century and a genius in his ability to touch people of all cultures and inspire many other writers. His name appears in all anthologies of Latin American Literature, as well as in the encyclopedias of world literature that are considered to represent the canon (an accepted standard). García Márquez is internationally recognized as a Latin American author of novels and short stories. He comments frequently, however, that he sees himself as a storyteller, first, and then as a journalist. García Márquez's career as a journalist began in 1948. Since then, he has written countless reports, essays, and documentaries. His work often starts as a journalistic piece. *The Story of a Shipwrecked Sailor* (1970), based on a true story, started as fourteen news articles he wrote for the Colombian newspaper *El Espectador* (The Spectator). Also based on a true story and using a journalistic style of reporting, *Chronicle of a Death Foretold* was published in 1981. Another journalistic work in documentary form that enjoys large readership is *Clandestine in Chile: The Adventures of Miguel Littín* (1986). In this book, García Márquez retells the story Miguel Littín told to him: it serves as a depiction of Chile after twelve years of dictatorship under Augusto Pinochet. In *News of a Kidnapping* (1996), García Márquez's journalistic reporting deals with a notorious drug lord, Pablo Escobar, and a wave of kidnappings. Among the kidnapped (ten in total) were important Colombian people from politics and the news media.

As a writer of fiction, however, García Márquez is always associated with magic realism. In fact, he is considered the central figure of magic realism. There is still some controversy over the term, probably because the Anglo reader, unfamiliar with the social and historical context of Latin America, seems to pay closer attention to the magic than the reality. In general terms, *magic realism* is nowadays used to describe fiction that juxtaposes the fantastic and the mythic with ordinary activities of daily life. The novel *One Hundred Years of Solitude* is especially regarded as a work of magic realism. However, this label sometimes limits the reception and understanding of Gabriel García Márquez's writing. Due to the common understanding of magic realism, the reader may fail to understand that behind the masterfully told stories lies a realistic universe where the individual and the community breathe, think, love, and live and die for ideals they consider just. García Márquez's fictional universe is the response to a Latin American literary tradition that can be traced as far back as 1492. García Márquez, for instance, considers *The Journal of Christopher Columbus* to be a work of fiction. The first masterwork of the literature of magic realism is the *Diary of Columbus*, he says (Palencia-Roth 251). However, from the end of the fifteenth century to the second half of the twentieth century, there are over 500 years of Latin American letters. Therefore, to place García Márquez within the literary milieu (environment) of his time, the reader should take into consideration the Latin American tradition to which he conforms.

It is commonplace in the United States to quickly associate the name of García Márquez with those of William Faulkner, Franz Kafka, Ernest Hemingway, James Joyce, and Virginia Woolf. For example, the English-speaking reader can find echoes of James Joyce and William Faulkner in García Márquez's *One Hundred Years of Solitude, The Autumn of the Patriarch, Leaf Storm*, or many of his other works. However, to stop there, without viewing García Márquez's works in light of a Latin American literary tradition, fails to pay tribute to the Spanish literary heritage that precedes him.

In 1967, the Argentine critic Ernesto Volkening discussed Gabriel García Márquez's literary models for the short story. Volkening mentioned James Joyce, Virginia Woolf, and William Faulkner—but only to comment that such observed models by some critics are inspired by a desire to invent a venerable genealogical tree for García Márquez. Those inventions are not based on a true appreciation of García Márquez's own merit as a narrator (Volkening 23–42). The analogies made by most critics between Faulkner and García Márquez seldom go beyond the obvious invention of a physical space: Yoknapatawpha, for William Faulkner, and Macondo, for Gabriel García Márquez. Both physical environments are dusty and seemingly forgotten by the outside world. Nothing seems to change because of a constant return to the same environment. However, beyond the invention of a physical space, there are other similarities between the writings of the two authors. The legendary character Colonel Aureliano Buendía can be said to find his alter ego (another side of oneself) in Faulkner's John Sartoris of *Sartoris* (1929). Another analogy mentioned by Volkening as a common trait cited by most English-speaking critics is the fact that both Yoknapatawpha and Macondo are viewed by their authors as the center of their fictionalized worlds. In effect, Volkening complains about a deep-rooted "colonizing" way of thinking, whereby the critic is prompt to judge, classify, and name the value of a writer based on supposed relationships with the literary movements of either Europe or the United States. Instead, he argues, a Latin American author such as García Márquez should be judged, first, in his individuality; second, in comparison with what the author has in common with other Latin American authors; and only then based on his possible affinities or similarities with authors in the rest of the world. To focus on the latter is a dangerous practice, "a delirium for relationships" to which critics and enthusiasts alike often succumb (Volkening 26). This simplification permits, whether intentionally or not, the creation of an artificial literary climate impregnated with secondhand experiences that do not converge with the author's own ideas as conveyed in his works (Volkening 26). As the reader of García Márquez may expect, Volkening finds similarities with other Latin American authors. Two of these are José Eustasio Rivera and Rómulo Gallegos, both known in literary circles and Latin American literature classes in the United States. However, says Volkening, García Márquez adds uniquely new ways of expressing life in the tropics.

From 1910 to 1950 most Latin American writers tried to describe their world in realistic fashion. To these realist writers, the problems they were faced with had a scientific explanation that could be documented, studied, and understood. The literature they produced was often schematic and sketchy. These novelists were interested in identifying a problem, finding its root, and then denouncing it. These often-didactic writers were interested in the portrayal of life with an emphasis on factualness, with no room for ambiguity, the supernatural, the world of dreams, or the absurd. This is the typical novel that preceded the writing of Gabriel García Márquez.

This type of literary realism is also often associated with *regionalism*. Regionalist novels put the emphasis, as did realism, on a faithful representation of the region they depict. In that sense, regionalism and realism are one and the same. Regionalism, indeed, is the type of Latin American novel that first interested European and American readers. Some of these novels are nowadays considered Latin American classics. Among the most commonly known are *Doña Bárbara* (1929) by Rómulo Gallegos, *Don Segundo Sombra* by Ricardo Güiraldes, and *La vorágine* (1924) by José Eustasio Rivera. Rómulo Gallegos wrote of the Venezuelan prairies and the local folklore, Ricardo Güiraldes described the Argentine pampas, and José Eustasio Rivera wrote of the South American tropical jungle.

This phase in Latin American literature can be considered, as some literary critics do, a necessary step in the development of the novel and the short story. While the writers of realism and regionalism focused on plot, those who came after, like Gabriel García Márquez, began to focus more on technique. They were concerned with the style and the methods in which they told their stories. *Leaf Storm*, García Márquez's first novella, set a precedent for this literary emphasis for future Latin American writers. This emphasis has been as influential in Latin America as it had been in Europe and the United States. This literary style in Latin America, however, was already being used by writers such as the Argentine Jorge Luis Borges; the Guatemalan Miguel Angel Asturias, who won the Nobel Prize in literature in 1967 (the same year García Márquez published *One Hundred Years of Solitude*); and the Cuban Alejo Carpentier; all of whom can be read in an English translation.

By the 1950s, critics were talking of the emergence of a "new Latin American novel," as if literary movements could begin and end abruptly rather than through gradual change or evolution. However, nothing could be further from the truth. While literary critics were debating about a "new Latin American novel" conforming to a style being used by Faulkner, Hemingway, Woolf, and Kafka's translations into English, García Márquez's writings, as well as those of Borges, Asturias, and Carpentier, were also being called "modernist." The term *modernism* (encompassing modernist authors) is often used in English to refer to the work of these Latin American authors, as well as to non–Latin American writers like James Joyce, Franz Kafka, William Faulkner, and Virginia Woolf. In fact, the term *modernist* has been applied to all authors who broke with established rules, traditions, and conventions and were experimental in form, style, and the use of language itself.

Readers of Latin American literature who are not careful may, unknowingly, confuse modernism with the term *modernismo*, although, indeed, the two terms have totally different meanings. (They are what linguists call false cognates: two words, in two different languages, that sound alike and whose spelling is similar but whose meanings are different.) Gabriel García Márquez is not a writer of the Latin American movement called *modernismo*. During the *modernismo* period, Latin American writers were consciously working to improve the usage of language with the intention of modernizing it. The *modernista* writers, who wrote around the turn of the nineteenth century and the first two decades of the twentieth, were mostly poets and essayists. This was a period of renovation and national pride. At that time the emphasis was not on the novel, but on poetry. The term was coined by Rubén Darío, a Nicaraguan poet, who was considerably influenced by the French Parnassians (poets who believed that art was an end in itself, not a means to an end; for them, poetry achieved the status of religion). French Parnassianism was an influential literary movement in France in the second half of the nineteenth century. While *modernismo* and the *modernista* writers may have been out of center stage by the end of the 1920s in Latin America, their influence continued into the 1930s and 1940s.

In Europe, meanwhile, in the early- to mid-twentieth century, *modernist* writers were paying particular attention to the psychology of character, that is, the inner world of the character. As is the case with any piece of literature, the social and historical context in which the text is written has an influence on it. World War I had an enormous effect on the modernist writers. The devastation of the war was reflected in much of their writings. Their fictional universe became fragmented, with disillusioned characters, and focused on the world of the unconscious. Hence, their affinity for, and use of, the stream-of-consciousness technique (interior monologue reflecting the thought processes). The leader of the movement, as was the case with the Latin American *modernista* movement, was also a poet: T. S. (Thomas Stearns) Eliot. T. S. Eliot was awarded the Nobel Prize in literature in 1948, the year when Gabriel García Márquez began his career as a journalist.

Whether or not Latin American writers such as Borges, Asturias, and Carpentier influenced García Márquez's writing, they clearly served as his models. Borges' use of cyclical time, the universe as a labyrinth, the concept of the *other*, the use of the absurd, and the role of an active reader who has to complete the story are often found in Gabriel García Márquez's writing. Borges, however, experimented with these literary techniques as early as 1923. Asturias and Carpentier's treatment of reality deals—like García Márquez's writing—with myths and an Afro-Indian folk tradition that blurs the demarcation between what is real and what is magic, as the term *magic realism* implies by definition. The *magic*, however, should not be so emphasized as to diminish the book's faithful representation of Latin American reality and culture. Magic does not mean the pure fantasy of a fairy tale, where everything is imaginary.

Leaf Storm, a book that has often been compared to the work of William Faulkner, was published in 1955, the same year the Mexican author Juan Rulfo published *Pedro Páramo*. There are many commonalities between the two works in theme, language usage, and style, but whereas García Márquez continued to write about the theme of death, solitude, war, and the violence of rural environments in many later books, Juan Rulfo never published again. Rulfo's *Pedro Páramo*, however, contributed substantially to the magic realism school of Latin America.

In an effort, perhaps, to associate and identify the work of writers as varied as Jorge Luis Borges, Alejo Carpentier, Italo Calvino, Günter Grass, Franz Kafka, and Salman Rushdie, along with García Márquez, Cortázar, and Asturias (among many others), the label of magic realism has been applied in a rather loose way. Of all these writers, however, García Márquez has emerged as the quintessential name associated with magic realism and *One Hundred Years of Solitude* has been identified as the magic realism book par excellence.

In magic realism, the mythical elements of oral tradition are incorporated into an otherwise realistic fiction. The social and economic problems that García Márquez disguises with a touch of magic realism are both past and present problems facing the individual and the community. If the reader fails to see through the disguise, it is because the narrative's emphasis is placed, not on the story, but rather on how the story is told. For instance, the countless wars that Colonel Aureliano Buendía fights and loses in *One Hundred Years of Solitude* represent the countless civil wars that Colombians actually fought throughout the nineteenth century. There is a similar analogy for the violence in *No One Writes to the Colonel*. Violence was everywhere in Colombia during the 1950s, but people could not speak out against the government. The dictatorship of President Gustavo Rojas Pinilla was so severe that much that Colombians did was indeed clandestine. In the novel, Agustín, the old colonel's son, is killed in 1956 for distributing clandestine literature.

By the time *One Hundred Years of Solitude* was published, Latin American novelists such as García Márquez had begun to enjoy worldwide recognition for their writing, in part, because of their use of magic realism, but mostly because of their commercial success, both in Spanish and in translation. These Latin American writers, including Julio Cortázar, Carlos Fuentes, and Mario Vargas Llosa, among others, were immediately grouped together, ignoring the fact that their writing styles were not alike, their concerns were different, and they were of different ages. They were not members of one generation nor of an organized movement or school, yet soon they were identified as writers of the "Latin American Boom." Although nondescriptive (other than in terms of book sales), the term stuck among literary critics, scholars, and the public alike. American and European universities began teaching courses on the Latin American Boom, and the works of this group of Latin American writers became well known in literary circles around the world. To date, the term continues to be used with an emphasis on chronology. Those writers in Latin America who began publishing in the 1970s and 1980s are often referred to as "Post-Boom" writers. The Chilean author Isabel Allende and the Mexican author Laura Esquivel are two such writers, both internationally known and associated with magic realism.

Gabriel García Márquez is a writer of the tropics. His writings are Latin American and, in particular, Colombian. His settings, which are frequently rural, resemble those found among the coastal towns of the Colombian northwest. When fully identified, the reader can identify Cartagena, Ríohacha, Manaure, Barranquilla, Santa Marta, Bolívar, Bogotá, and Medellín. Otherwise, the dusty isolated towns are described merely as being along the Magdalena River or close to the Caribbean Sea.

As if to go back to the roots of a constant political discontent, national instability, poverty, and abject solitude, Gabriel García Márquez first published a trilogy covering some of the most important moments of Colombian history (from the nineteenth century up to the 1960s). These three works are *Leaf Storm* (1955), *No One Writes to the Colonel* (1961), and *In Evil Hour* (1962). This trilogy establishes both thematic and technical elements that are recognizable in all of García Márquez's work. The trilogy also contains the seeds of *One Hundred Years of Solitude* (1967). Whether readers of García Márquez see him as a modernist, a boom writer, or a magic realist, the literary contexts of this Colombian author are determined, not by the effects of World War I, as was the case for European and American modernist writers, but by the social, political, and historical events that shaped the country of his birth. His works are, indeed, universal inasmuch as they touch the lives of readers around the world through his detailed development of both character and plot. Most, if not all, readers can also identify with the solitude suffered by the individual in modern times as described by García Márquez. However, the solitude of García Márquez is the solitude of Latin America; in that sense it is object specific, as is his literature. No reader can confuse the settings. They are tropical, near the Caribbean Sea or the Magdalena River, or located somewhere in rural Latin America. The impotence that readers may feel in the presence of death and the discontent and repudiation they may experience in reaction to the arbitrariness and abuses of corrupt, petty officials are indeed universal, but García Márquez's literary contexts are undeniably Colombian.

García Márquez's works are read as fiction, but his sources are factual. The absurd and inexplicable events of his short stories and novels are ironic representations of the absurdity of life. The literary context of García Márquez can be found in the history of Colombia, his private life, and that of his parents and grandparents. Aracataca, the place where he was born, appears either as Macondo or a nameless town close by a river. The references to the banana boom and the aftermath of the slaughter of the banana strikers in Ciénaga, the capital of the Colombian banana-producing zone in the 1920s, are prominent in *Leaf Storm* and *One Hundred Years of Solitude*. Echoes can also be heard in *No One Writes to the Colonel* and *Love in the Time of Cholera*, as well as in some of García Márquez's short stories. The images of power, religion, and celebrations all seem to have an origin in the oral traditions or the social and historical culture of Colombia. The events in *Big Mama's Funeral*, for example, can be traced back to a three-day festival that takes place in Ciénaga during the last week of January. *One Hundred Years of Solitude* and *Love in the Time of Cholera* are both based, although not entirely, on what the author was told about his parents and grandparents, and particularly what his grandmother passed on to him.

If García Márquez's works seem foreign to English-speaking readers, it is because his fiction includes not only a European component, but also a pre-Columbian (native Latin American Indian) and an African component. The tradition of Latin America is, of course, Spanish, but it is also Muslim and Jewish. The Muslim component of García Márquez's works is most evident in *Chronicle of a Death Foretold*. Latin America is a multiracial civilization, where Indians, Europeans, and Africans have created a distinctly Latin American way of life in all its forms (literature being one of them). By the time of independence from Spain, between 1810 and 1824, most Spanish-speaking countries had integrated a myriad of cultures into one. This was a nationalistic experience that precipitated countless civil wars in the newly formed republics. *One Hundred Years of Solitude* is the novel that best plays out this drama.

However, the history of Colombia in the penmanship of García Márquez would not be complete had he not chosen to write about Simón Bolívar. In *The General and His Labyrinth* (1990) the reader witnesses the last days in the life of one of Latin America's greatest figures, who was a general, politician, and liberator. Through his military effort, Colombia became fully independent from Spain in 1819. At that time, Colombia was made up of Venezuela (Bolívar was born in Caracas), Colombia, Panama, and Ecuador. In 1821 Venezuela claimed independence from Colombia, and a year later Ecuador did the same. By 1903, Panama, too, had separated from Colombia. *The General and His Labyrinth* is a somber, sad, but humanistic study of a disillusioned figure of a man, not of a mythic historical hero. In the account, Simón Bolívar dislikes the centralized power of Bogotá as much as any of the liberal characters in García Márquez's fictional works. By 1903, the year he dies, the character of Bolívar can remember twenty years of useless wars.

The wars and constant violence in García Márquez's works represent the fictionalized reality of many historical events. In the nineteenth century and the first two decades of the twentieth, the protagonists of the wars were generals, politicians, armed forces, and people at large who pledged allegiance to either the Conservative or the Liberal Parties. Both parties were fighting for a single thing: power. This historical context is clearly depicted in *One Hundred Years of Solitude*. Colonel Aureliano Buendía is a liberal who fights against the Conservative Party. The peace of Macondo, in *One Hundred Years of Solitude*, is altered when Apolinar Moscote and his family arrive in Macondo. He has been sent by the Conservative Party, the central government in Bogotá. He brings an armed police force to maintain law and order. He even wants all the houses painted blue, one of the colors of the Colombian flag and the color of the Conservative Party. However, the Buendía family, the founders of the town, wants the houses to stay white. Ironically, disorder and chaos break out.

Its repercussion is found in *No One Writes to the Colonel*. In this novel, on the one hand, the colonel is suffering the negligence and corruption of a bygone era, the wars of the nineteenth century. On the other hand, the violence of the 1950s is also portrayed when the colonel's son, Agustín, is killed by the police. The year of Agustín's death, 1956, clearly refers to the violence Colombia underwent from 1948 to 1958. The violence began with the death of Jorge Eliécer Gaitán (in 1948), a populist Liberal leader who was loved by the masses. His death, once again, caused new civil wars to erupt, again in the pursuit of power. Ironically, Jorge Eliécer Gaitán was not killed by members of the opposing party, but by other liberal leaders who were envious of his popularity and its populism. To end the constant bloodbaths, the two political parties agreed to a cease-fire and formed an alliance. This aristocratic pact between the Conservative and Liberal Parties, known as the Frente Nacional (National Front) was instituted in 1958.

Meanwhile, the decade between 1948 and 1958 witnessed a massive migration of people from the rural areas (Macondo, in the short stories and novels) to the big cities, such as Bogotá, Medellín, and Cali. This, too, is explored in *No One Writes to the Colonel* and other works. Sabas, the fat, rich, diabetic character of *No One Writes to the Colonel*, gets rich by buying the land, at a low price, of those who were persecuted and driven away by the mayor.

The National Front, as instituted in 1958, provided a civil and peaceful sixteen years but served to further fracture the democratic political life of Colombia. The presidency would shift every four years, from a Liberal to a Conservative regime and vice versa. During the 1960s the main cities grew exponentially, and the social phenomena of guerrillas began to gradually develop and expand to what they are today.

The drug culture portrayed in García Márquez's nonfiction *News of a Kidnapping* (1996) had its beginnings in the early 1970s. The central figure of *News of a Kidnapping*, drug lord Pablo Escobar, is an unknown drug dealer in the 1980s. His power and fortune, however, grow to unimaginable proportions. The kidnappings of the book are all masterminded by Pablo Escobar to fight his extradition to the United States. The people he is kidnapping to pressure the Colombian government to stop the process are involved in politics and the news media.

The old wars of the Liberal Party were back: in the Colombian social/ political landscape and in García Márquez's writing. The difference was that this renewed Liberal Party was now fighting against the drug lords of the Medellín cartel, not against the Conservative Party. Maruja Pachón, abductee and informant for *News of a Kidnapping*, was the sister-in-law of the founder of the New Liberal Party, founded in 1979. The New Liberal Party forcefully fought against drug trafficking and was very much in favor of extraditing drug criminals to the United States.

The literary context of Gabriel García Márquez's characters is both real and imaginary. His grandparents are the inspiration for the strong, centered, solid, patient women, on the female side, and the stubborn, strong-willed dreamers, on the male side. His maternal grandparents served as models; but when García Márquez fictionalized them, they became symbols of the social world in which they lived. His grandfather, Nicolás Márquez Iguarán, was a colonel in the civil wars of the nineteenth century. His grandmother, Tranquilina Iguarán Cotes, was a matriarch who ruled the house and passed on to García Márquez, her first grandson, stories about ghosts, women who run away, and men who go to war. Strong, iron-willed women are typical in García Márquez's writings, as are colonels, especially in the early years (up to 1967, with the publication of *One Hundred Years of Solitude*). García Márquez's grandmother understood the character and psychology of the people of Aracataca (Macondo in the novels). She passed it on to García Márquez through the art of storytelling. Thus, from childhood on, García Márquez has considered himself a storyteller.

One of García Márquez's literary traits is the frequent use as characters of real peoples' names or personas. This can be observed in nearly all his novels and some of his short stories. However, he rarely gives them major roles, and when he does, he changes their names. In *Chronicle of a Death Foretold* he uses his wife's name, Mercedes Barcha, in full and mentions the occasion when he proposed to her. She is too young (she is in primary school), reads the narrative, so the narrator (García Márquez himself) has to wait twelve years. This same incident from García Márquez's own life is first introduced, in fictional form, in *One Hundred Years of Solitude*. In that novel, however, there are two alterations: the little girl of singular beauty bears the name of Remedios Moscote and the one proposing to her is none other than Colonel Aureliano Buendía. The colonel refuses to wait, however, and marries her immediately.

In *Chronicle of a Death Foretold* the reader finds two of García Márquez's siblings plus his mother. His younger brother, Luis Enrique, appears by his full name and a sister, Aida, shows up as a nun, although she is not described by a proper name. (Aida is a former nun.) The mother of the novel's narrator is Luisa Santiaga; the author's own mother was Luisa Santiaga Márquez. *One Hundred Years of Solitude* introduces García Márquez and his friends Alvaro, Germán, and Alfonso as secondary characters. These secondary characters are lovers of literature, as are García Márquez and his friends in real life. In the novel they are friends of Aureliano Babilonia, the last of the Buendías, another literature lover, who translates the parchments written by Melquíades. Alvaro is Alvaro Mutis, Germán is Germán Vargas, and Alfonso is Alfonso Fuenmayor. In the novel, García Márquez uses his own name, but without *García*, to describe the fourth friend, who appears as Gabriel Márquez. Alvaro, Germán, and Alfonso also appear as friends in *No One Writes to the Colonel*. The three are friends of Agustín, the son of the old colonel, who plays a major role in the novel.

Perhaps the most interesting and beautiful depiction of the use of real peoples' personas in García Márquez's character development can be found in *Love in the Time of Cholera*. His experience with real-life characters is the basis for the love story in the novel, although the names are all fictitious. In an interview available in videocassette as *Tratos y Retratos* (in English, *Relations and Portraits*), he assures the viewer that the story is a true and literal retelling of the love story of his parents. His father, Eligio García—like Florentino Ariza in the novel—had to overcome the hostility of his beloved's parents. Florentino Ariza, like García Márquez's own father, plays the violin and writes poetry. García Márquez's mother, Luisa Santiaga, was an only child, as is Fermina Daza in the novel. Also like García Márquez's own mother, Fermina has a strong character. While García Márquez's mother had eleven children, however, in the novel Fermina has only two. However, Gabriel García Márquez has two children. García Márquez's father, Eligio García, was the town telegraph operator, as is Florentino Ariza in the novel. That in itself was reason enough for his mother's parents to reject him. On top of that, however, Eligio García was a conservative. In real life, Eligio García and Luisa Márquez did get married, but to keep up appearances they had to move out of town. (They settled in Ríohacha.) In the novel, Fermina Daza's father never accepts Florentino Ariza, but the young man stays in town and never marries Fermina Daza. Nonetheless, in the end, true love prevails.

To paraphrase García Márquez, his readers cannot separate reality from fiction; they are inseparable. Where reality ends and fiction begins is impossible to say. His work must continue to be read as a parchment that each reader must decipher individually.

3

Leaf Storm
(1955)

García Márquez's first novella, *Leaf Storm*, was translated into English in 1972, eighteen years after it was published in Spanish and two years after the English-speaking public first read his acclaimed masterpiece *One Hundred Years of Solitude* (referred to in this chapter as *Solitude*). As might be expected, some critics in the United States used *Solitude* as the model against which to compare this novella. In a novella (which is generally shorter than a novel), as in the short story, a fictional narrative is restricted to a single event, situation, or conflict. As the British author and literary critic John Anthony Cuddon noted, while this often

> produces an element of suspense and leads to an unexpected turning point so that the conclusion surprises even while it is a logical outcome, the *novella* is also characterized by its length, which although indeterminate, nevertheless lies between a short story and a full-length novel. (Cuddon 642)

As examples of novellas, one may think of *The Old Man and the Sea* (1952) by Ernest Hemingway, as well as two others by García Márquez: *No One Writes to the Colonel* (1961) and *In Evil Hour* (1962).

La hojarasca (as it was published in Spanish in 1955) appeared in English as *Leaf Storm and Other Stories*. Some critics were initially unable to appreciate *Leaf Storm*. A reviewer for *Time* magazine, Martha Duffy, wrote that *Leaf Storm* was in most ways a disappointment, as she found it filled with "undifferentiated nostalgia for old values, old vitality, and old civility" (Duffy 25). However, *Leaf Storm* did not disappoint all critics. From a more literary perspective, Kathleen McNerney believed that *Leaf Storm* anticipated the fiction that was yet to come. She explained: "*Leaf Storm* contains elements of enough other works by García Márquez to qualify it as a microcosm of the body of his oeuvre" (McNerney 104). As if it were a seed or an embryo, *Leaf Storm*'s theme and techniques are developed more fully in later works. The author has offered his own endorsement. Gabriel García Márquez stated that "of all the books he had written [as of 1973], *Leaf Storm* was his favorite because he felt it was his most sincere and spontaneous" (McMurray 1977, 3). *Leaf Storm* also reveals the beginnings of a serious writer, who is attentive to form and technique and responsive to the literary traditions that preceded his work—Latin American, classical, and European. One example of this form is the placement and origin of the epigraph (a quotation placed at the beginning of a work, which alludes to common themes) that opens the novella and links it thematically to the classics of Western literature, and specifically to Sophocles' *Antigone*. The relationship between the classical *Antigone* and *Leaf Storm* will be examined later in the chapter.

Another example is a prominent technique employed, stream of consciousness, which reveals an influence, or perhaps a coincidence (as Mario Vargas Llosa pointed out), with William Faulkner's *As I Lay Dying*.

However, before entering into the thoughts and feelings of *Leaf Storm*'s main characters, the author prepares the reader with two devices. First, a foreboding of the theme of death and the dispute to the rights and rites of burial is initiated by the epigraph from Sophocles' *Antigone*. This is followed by a prologue in the voice of an omniscient narrator writing in the first person plural. The prologue's writer is located in Macondo, in the year 1909. The reader learns that Macondo is undergoing three historical events: the arrival of a banana company (the United Fruit Company); the coming of the people that the banana company attracted, known as "la hojarasca" (the leaf storm); and the end of a Colombian civil war.

The nature of these three events not only defines the background of the novella, but also establishes the presence and importance of the community, which is partly composed of "la hojarasca." Macondo, the physical space where the novella takes place, may have been inspired by the name of a plantation near where Gabriel García Márquez grew up, but the Macondo of *Leaf Storm* is fictional; there is no town named Macondo in Colombia.

Against this background, the author uses the stream-of-consciousness technique to explore themes such as death, war, the double, the other, and solitude. The stream of consciousness technique "seeks to depict the multitudinous thoughts and feelings which pass through the mind" (Cuddon 919). In *Leaf Storm*, specifically, this literary device can be seen through the inner thoughts of the colonel, his daughter, Isabel, and Isabel's son. All tell the story of the burial of a stranger hated by the townspeople, the doctor. The stream of consciousness of the ten-year-old child, the twenty-nine-year-old Isabel, and the respected old colonel engage the reader in the moral, religious, and political struggles of a family within the community of rural Macondo.

PLOT DEVELOPMENT

The events announced in the prologue spark both curiosity and suspense in the reader. The curiosity to know about these newcomers, these outsiders referred to as *a whirling leaf storm* and identified as "a swirling crowd that smelled of skin secretion and hidden death" (2). The ominous description will intrigue the reader, who is told that this diverse group of people has come to dominate the everyday life of Macondo. The omniscient narrator of the prologue, a member of the founders, laments this fact when he says that "the first of us came to be the last; we were the outsiders, the newcomers" (2).

The plot can be summarized as the efforts of an old colonel to give a Christian burial to an outsider who was hated by the townspeople—a French doctor. No one in the community, other than his own daughter and grandson, supports the old colonel. As a part of the plot, the child's stream of consciousness allows the reader to pose the question: Why does this happen? This question can be seen as open-ended due to at least four different possibilities. The child, up until now, has never seen a corpse; hence he is unfamiliar with the concept of death. He wonders why he is all dressed up as if it were Sunday; he questions why he has been brought to the doctor's wake; and indeed, he wonders why no one else comes to the wake other than himself, his mother, his grandfather, and four Guajiro Indians who work for his grandfather. The child's viewpoint reveals his own concept of social class when he describes his own house as faded and run-down, but as "the perfect" imaginary house. He believes in ghosts and local omens. Although it is much too early for a boy not yet eleven years old, he has become sexually active as a voyeur, getting sexual pleasure by viewing Lucrecia's nude body (78).

Isabel, the boy's mother, would have preferred not to come to the wake. Like her son, she also asks herself the rhetorical question, Why is this happening? Despite the fact that she is nearly thirty years old, she finds herself hopeless and lacking free will. Isabel's continuing blind obedience to her father is her downfall. As an act of obedience, she marries Martín, whom her father has chosen as a husband. Martín, she says, "seemed to be linked to my father by a deep and solid friendship, and my father spoke of him as if it were he and not I who was going to marry Martín" (62). However, after two years, Martín leaves her and their son.

Isabel's viewpoint gives the novella a traditionally feminine approach. Through her, the reader penetrates the psychology of the women in the community. Isabel talks about the Indian ways of the woman Meme, who, she says, "was at the same time both open and reserved; a mixed-up combination of innocence and mistrust" (18). Isabel pays attention to dress codes and styles, and she passes judgment on what is cheap, ridiculous, elegant or otherwise. It is through her viewpoint that the reader learns of love affairs and betrayal. Isabel's friendship with Meme provides the former with the history of her family and that of Macondo. Meme, says Isabel, "Spoke to me about the journey my parents [they were first cousins] had made during the war, about the pilgrimage that would end with settling in Macondo" (24). Meme knows about Isabel's personal history, literally—she knows where, Isabel and her family come from.

Isabel's awareness of daily life and the declines of social interactions provide her with a knowledge of law and order, as based on social class and race. Isabel's awareness of social class comes from living in a country mansion, having Indian servants, and watching her father impose his will on the town's mayor, who presumably represents the community at large.

Moving from Isabel's point of view, the narrative perspective shifts to that of the old, lame colonel; this allows the reader to enter the institutional community, particularly the law and the Church. As only he can, the colonel recounts the present and the past of Macondo—its movie house, its whorehouse, its shops, and public life in general. His stream of consciousness brings the story together. What he knows about the doctor forces him to go against the wishes of the whole town, which opposes the Christian burial of the foreign man (who is probably of French origin). He acts out of pride, moral values, and ties of old friendship. The ties are with none other than Colonel Aureliano Buendía, son of José Arcadio Buendía, the patriarch and founder of Macondo in *Solitude*. At least twenty-five years before the novella begins, Colonel Buendía had given the doctor a letter of recommendation to the old, nameless colonel of *Leaf Storm*.

Through the stream of consciousness of the colonel, readers witness the rise and fall of a community and its institutions as they pass from the late 1800s to the second decade of the 1900s. Astoundingly, all these events occur within the short time frame of a half-hour and inside the four walls of a room on Wednesday, September 12, 1928, around 2:30 on a hot and sunny afternoon of a leap year, in Macondo.

GENRE AND NARRATIVE STRUCTURE

In *Leaf Storm* García Márquez begins with a technique more commonly used in the movies: he begins in medias res (Latin for "in the middle of things"). When an author uses this technique, the narration can start in the middle or at any other point in the story. Thereafter, the writer brings interrelated events together without having to follow a linear time line and sometimes, as in *Leaf Storm*, working in a circular and repetitious way. In the case of *Leaf Storm* the reader is present, from the very start of the narration, at the doctor's wake, which happens to occur at the end of the story. Who is this dead man? What did he die from? How old is he? Why is a strange child telling the story? From the start the reader has to pay close attention to events, because any information that the main characters provide is given only in small increments and at unexpected times.

Rich in technique, *Leaf Storm* seems to be a most experimental work for someone who was publishing for the first time. The reader may have the illusion of listening to the narrative voice of the child, but what is really heard is his inner voice or thoughts. What is heard is, actually, his stream of consciousness. Dressed up in an uncomfortable green corduroy suit, the child wonders why he has to be there, all dressed up "as if it were a Sunday," knowing that he should be in school because it is actually Wednesday. Although his language reflects his childlike point of view, at times he sounds too precocious and his language is not that of a child. Before the narrative point of view shifts to his mother, the child hears a train whistle in the distance and thinks, "It's two thirty" (7). He thinks of his friend Abraham, and how, at that time, the boys in school would be lining up for the first class of the afternoon. These imaginative leaps in time and space seem effortless, and they lead the reader to surprises time and time again.

Shifting to the mother's point of view, the reader learns that she worries about the townspeople's opinion. She reacts to public opinion: she finds burying the doctor to be ridiculous and shameful because everybody in town wanted him dead. She also hears the train whistling and confirms that it is 2:30 on a hot afternoon in September. In Macondo, this is the time for a siesta, and she thinks of Father Angel dozing, sitting in the sacristy. Isabel's stream of consciousness seems to be the most disjointed; she thinks of Meme as dead; looks at her father and thinks, "he's cold-blooded about the burial"; and thinks about what other people may think of them. She worries about time and about her dress; she decides that being at the burial was her destiny. All this was supposed to happen to her in this fateful leap year, after the doctor committed suicide by hanging himself.

In journalistic style, García Márquez unfolds details, one by one, to construct an atmosphere that can be better seen as the reader moves through the novella. Unlike in journalism, however, the facts are passed on as if in oral form, as if the characters were talking, perhaps telling the reader something he or she already knows. As is the case in oral tradition, the news is passed on by word of mouth in a circular and repetitive way. The point of view shifts back from Isabel to the child and then from the child to the old colonel. At this point, the reader experiences both a dialogue with the mayor, with whom the colonel discusses his right to bury the doctor, and the colonel's own stream of consciousness. Through the former, the reader learns that the mayor shares the anger of the town against the doctor. The town's anger has turned to hate because the doctor had refused to take care of some wounded men. Having refused to do what the town considered a charitable act, the townspeople turn their back on the doctor for the next ten years. The doctor had not even drunk the water in his well for ten years for fear that it might be poisoned.

By the end of the first chapter of *Leaf Storm* the reader has been given most of the facts that sustain the novella. The breakdown of time and the disjointed order of events suggest the random nature of the thought processes of the three main characters: Isabel, the colonel, and the child.

CHARACTER DEVELOPMENT

Leaf Storm, like most of García Márquez's fictional works, leads the reader to envision a whole town and its people interacting with one another as if they were all fully developed characters. This illusion is due to the fact, on the one hand, that García Márquez's fiction is filled with characters that come in and out of the story as a mere enunciation—as a spoken reference or part of the social scene, often with a first name and sometimes even with a last name. The main characters, on the other hand, may appear fully developed yet lack names. This is the case for some of the main characters of *Leaf Storm*. Of the four main characters who dominate the story, three have no name: the colonel, his grandson, and the doctor; we learn only the name of the colonel's daughter, which is Isabel. Both the colonel and Isabel tell the story of the doctor, making it the axis around which several other stories are told. Among the most important are the love affair of Meme and the doctor and the arrival of the town's priest, Father Angel, accompanied by flashbacks of the old town.

Of the old colonel the reader is told that he wears glasses, uses a cane to walk, and has a lame leg that he has to keep stretched out when he sits down. The narrative focuses on a few salient physical characteristics, just enough to enable the reader to visualize the character. The colonel is fully developed, not only by how other characters see him, but also by the way he sees himself. He, as much as Isabel, shows a tremendous self-awareness of what the town thinks of them. The mayor of Macondo, for example, thinks of the colonel as a respectable man, and the colonel in turn seems convinced of the mayor's respectability, for he fought alongside the colonel's former commander, Colonel Aureliano Buendía. He is a member of the town founders and therefore disdains the newcomers brought to town by the banana boom. They are the despicable people whom he calls "the leaf storm," which gives the name to the novella. Few people escape his disdain other than the doctor, the priest, Meme, and, curiously enough, the total stranger, Martín.

Although a newcomer, Martín wins the colonel's trust to the extent that Martín ends up marrying his only daughter. The colonel, like the doctor, leads a life apart from the community. The colonel rules his life by his own principles and so defies the Church, the state, and the community.

The doctor behaves in a similar way. However, unlike the colonel, who receives respect, the doctor receives hatred. The townspeople and the Church justify their hatred in different ways. The people of Macondo hate the doctor for refusing to care for some of their men who were wounded in war. For this reason, they do not want the doctor to be given a Christian burial. The omniscient narrator knows that Father Angel "had been a colonel at the age of seventeen and that he was intrepid, hardheaded, and against the government" (32). Father Angel also denies the doctor a Christian burial when he says, "I won't let them bury in consecrated ground a man who hanged himself after having lived sixty years without God" (15).

The doctor is a well-developed character whose persona, from the moment of his arrival in town, defines him as a social outcast. He can be seen as a man standing against the community, like the colonel, but his decision throughout the story is viewed as egotistical. The colonel's decision to go against the town is not viewed as egotistical but it is, nevertheless, defiant. His is the decision of a man who views himself as self-righteous, respected, and loved.

Isabel is a character who is identified by her beauty and her passivity, which is also shared by Adelaida, her stepmother. There is nothing about Isabel's persona that shows independence and free will, even though she is a mother, and nearly thirty years of age. This can be said because Meme, her Indian nanny, is the only woman in the narrative who makes decisions for herself against the will of others: she stands against the paternalistic colonel, against her own lover (the hated doctor), and against the town. Isabel's life is marked by a series of unfortunate incidents. The most important life events are marked by tragedy, beginning with her birth, which causes her mother's death. A year later, her father marries again, to Adelaida.

The characterization of Meme seems shortened and left to the townspeople's imagination, as well as to that of the community of readers of the text. For Meme, Isabel feels love but not admiration. Meme, like the four Indians present at the wake, grew up in Isabel's home as part of the family, but she is considered more a possession than a member of the family.

For Genoveva, a young woman who ran away with her lover—the head of a company of puppeteers—and later returns, Isabel feels sad (83). Either for love or because she simply wants to escape Macondo, Genoveva leaves. Later she returns with six children, and nothing more is said of the puppeteer.

Characters such as the mayor and the four Guajiro Indians, along with the stepmother and Genoveva, among others, appear as character types. They seem to complement the main characters by providing continuity to what they have to say, as opposed to expressing their own point of view.

It is interesting to note the characterization of the child, Isabel's son. His viewpoint, above all others, is the only one that needs no interaction. His world is totally autonomous. He does not worry about the community, and he looks at death with the same curiosity that he sees life.

He never loses track of time and wonders, instead, what his friends at school are doing at that moment.

The careful development of characters in *Leaf Storm* serves to depict a rural Latin American community where the main character is not the colonel nor the doctor, but the community itself—the town of Macondo. The narrative voice of the omniscient narrator announces that fact from the beginning, in the prologue. The reader, however, gets immersed in the stream of consciousness of the main characters. It is indeed the community that both the omniscient narrator and the colonel call "the leaf storm," which supplies the story's title. Unlike single characters developed in a detailed way, the community as character can be better understood if the reader thinks of it as atmosphere. The community as character can be seen through the mood, the feelings, the interpersonal relations between the townspeople, and the relationships between the townspeople and their institutions. Macondo thus becomes a physical place, although imaginary, in the mind of the readers. At the end of *Leaf Storm* the reader will have the impression of dwelling in a rural Latin American town and its people.

THEMATIC ISSUES

The doctor's death and his self-imposed solitude, which is shared by others as well as by the town as a whole, comprise the central theme of *Leaf Storm*. In fact, the two themes combined can be seen as one—as solitude, a theme that has always interested García Márquez.

The epigraph that precedes the story, a quote from Sophocles' classical Greek play *Antigone*, establishes the connections that add meaning to *Leaf Storm*. In *Antigone*'s plot, readers come to know about an individual who knows the life-threatening consequences of her actions yet nevertheless, chooses to defy the state's decrees and obey a higher, moral law. Creon, the reigning king, announces that no one may bury Antigone's brother, Polyneices. Anyone who attempts to bury him "will die by public stoning in the town." In *Leaf Storm*, the colonel does not face certain death but only the town's veiled menace. He does not defy a written law, although he risks the community's opprobrium (disapproval). Unlike Antigone daring to bury her brother, the colonel seeks to bury a stranger recommended to him by Colonel Aureliano Buendía, once his superior officer from a distant time and place. The act of defiance, by both Antigone and the colonel, is carried out by an individual acting alone and in response to death.

Like the solitude of death, a feeling of solitude haunts all the characters. The town itself suffers the solitude that comes from isolation. However, although the colonel, the main characters, and the town are all isolated, nobody suffers solitude more than the doctor. He comes to Macondo without knowledge of the culture. He chooses to live like a hermit, bound and insulated in his own life, and acts as if there were no need for anyone special in his life. He loves no one and needs no one. He makes no effort to be connected to anyone or anything. Once he has left the colonel's house, he closes the door of his house and literally never leaves for ten years. The doctor's solitude ends with the loneliest act of all, his suicide.

The solitude of the characters is emphasized, as critic Kathleen McNerney points out, by the technique of interior monologue: "each narrator is turned inward, and what little dialogue there is is always a quotation within someone else's monologue" (McNerney 104). All the characters are far removed from one another and also far away from themselves, immersed in their own thoughts. Both the child and his mother wonder to themselves why they have to be at the burial and wish they were elsewhere. The solitude of the colonel is well marked by the fact that a letter of recommendation from far away is enough to open his house to a complete stranger. By this act the colonel shows loyalty to a time and place other than his own at the time of the story.

The theme of solitude permeates nearly all García Márquez's works, either overtly or covertly. The solitude of *Leaf Storm* may seem concealed, as opposed to its use in his masterpiece *One Hundred Years of Solitude*, in which solitude is mentioned in the title.

Although solitude and death are the two most prominent themes in *Leaf Storm*, several other themes merit mention and further study for their relevance to García Márquez's work: war, the double, and the other. These themes seem to create the atmosphere of *Leaf Storm*. Regardless of the fact that the narrative itself starts with the doctor's corpse, by the end of the first chapter the reader has learned that the doctor came to Macondo twenty-five years before. He arrived at the colonel's home with a reminder of the colonel's days at war. In fact, the colonel remembers this war as the Great War. The use of the superlative makes the reader assume that there were indeed other wars as well (17).

The theme of war, as most readers of García Márquez can attest, is recurrent in nearly all his works. In *Leaf Storm*, there are several other indications that the town has suffered the effects of war. The reader knows, for example, that Macondo has experienced some civil unrest when reading that the doctor has refused to tend some men wounded in war. Nonetheless, the theme of war may pass almost unnoticed for some readers.

The theme of the double appears even less developed than the theme of war; it appears to be almost latent, as if waiting to appear again in a different story. In fact, the theme of the double is front and center in *Chronicle of a Death Foretold* and *One Hundred Years of Solitude*. In *Leaf Storm*, however, it is there only in embryo. The reader is told that the doctor and the priest of the town, "the Pup," can almost pass for brothers, due to a strong physical resemblance, but no one is confused as to who is who. This is not the case with the identical twins who do the killing in *Chronicle of a Death Foretold*.

The theme of the other appears inverted. To the colonel, most everybody is the other. The prologue reads that with the arrival of the banana company, waves of people came and settled. All of these outsiders, seen as the other, become the majority, and therefore the colonel is turned into the other, thus inverting the concept. The doctor, as Michael Bell writes, "provides its principal focus" (13). Not even the colonel's family ever fully accepts him, even though he lived with them for nearly ten years. The doctor was always the other. His status was always that of a stranger, a real outsider. His otherness is even obvious in the strange ways in which he eats and sleeps.

Like the themes of war and the double, the theme of the other recurs in García Márquez's writing. Bell notes "the arrival of a stranger [the doctor, for example] is a frequent catalyst in Márquez's fiction since his theme is often the incapacity to assimilate the outsider" (Bell 13). Often, but not always: Martín is not only a stranger who is assimilated, but he is given the colonel's daughter in marriage.

SOCIAL AND HISTORICAL CONTEXT

Leaf Storm does not reflect the Colombian political turmoil of the 1950s, the decade in which it was published. The novella mentions nothing about the dictatorship or the dictator in power, Gustavo Rojas Pinilla (see Chapter 1). It re-creates, instead, life during the first two decades of the twentieth century in an impoverished, sleepy town, where the law is corrupt, social order is rigid, and social mobility does not exist. Even today, for many people, this image describes rural towns in Latin America. Therefore, although the novella is not overtly political, it has an underlying tone of protest, a recognizable trait of García Márquez's writing and of Latin American prose in general. This can be observed in the mayor's refusal to allow the old colonel to bury the foreign doctor, for example. The old colonel defies, not so much the town's mayor, but rather the institution that the mayor represents.

The narrative portrays the problems suffered in a rigid society where there is a strong division of social classes. The colonel and his family represent the upper class. His military rank and the fact that he is a member of the "old families" of Macondo give him the strength and power to defy the mayor. The priest, who is a friend of the colonel, is also a member of the upper class due to the power and influence he exercises through his position in the church. The townspeople—*la hoja-rasca*—represent the working-class poor. Except for a projected, vague, and foreboding menace attributed to this group, it is essentially power-less. The Guajiro Indians belong to the lowest class of the region and are portrayed as servants. One of these is Meme, the doctor's lover. She is considered unworthy of marriage to the doctor because she is an Indian.

The prologue provides the reader with enough information to under-stand the social and the historical components of the novella, but it does not explain it. The reader has to assemble the story piece by piece, as with a puzzle. This makes the reading difficult because of the constant shift of voice, or viewpoint, from the child to his mother, to the colonel, back to the mother, and so on throughout the narrative. There the child's point of view closes the novella. If it is valid to say that the reader has to fit the pieces of the story together, it can be added that at the end of the story, the reader will continue to be puzzled by certain inexplicable events. The colonel's behavior, for example, seems very inconsistent: he acts loyally and morally toward the doctor but inconsiderately toward his own daughter. He defies the whole community and fulfills his prom-ise in insisting on the sacred right to bury the doctor, yet he marries his only daughter to Martín, a stranger. Martín is a nobody, perhaps even a swindler, who, in fact, leaves town, his wife, and his two-year-old son, never to return. *Leaf Storm* is not a nostalgic, complacent look at the past, but a critical and thought-provoking account.

ALTERNATIVE READING: ANALYTICAL CRITICISM

Analytical criticism is a term used by scholars who view a text as a self-contained work, which can be examined in its own terms without ref-erence to other texts. They believe it is possible to reveal the meaning and nature of a text by objectively and logically analyzing its parts and their organization (Thrall and Hibbard 17). Analyzing the relationship of form and theme helps the reader understand a text. Form, in analytical criticism, is also known as technique. In *Leaf Storm*, Gabriel García Márquez uses a technique called stream of consciousness, sometimes referred to as interior monologue. This technique has been used in the twentieth century by other authors such as William Faulkner, James Joyce, and Virginia Woolf, among others.

When reading a work of fiction, literary critics examine the role of the narrator. They want to know who, inside the fictional work, is speaking—who is *telling* the story and from whose point of view does the reader understand the story. A real author, of course, has written the work, but the story being told does not necessarily reflect his own point of view, for the characters possess their own viewpoints. For example, we know J. D. Salinger is the author of *The Catcher in the Rye* (1951). However, in *The Catcher in the Rye*, the fictional character of Holden Caulfield appears to describe his own feelings and experiences in his own colorful language and humor.

Scholars have identified at least three major kinds of narrative voice, or, as the French critic Gerard Genette refers to it, *focalizations* (a term derived from Cleanth Brooks and Robert Penn Warren's earlier phrase, *focus of narration*). One kind of narrative voice is an omniscient narrator. This narrator is the one who knows everything that happens to all the characters and can comprehend what all the characters are thinking. Genette calls this a *nonfocalized* narration. Many folk tales and myths, though not all, are related in this way. The narrator understands all the important events in the story, can report dialogues between different people, and explain the characters' motivations, fears, and wishes, as if reading their minds. For example, in the story of "Snow White and the Seven Dwarfs," the narrator tells the reader as much about the stepmother as about Snow White.

A second kind of narrative voice is called external focalization. Here the narrator does not know or reveal the characters' inner thoughts. Many mystery stories use this kind of narrative voice in order to conceal what the characters are thinking. For example, an Agatha Christie (1890–1976) novel relies on the observational powers of Hercule Poirot (a Belgian detective who appears in as many as twenty-five novels and many short stories) to notice physical clues, which are only gradually revealed to the reader.

A third kind of narrative voice is what Genette terms internal focalization; this is the type of narration that characterizes *Leaf Storm*. The narrative point of view is restricted to what a single character may know, and the reader's knowledge is then limited to this character's feelings, ideas, and ability to observe. As is the case in *Leaf Storm*, the internal focalization may be variable; that is, the reader alternates in hearing interior monologues of three distinct characters: the child, the colonel, and his daughter, Isabel. When an author uses internal focalization, or interior monologue, no outside narrator intervenes between the reader and the character's most intimate thoughts. The reader knows, for example, that no one else knows what the child, his mother, and his grandfather (the colonel) are thinking. Only the reader, outside the work of fiction, knows. The reader's awareness of the hour: "two thirty in the afternoon," for example, comes from the awareness of each character. To the reader it is repetitious, but for the characters it is not. Nor does each character structure his or her thoughts and words as if trying to be understood by another, as might happen in a conversation. Each character is "talking" to him- or herself with an internal association of ideas, or stream of consciousness. Thoughts, colored by feelings, may be fragmentary, and one idea, image, or word may lead to another based on the character's experience, desires, or fears. This is how, in *Leaf Storm*, the reader comes to have access to a childlike world, the stories of women, and the social history of Macondo. The reader not only sees the fictional world from the character's perspective but also has a direct experience of the character's innermost being, which the rest of the characters in the novel may not learn about. The colonel, for example, never knows that Isabel is critical of the fact that he is more interested in her marrying Martín than she is.

In *Leaf Storm*, only the reader comes to know the three main characters: the colonel; his twenty-nine-year-old daughter, Isabel; and his ten-year-old grandson. The readers learn of their reactions to the death of the doctor and what they know of the doctor's history through the characters' interior monologues.

After a prologue that sets the social-historical context of the novella in Macondo, a small, out-of-the-way Latin American village, the first chapter opens immediately with the interior monologue of the ten-year-old:

> I've seen a corpse for the first time. It's Wednesday but it feels
> as if it was Sunday because I didn't go to school and they
> dressed me up in a green corduroy suit that's tight in some
> places. (5)

The narrator is the "I" who is thinking and feeling: "I've seen" and "I feel." In the first sentence the boy (and through him the reader) confronts a dead body. A reader might expect that the second sentence would be a direct reaction to the corpse. Instead, the boy refers only indirectly to the mystery of death and its sacred aspect. Without stating it directly, he associates the mystery of death with a Sunday, a day for religious activities. This is a reference to his own experience of time. Although this may be a Wednesday, he did not go to school, as if it were Sunday. His stream of consciousness connects Sunday and this Wednesday with the physical discomfort of his clothing; the green corduroy suit that is too tight (and in the heat, probably much too warm).

Because the narrative "I" moves quickly from the sight of a dead body to the feeling of a religious day, Sunday, to the discomfort of clothing, the reader experiences the thoughts and feelings of the boy just as he himself does, as they occur to him in the quietness of his mind. What García Márquez has used is the internal focalization of a young child to confront the reader with a corpse, its inherent sacred quality, and the discomfort of the day. Through the use of the stream-of-consciousness technique, the boy appears enclosed in his thoughts, and thus separate from the others, as if in solitude.

The boy, his mother, and his grandfather think about each other but rarely communicate. Isabel reflects to herself, "I shouldn't have brought the child. A spectacle like this isn't proper for him" (9). The use of the word *spectacle* emphasizes that she is concerned with what the boy will see and how that will affect his way of seeing things and his perspective. Later the grandfather thinks the same thing, but without communicating it to his daughter. The lack of communication does, indeed, produce the sense that the story is disconnected, but the repetition from the different focalizations and the variations in accuracy of the same event provide the reader with the cohesiveness by which to understand the story. In a single afternoon in the doctor's house, the three main characters remember fragments from the past and speculate about the future. These memories do not occur necessarily in chronological manner (in the order in which they originally happened), but rather in overlapping, remembered fragments of time—in flashbacks.

In *Leaf Storm*, there is little plot or physical action. Rather, Isabel and her son passively remain with the colonel while he, in turn, waits for permission to bury the doctor. They all stay with the corpse in his house and watch while the Indians place it in the coffin. The suppression of physical action highlights the interior monologue of the characters. The most important changes are not in the sequences that might compose a traditional story, which changes from one action to another, but in the change of consciousness—the shift from one interior monologue to another. This emphasizes the interior monologue, which has the effect of seeming to enclose each of the three main characters in their own private space, thus isolating them. Through the device of interior monologue in the narrative voice, which becomes interior and separate, the novella stresses the theme of solitude.

Not only is each of the three main characters alone with their thoughts and feelings that afternoon, isolation and solitude seem to distinguish all relationships in the novella. By attempting to bury the doctor—a promise the colonel made to him some three years earlier—the three are setting themselves apart from the community. In their hatred of the doctor, the community wishes to prevent his burial in the cemetery. Isabel, worrying about the town's reaction to the burial, thinks to herself that maybe the townspeople would wait for them to come out with the corpse and then throw excrement at them for "going against the will of the town" (10).

In *Leaf Storm*, a form of solitude is present at many levels. In interviews, Gabriel García Márquez has commented on the importance of this theme in his work. "The only subject I've written about [is solitude]" (Guibert 76). The author is not just writing about the solitude of an individual within a family, as exemplified by the three members of the colonel's family, who appear isolated in their monologues. Nor is he writing merely about the solitude and isolation of individuals from their community, as the doctor experiences in being rejected by, and isolated from, the people of Macondo. As García Márquez makes clear in the prologue, Macondo itself is isolated from the larger world. It has been used and discarded by a big international company, the United Fruit Company.

The isolation of Macondo in *Leaf Storm* may represent, on a different scale, a larger social, political, and economic reality: the solitude of Latin America. As García Márquez indicated in his Nobel acceptance speech, "superpowers and other outsiders have fought over us for centuries in ways that have nothing to do with our problems. In reality we are all alone" (quoted in Simons 1991, 78).

4

No One Writes to the Colonel
(1961)

No One Writes to the Colonel may seem unassuming, for the story line is simple and nonexperimental in technique. However, its narrative exposes a corrupt town and its institutions. *No One Writes to the Colonel*, to date, continues to be considered one of Gabriel García Márquez's best works. (In 1999, Mexican movie director Arturo Ripstein released it as a film, which was entered in the 1999 Cannes Film Festival.) The trilogy of *Leaf Storm, No One Writes to the Colonel*, and *Chronicle of a Death Foretold* emphasizes the theme of the individual against the government, along with the themes of war and solitude.

No One Writes to the Colonel has been praised for its economy of language. The García Márquez reader will immediately recall the colonel in *Leaf Storm*, for the two novellas both portray an old colonel as the main character. Their differences, however, are clearly depicted. The two books, along with a third one, *In Evil Hour* (1966), hint at La violencia (the Violence), a bloody two decades of gunfire in Colombian history that started in 1948. This literary trilogy can be seen as the embryo for *One Hundred Years of Solitude. No One Writes to the Colonel* was first published in the magazine *Mito* in 1958. Three years later it was published again in book form.

PLOT DEVELOPMENT

The story opens with a series of incompletely explained occurrences. The morning when the colonel awakens is a difficult one for him, even though he has been waiting for nearly sixty years, states the narrative voice. The narrator, however, does not reveal what it is that the colonel has been waiting for. His asthmatic wife is introduced, but only to add more suspense to the story. Who are these people? Why are they not given proper names? As if the reader were not already sufficiently confused, the couple starts talking about some person's funeral, for whom the town's church bells are ringing.

The plot's suspense now increases as the wife talks about the dead person. The colonel gets dressed and some children come through a hole in the fence to look, as if in awe, at the rooster in the back yard. The rooster, a fighting cock, captures the reader's attention. The plot then brings to the foreground a piece of information that further adds to the suspense. The colonel and his wife comment that their son, Agustín, is "probably talking roosters" (121) with the dead man for whom the bells are tolling—but where is their conversation taking place? The reader is faced with numerous questions, yet the colonel has not even left the house. As if in telegraphic speech (a form of speech in which the speaker uses brief and abbreviated language that the reader must "decode"), the plot continues to present information that the reader must keep in mind to understand the apparently simple, yet deceivingly complex, plot. The dead man is the first to die of natural causes in many years and that, in itself, makes his death a "special event" (122). The increasing confusion felt by the reader is finally diminished upon learning that the town is under martial law. As a result, the funeral march cannot pass in front of the police barracks (125), so the cortege changes direction and continues to the town's cemetery, where, the reader learns, the mourners will bury a poor musician loved by the town.

No One Writes to the Colonel, the reader eventually discovers, contains several intertwined plots. In addition to the plot concerning the colonel's son Agustín, another deals with the political tensions of the town, and a third centers on the colonel himself. The plot involving the colonel, however, encompasses all the other two and dominates the narrative.

The feeling of having to wait, as if everything were suspended or trapped in a freeze-frame, pervades the entire plot of the story. For fifteen years, the poor, destitute colonel has been waiting for "mail," a piece of mail that the narrative voice emphasizes is of sizable importance. Readers first learn of this long wait when the colonel leaves his house to go to the town's harbor to wait for the launch that brings the mail to town every Friday. The plot surrounding the colonel revolves around waiting for this piece of mail. The title of the book foreshadows what the colonel confirms the first time readers see him go to the harbor. When the postmaster announces that there is nothing for the colonel, the colonel replies, "No one writes to me" (129).

While the reader's attention may focus on the colonel, the town's political tensions also play an important role. The country at large should be having elections, but no one except the naive colonel thinks this will happen, as the town is under martial law. The colonel's wife summarizes it well when she says, "the world is corrupt" (130). The corruption mentioned by the colonel's wife is also mentioned in other books by García Márquez, such as *In Evil Hour* (1966). The economic conditions of the colonel and his wife are very poor indeed, as is their health. The colonel suffers from intestinal problems and constant fever, and his wife has asthma.

The doctor, who is young and handsome, looks after the colonel and his wife with much compassion and understanding. He brings "health" to the old couple as well as clandestine information for the colonel to pass on (133). The doctor charges nothing for his visits, jokingly saying he will bill them when the colonel's rooster fights and wins. The rooster indirectly ties together the three different plots of the book. Seen as a symbol, the rooster is supposed to bring well-being to the colonel, his wife, the schoolchildren, and the town at large. The colonel prefers to provide for the rooster rather than for his wife and for himself. His wife begrudgingly tells him to buy corn for the rooster, although she adds that God knows how the two of them will manage (136). However, the rooster also suffers from the colonel's dire circumstances and goes without corn for two days. The rooster suffers the same hardship that the colonel and his wife are going through, and just like the old colonel, the rooster shows pride by not eating what he does not like. The colonel's wife wants the colonel to get rid of the rooster. She thinks roosters are accursed and that her husband's rooster caused the death of her son, Agustín. However, the colonel insists that it is best to keep the rooster to honor their son's memory and to sell it after the fight for a better price (147).

In the meantime, the wife, who is frail and asthmatic, fears they may die of hunger. She believes she has found the solution to their problems when she decides they can sell their wall clock for forty pesos to Alvaro, the same person who bought their son's sewing machine from them. (The colonel's son was a tailor, who used to work for Alvaro.) Again, however, the colonel's pride gets in his way. Agustín's friends are at the tailor shop when the colonel arrives to sell the rooster, and so the colonel is too ashamed to say what has brought him to the store. Agustín's friends, however, decided to feed the rooster after the colonel tells them he does not want to take care of it anymore, telling them, "I'm too old for that" (151).

On the second Friday, the colonel goes back to the harbor and waits, once again, for the anticipated piece of mail. The doctor gets his news-papers and personal mail, and when he asks the mailman if there is something for the colonel, the mailman emphatically answers: "No one writes to the colonel" (138). For fifteen years the colonel has been waiting for his pension as a veteran of war. In an attempt to solve this problem, the old colonel goes to see his lawyer, who insists that he be patient. At this point, the old colonel decides that he needs to hire a new lawyer.

On the third Friday, while the colonel is maintaining his pride by returning to the harbor, his wife tries to get a loan from Father Angel but fails. She then tries to sell the wall clock, only to find out that most people already own a better one. When she tries to sell the painting off their wall, she finds that nearly everybody has the same one. Her efforts to bring money home only upset the colonel, who bitterly replies, "so now everyone knows we're starving" (159). His wife answers, "you should realize that you can't eat dignity" (160). The colonel's dignity might also be seen as lack of character, as his own wife tells him (163). He finally decides he must sell the rooster. However, when he arrives at the home of the rich man in town, Sabas, in order to do so, "he wished he had arrived an hour later and missed Sabas" (165). The young doctor is in Sabas's home when the colonel arrives. Sabas offers to buy the rooster at a price that the doctor feels is less than half what the rooster is worth. The doctor seems to understand Sabas's greed, ambition, and corruption better than the colonel. Sabas's fortune, the doctor explains to the colonel, was created through his questionable connivance with the town's mayor. When landowners were persecuted by the mayor's armed forces—the same armed forces that killed the colonel's son—Sabas bought the landowners' properties at half their value just before they were driven out (168).

The colonel, however, wants to see Sabas in a different light. His dig-nity allows him to ignore Sabas's material wealth and disregard what others say about him. The colonel lives in a world of make-believe, but he appears to be respected by people, nonetheless. At the town's pool hall, he is shown considerable respect when the same policeman who killed his son catches him with a clandestine lampoon in his pocket. The policeman aims his rifle barrel at the colonel, but the colonel "gently push[es] the rifle barrel away with the tips of his fingers" and excuses himself, as if to ask the policeman to clear his way; surprisingly enough, the policeman answers, "you may go Colonel" (170).

As the reader approaches the end of the story, the colonel's wife still looks at the rooster with disdain and cannot wait to get rid of the "evilomened bird," as she refers to him (170). The colonel continues to go to the harbor every Friday to wait for his mail, and the townspeople continue to cheer for the rooster. In fact, the rooster goes for trials at a local pit and, like a gold-medal athlete or a superstar soccer player, he is greeted with applause and loud shouting. The loud, frenetic applause for the rooster has an impact on the colonel's psyche. He believes, with the townsfolk, that the rooster belongs to everybody, just as a pop star, movie actor, or folk hero belongs to the masses. The colonel himself takes the rooster back to the pit for trials and hopes for the quick arrival of January 20, the date when the rooster will fight. The colonel, in the end, seems to take complete control of his life. He cannot envision the rooster losing and thinks his pension from the civil war will eventually come. His wife, however, remains skeptical and does not believe any of this. When she finally finds herself running out of possible arguments, she loses control, grabs the colonel by the collar of his shirt, and shakes him hard while demanding "and meanwhile what do we eat?" (181). The colonel, without losing his composure, and obviously feeling rather invincible, quietly answers "Shit" (181).

GENRE AND NARRATIVE STRUCTURE

No One Writes to the Colonel was the second book published by Gabriel García Márquez. Like the book that preceded it, *Leaf Storm* (1955), *No One Writes to the Colonel* is also a novella, a fictional narrative most commonly identified by its length, which is generally between that of a short story and that of a full-length novel (see Chapter 3 for a more detailed definition). Unlike *Leaf Storm*, *No One Writes to the Colonel* is not an experimental work focused on form and technique. The plot unfolds in straight, chronological order; this type of narrative is referred to as linear narration. *No One Writes to the Colonel* is structured in seven discrete, unnumbered chapters. The first three chapters of the novella pay particular attention to the colonel's anguishing wait for the mail and close with his decision to change lawyers to better appeal for his veteran's pension. To carry the narrative through to its dramatic end, the story of the rooster is added as a parallel narration in the present and as a symbol of hope for both the colonel and the townsfolk. The seemingly unassuming and compact narration of *No One Writes to the Colonel*, however, requires a careful reading. A superficial or hurried reading may leave readers with the idea that the whole story is trivial and nonsensical, or even superfluous, absurd, or totally irrational. Such a reaction, unfortunately, perpetuates a stereotype that *No One Writes to the Colonel* actually mocks in a most ironical way.

In almost traditional style, the narrative structure of *No One Writes to the Colonel* has an omniscient narrator outside the story line (not a participating character). The narrator is easily identified throughout the novella in scenes where, for example, the colonel took the top off the coffee; his wife raised the mosquito netting; we are told it was seven-twenty when the colonel finished winding the clock; and others.

The story line about the seventy-five-year-old colonel, his asthmatic wife, his dead son, and the rooster upon whom the colonel pins all his hopes is only interrupted by references to the past made by the omniscient narrator. The narrative structure of *No One Writes to the Colonel*, stated William Plummer, a critic of North American and Latin American literature, shows an overhauled prose, stripped of extravagance and thus made more efficient (Plummer 39). This comment Plummer makes also encompasses the novel *In Evil Hour* (1966) and the short stories (see Chapter 5).

Although linear narration is usually seen as traditional and nonexperimental, as a form that presents mostly one viewpoint—that of the omniscient narrator—García Márquez reveals a unique design for the use of time. To paraphrase the American literary critic Richard D. Woods, García Márquez's frequent indication of the exact hour and minute or a recurring mention of the day or the month (or both); a suggestion that time is static; and, finally, an occasional reference to clocks proves how effective the concept of time is for the development of both personality and theme (Woods 87). The narrative structure of the novella pays particular attention to the present time. The story starts on October 27 and ends on December 7, a period of six weeks. The narration, however, expands over a much longer period of time. From the very start, the reader is taken back in time when the colonel's wife recalls the year their dead son was born, 1922. In fact, their son was born on March 7, 1922, and was killed by the police nine months before the start of the story on January 3, at a cockfight, where he was distributing clandestine literature. Their son, Agustín, worked at a tailor shop and was a cockfight fanatic. The omniscient narrator then recalls an incident when the family was happy and their son Agustín was eight. This makes the year 1930, but readers, in this instance, only get the reference to the incident, not the exact year when it happened. The present tense of the narrative elapses only one week before the colonel gets ready to go pick up the mail. Once again, however, a regression in time is noted by the omniscient narrator: "fifteen years of waiting had sharpened his intuition"

(128). The colonel receives nothing that Friday, nor the following. The narrative structure refers to the past again, to August 12, 1949, to inform the reader that the colonel was put on the rolls to receive a pension on this date. Congress had passed the law to award pensions to those who fought to defend the Republic nineteen years ago, but it took eight years to prove the colonel's claim and then six years to get him included in the rolls. The narrative structure moves in a linear fashion, both in the past and in the present. In relation to the past, it starts with the birth of Agustín in 1922 and moves on to 1949. The present time of the six weeks of narration moves from the end of October to the first week of December, although the year is never mentioned. The reader, if interested, has to play detective and pay attention to dates and incidents, piecing together disparate allusions to complete an accurate time line. Some dates are indeed those of historical events intertwined within the narrative's fiction. The supposedly unassuming linear structure of the narrative is not as simple as it seems, however. The constant regressions in time by the omniscient narrator, although objective and insistently emphasized, contribute to the reader's sense that the novella is most focused in nostalgia and the past rather than in the present. Nonetheless, the opposite is indeed the truth. The narrative structure and the treatment of time contribute to the plot. The current time of the novella, 1956, was a time when Colombia was undergoing a wave of violence referred to by historians as La violencia (the Violence); hence, the significance of the date when the colonel's son was killed (January 3, 1956).

The language of the narration is as austere as the life of the colonel and the townsfolk. The use of language is also a harbinger of much discontent, for in this nameless Colombian coastal town, the only certain thing is death. As the postmaster tells the colonel, who thinks that by changing lawyers his pension might then be made to come, "the only thing that comes for sure is death, Colonel" (156). In a previous scene, Sabas cries, "this town stinks" (153). This is a very sanitized translation of the original Spanish, "este es un pueblo de mierda" (this is a shit town).

CHARACTER DEVELOPMENT

Character development in *No One Writes to the Colonel* depends on the consciousness of the omniscient narrator and the consciousness of the characters as they interact with one another as the plot unwinds. The main characters of the novella are the colonel, his wife, and the rooster.

None of the three, however, is given a proper name. The secondary characters are numerous: they include Sabas; the doctor; the postman; the lawyer; the town's mayor; Father Angel; Agustín's friends, Alvaro, Alfonso, and Germán; Sabas's wife; Moses the Syrian; and Agustín. With these main and secondary characters, García Márquez creates the illusion that a whole town is present as the reader moves through the story. The consciousness of the omniscient narrator reveals the characters' past, and the consciousness of the characters adds to their own personalities. In this manner, a character who is never present—never depicted in the text—becomes the most important of the secondary characters. Agustín first emerges as a mere reference but gradually evolves to become an important symbol of guidance and subversion.

Of the three main characters of the narrative, the colonel is the most important. The colonel, however, is developed in opposition to his wife. The husband and wife complement one another as if they constituted one whole made out of two parts, like two sides of one coin. However, they are indeed two different characters. The colonel cannot see things the way his wife does, but neither can she understand the way he thinks.

The seventy-five-year-old colonel is part of a group of veterans who fought for their country at the end of the nineteenth century, and he now waits for his promised pension. The majority of this group of veterans has died or fled the country. The old colonel, nevertheless, continues to wait as the novella unfolds. In fact, waiting for his pension is what keeps the colonel going. The reader senses that the colonel should not have such high hopes; therefore, the irony of his wait becomes obvious, if not absurd. From the start, he is a character drowning in extreme poverty; the opening lines picture him scrounging to prepare himself a small cup of coffee in a country known for its coffee plantations. His umbrella is nearly completely destroyed by the moths; he has to shave by feel since he does not own a mirror; his house is mortgaged; and he and his wife often boil stones in the cooking pot to fool the neighbors into thinking they are not as destitute as they really are. What, readers may ask themselves, keeps the colonel hopeful when everyone else seems to have given up? Is it because he has hope that the letter, to confirm his pension, will be a form of recognition for his merit in war? These two rhetorical questions can be answered with one word: he has dignity. In fact, dignity is all that the colonel has left. He is not only poor, but the system that has impoverished him financially has also killed his only son.

From the age of twenty, the colonel has been going from one frustration to the next. His wife no longer trusts him or his decisions, for all have been failures. The country's authorities are totally indifferent to his situation. The colonel, at first glance, appears pathetic. His wife, for example, is always reproaching him for his lack of character, for his stubbornness to keep the rooster, for his insistence in hoping for a letter that never arrives. His destiny, if there is one, seems to be a miserable one, yet he conquers all. His personality seems to be like that of Don Quixote. His dream, like Don Quixote's, may also be impossible. The colonel continues to fight, never loses hope, and truly believes that, in the end—through the cock fight—he will finally win.

The colonel is redeemed because he never gives up. He keeps his son's tradition alive by passing on clandestine literature, by keeping the rooster, and by never losing his sense of pride. To the end the colonel is the idealized strength that can face the misery of everyday life with a spiritual richness. He is never defeated, because he never gives up. He is far removed from the reality that surrounds him, but not blind to what he experiences. The ominous present does not stop him from dreaming of a better future.

In contrast, the colonel's wife is not a dreamer or idealist. Her world is as real as her asthma and the routine of her everyday life. She is simple, strong, faithful, hard-working, long-suffering, and a true religious believer. She is small, thin, and asthmatic. If she undergoes a flare-up in her asthma, she simply waits until the crisis is over. When the crisis is over, she cleans the house and keeps it as best she can. She is capable of performing the miracle of multiplying the bread, says the colonel. She can also sew, mend, and restore. It is as if she had found a key to sustaining a domestic economy where money is nonexistent. She adapts to their poverty, although it begets misery. However, little by little she starts to question her husband until finally she rebels against the situation into which they have fallen. She rebels with a voice filled with anger, stating that she is up to her tonsils with resignation and pride. This state of affairs reminds her of the conditions that destroyed the town's economy. She remembers the time when senators would make a thousand pesos a month for twenty years without doing anything. She remembers their friend Sabas, a man who came to town selling medicines on the streets with a snake around his neck and who now lives in a two-story house and enjoys great wealth. She screams all this at her husband to convince him that dignity cannot feed them.

The colonel's wife has a harsh and strong temperament. This makes her inflexible, especially in the face of adversity. The death of their son caused her to shed not a single tear, but the unjustified situation in which they live makes her scream, against her own husband and against society as a whole. Unlike the colonel, she is forceful and decisive. Her decisions are all practical. Also unlike the colonel, however, she is the one who suffers most from reality.

The rooster's presence throughout the novella seems both obsessive and symbolic. The rooster catches the reader's attention in the same way that it becomes the focus of the colonel's life. Its symbolism depicts the absurdity of a reality that combines hope and despair. However, the rooster is not an ordinary bird. It is an inheritance from the colonel's son; it is a fighting cock; and it is the talk of the town. In fact, the rooster's success as a breeding stud is compared, by the colonel, to that of Colonel Aureliano Buendía (157). To emphasize the absurdity of the novella, the rooster is the sole hope of the colonel, the doctor, the children, and everybody else—except for the women. The colonel's wife finds the rooster ugly. To her, it looks like a freak: "his head is too tiny for his feet" (127). The rooster, in short, goes through a personification; that is, the rooster is given human attributes. For example, according to the narrative voice, the rooster seems to be aware of the colonel's poverty and also of the townsfolk's near-delirious expectations (173).

Of the secondary characters, it is interesting to note that the most important one is somehow outside the text. Agustín is already dead by the time the narrative takes place, yet his memory is more influential in determining the course of events than the interaction of most characters within the novella. Once again, like the rooster, Agustín is a symbol. His influence is passed on to the friends who survived him, Alvaro, Alfonso, and Germán. His heritage is passed on to others through his rooster. Agustín, at the time of his death, was raising the rooster for a cockfight. The rooster is Agustín's inheritance to his family and his friends. Symbolically, it is the inheritance of rebellion: the rooster is a fighter in the same way that Agustín is remembered for inciting the town to rebellion. The rooster, in the end, belongs to everybody. In the same way, the clandestine literature that is passed on to others by the colonel, the doctor, and those who go to the tailor shop is a form of Agustín's heritage. The police shot Agustín for distributing such literature. His death, however, gives relevance to the novella as a symbol of the repression perpetrated by the regime of the time. The head of state, General Gustavo Rojas Pinilla, ruled Colombia in a totalitarian dictatorship during which hundreds of people who opposed his rule were killed. Pinilla's totalitarianism exercised absolute control over all aspects of life in Colombia. His dictatorship outlawed any form of opposition. Agustín is not a character within the narration, but he is as visible as the violence that permeates the novella.

Agustín's character development is analogous with the life of Saint

Augustine. He, too, lived a life of rebellion against his mother's will. Agustín rebelled against the town's police and incited his friends to do likewise, as did Saint Augustine, who incited his friends to fight against those who were taking heaven by force (Wallace 125). The leadership of Saint Augustine was passed on to the order he founded, the Augustinian Order. Agustín's legacy in the novella is passed on to others and left open-ended. His father, the old colonel, decides both to carry on the cockfight tradition (by keeping the rooster) and to distribute clandestine literature.

Sabas is one of the few characters with a proper name in *No One Writes to the Colonel*. He represents the sector of society that has benefited from the violence suffered by the townsfolk. He is the only member of the colonel's political party who escaped political persecution, which he did by siding with the government forces through his friendship with the town's mayor. His house is a new building reflecting his newfound wealth. Sabas is a person without scruples, dedicated to business whether honest or not. He comes across as a hateful character; not by coincidence, the narrative describes him as fat and physically ill. Sabas represents the new ruling class.

The humanitarian qualities of the doctor are the antithesis (direct contrast) of Sabas. Through him, the reader gets a fresh and critical viewpoint of the outside world. It is through the doctor that news from abroad comes to town, and he passes it on along with subversive literature. To the needy, like the old colonel and his wife, he charges nothing for his services. His likable characterization is a precursor to the character of the doctor, Juvenal Urbino, in *Love in the Time of Cholera* (1985).

The lawyer is depicted as the bureaucrat representing the political system in the town. In fifteen years he has not accomplished what he was hired for, to make sure that the colonel received his pension. The lawyer is shown as disinterested, only capable of arguing in terms of names, dates, and excuses. The town's mayor is another petty official whose authority is exercised in a dictatorial manner. When he persecutes people, they either die or leave the town. His accomplice in crime is Sabas.

Father Angel adds the moral censorship of the Church to the already repressive system. He announces, by ringing the church bells, which movies are appropriate for the public and which are not. However, Father Angel does not decide on his own. He receives, from the central government offices in Bogotá, a list of films that are morally approved for the townsfolk. In nearly a year's time, not one movie has been approved. The colonel's wife, however, seems to agree with the classification of films and is heard saying, "the world is corrupt" (130). Sabas's wife is the antithesis of the colonel's wife. Her husband, who finds her useless and thinks she talks too much, verbally abuses her. She is described as superstitious and preoccupied with death. Unlike her pragmatic husband, she lives in a world of dreams. Moses the Syrian seems to add to the background of the novella. His role is as vague as that of the postman. He is supposed to be a member of a group of merchant Syrians.

All characters, main and secondary, are developed in relation to the community, and the community is viewed through the interaction of characters. However, the violence within the community and the decadence shown by the petty officials is dictated from the outside by a head of state whose name is never disclosed. Thus, in the end, the reader may have to accept that the careful development of characters is intended to create atmosphere. An atmosphere of violence, poverty, corruption, and solitude is created through the depiction of the most important character of all—the community itself, or the town.

THEMATIC ISSUES

It is obvious that corruption is the main theme of *No One Writes to the Colonel*. The colonel's naive hope leads him to fight yet one more battle, the humiliating battle of having to wait for a veteran's pension that never comes. Through the open-ended theme of corruption, the novella also explores themes such as violence, hope and despair, the injustices suffered by the townsfolk, the disparities of wealth among the country's people, and the theme of solitude.

The corruption and violence that Colombia has undergone from the civil wars of the nineteenth century right through to the twentieth century are portrayed in *No One Writes to the Colonel* through two generations. The old colonel, his wife, and those in power represent the older generation, and Agustín and his friends, the younger generation. As the younger generation protests the dictatorship of the 1950s, the old colonel, with indignation, remembers the last war of the nineteenth century and points out the corruption of the bureaucracy and its chief officials that accompanied it. At that time, the old colonel was a very young man living in Macondo. The Treaty of Neerlandia had been signed, yet the colonel had to wait for ten years to see the promises of the treaty fulfilled. Meanwhile Macondo was inundated with people from out of town who came there to work in the booming economy of the banana plantations. This new social and economic wave forced the proud and dignified colonel to leave Macondo. It also marked the beginning of a period in which the country was engulfed by despair, frustration, oppression, corruption, solitude, violence, and death. The colonel's misfortune, which began when he left Macondo, permeates the entire book. Initially he was still young and strong and believed that things might change for the better. The colonel was, and continues to be throughout the book, hopelessly optimistic, yet life in the story only gets worse. The young colonel and his wife grow old, physically decrepit, weary, sick, and shamelessly poor; moreover, the violence of the time of the narrative is so pervasive that their only son is killed by the police for distributing clandestine literature. In fact, the magnitude of the violence at the time of the narrative can be measured by the fact that the burial that occurs in the opening chapter is the town's first burial for natural causes in many years.

The theme of hope versus despair is best exemplified by the rooster, which is a symbol of both forces. The narrative introduces the story of the rooster to counterbalance the mostly nightmarish reality and hopelessness of the historical facts of the backdrop of *No One Writes to the Colonel*. The town's doctor, the old colonel, and the townsfolk at large all put their hopes on the rooster. Thus, it serves to partially offset the tension brought about by the police and the town's martial law. But will the rooster win the fight that is yet to take place and thus "save" the town? The reader has to decide independently because the story ends before the rooster is scheduled to fight, at the point when the old colonel decides to keep the rooster even if it means that he and his wife must do without. The abrupt end seems absurd, but it is an absurdity that calls for examination on behalf of the reader. The old colonel—and all those who pin their hopes on a victory by the rooster—are simply looking for a form of victory against the oppressive government forces that control their very existence. When the old colonel closes the book's narrative, he feels pure and invincible at last—at seventy-five years of age—because he thinks he can finally win his battle. His rooster "can't lose" (181). His victory is certain; at last he is on the verge of victory, at the end of both his life and the book.

Another theme, the injustices suffered by the townsfolk, can be immediately seen in the poverty in which the old colonel and his sick wife exist. Their house and their lives are pathetic; they seem to be dying in quiet desperation. Theirs is not a really even life, but an agony that the reader must feel as well. They lack money, possessions, and essentials. They lack health and everything else; as the colonel says, they "are rotting alive" (122). As the reader might imagine, the injustices that they suffer are also suffered by most of the townsfolk. This is certainly the case for the people at the tailor shop, the children who come to see the rooster after school, and the cockfight fanatics who save their money to bet on the rooster. The crises that the poor endure are more like a purgatory than a life. One example is the fact that the townsfolk are not free to walk by the police barracks during the procession to bury the poor musician. The townsfolk are both economically and socially oppressed. Sabas is the only leader of the colonel's party (the Liberal Party) who escapes political persecution and continues to live in town. The injustices of the poor in general are exemplified by what happens to the old colonel. He is not merely poor, he is impoverished and let down by a social and political system that fails to pay what is legally his, his pension for having served the country. Other members of the middle class who are shown as impoverished complement the poverty apparent in the portrait of the colonel; these include the doctor and the black, toothless lawyer. The poverty of these three middle-class characters is a microcosm of the poverty of the town, a sample of the injustices of a government that is incapable of providing, or unwilling to provide, for its citizens. The injustices suffered by the townspeople, in turn, are a constant reminder of the Colombia of the period when *No One Writes to the Colonel* was written.

Disparity of wealth, as a theme, can be recognized in the descriptions of a relatively small group of government officials, a few men who have umbrellas to protect themselves from the rain, and, most obviously, Sabas. At the time of the burial, the town's mayor is still in bedclothes, a sign that he does not need to be at work to earn his money. He is described as standing on the balcony of the barracks, unshaven and swollen in the face. The men with the umbrellas, also attending the musician's funeral, are members of a social class that can afford to dress in white with black ties (123). However, of all people, the one who has benefited the most from knowing how to manipulate the system is Sabas. The English translation omits the social title that Sabas goes by in the original Spanish: Don Sabas. The word *Don* before his name is an appellation of economic success. He is not just Sabas, as the English translation goes, he is Don Sabas. A translation using Mr. Sabas would not do justice to what Gabriel García Márquez intends. His Don Sabas is someone who is economically and socially special. He lives in a new, two-story house with wrought-iron window gratings (126). Although the colonel and Sabas live in the same town, they lead as separate a reality as they would if they lived in two different latitudes. As the colonel and Sabas watch the rain come down, the colonel says that the rain from Sabas's window is like watching it rain in another town (153). Sabas has an office in his house in which to conduct business. He employs a foreman and a group of men to take care of his ranch and animals. His new wealth is such that he requires the use of a safe. Don Sabas, or Sabas as the English translation calls him, is the economic antithesis of the colonel. Sabas was not born rich. Both he and the town's mayor have become rich by taking advantage of the political turmoil that prevailed at a time before the narrative begins. The townsfolk who were persecuted had to choose between death and immigration to the urban centers. The mayor at the time threatened those who were persecuted with the loss of their property. To avoid this fate, they were forced to sell their lands. People like Sabas benefited by buying their properties at half-price. Sabas has gotten so used to taking advantage of the less fortunate that he tells the colonel that he could sell the rooster for 400 pesos, less than half what he had originally offered. The doctor warns the colonel that the rooster is worth a lot more than what Sabas has offered. Sabas, reveals the doctor, is the epitome of corruption; he enjoys a "sweet deal," along with the town's mayor. The colonel defends Sabas by saying that he had to side with the mayor and the Conservative Party (which is in power) to save his own life, but the doctor insists that Sabas is more interested in money than in his own life.

The final theme that is presented to readers in *No One Writes to the Colonel*, once again, is the theme of solitude, a theme that ranges throughout García Márquez's works. There is the solitude inflicted upon the town by its geographic isolation. Its only contact with the outside world takes place once a week in the form of mail. The long wait of the colonel is another act of solitude. He is an individual acting alone, in the same way that the colonel of *Leaf Storm* acts alone to bury the foreign doctor of the novella, against the will of the townspeople. If the colonel's wait is an act of solitude, his wife's lifestyle is even more so. She only leaves the house once, to try to sell the clock and the painting (the only two possessions, other than the rooster, that they have left). The two of them form a couple that lives in solitude. The solitude of this old couple also evokes the solitude of the old couple in *Love in the Time of Cholera*.

SOCIAL AND HISTORICAL CONTEXT

The social, political, and economic events of *No One Writes to the Colonel* take place in an anonymous fictional town in Colombia in the coastal northwest part of the country. The action of the novella symbolically, yet realistically, depicts the extreme poverty of the majority of the population of all Colombia compared to the wealth of Colombia's very small elite in the 1950s. The town is under martial law and almost everything is either censored or controlled by the state or the Church. *No One Writes to the Colonel*, like most of Gabriel García Márquez's works, shows concern with the Colombian civil wars that had afflicted the country at the end of the nineteenth century. As if to sketch the social and historical events that unfold later in García Márquez's seminal work, *One Hundred Years of Solitude, No One Writes to the Colonel* deals with several historical events that might normally pass unnoticed. The three most important events as they appear in the narrative are the War of a Thousand Days, La violencia (the Violence), and the banana strike of 1928.

At the start of the novella, the War of a Thousand Days is the first reference to appear. The narrative implies that the colonel participated, nearly sixty years before the time of the narrative of *No One Writes to the Colonel*, in "the last civil war" (119). This reference alludes to the civil wars of 1899 to 1902. This period, referred to as the War of a Thousand Days, resulted from a fragile and divided political structure between the Liberal and Conservative Parties. The origin of the War of a Thousand Days may be dated back to 1863, when the Liberal Party was dominant but the Conservative Party was favored by the federalist constitution instituted in that same year. In Colombia at that time, it was difficult to even talk of the constitution as a single document. Between 1821 (eleven years after Colombia gained its independence from Spain) and 1945, Colombia formulated eleven national constitutions. The cease-fire of the War of a Thousand Days ended with the signing of several peace treaties. The Treaty of Neerlandia mentioned in *No One Writes to the Colonel* was signed in 1902 by General Juan B. Tovar of the Conservative Party and Rafael Uribe Uribe of the Liberal Party. In November of that same year, two other peace treaties were signed, but they are not mentioned in the novella; they were the Treaty of Wisconsin and the Treaty of Chinacota. As is the case in most of García Márquez's work, fiction and fact are combined in the novella. García Márquez's grandfather, Colonel Nicolás Márquez Iguarán, was a colonel who fought in the civil war of 1902. Although the old colonel in *No One Writes to the Colonel* is modeled after García Márquez's own grandfather, Colonel Aureliano Buendía is pure fiction. (Colonel Aureliano Buendía is the same colonel who features prominently in *One Hundred Years of Solitude*.) Although the town of Macondo is fictional, the historical events that occur there are based on events of the nineteenth century combined with those that García Márquez witnessed himself from 1948 to the time of the publication of *No One Writes to the Colonel*.

The second important event, the killing of Agustín, the colonel's only son, is García Márquez's way of aesthetically writing about the violence that engulfed Colombia during the 1950s. Agustín is killed in 1956, while the fictionalized town is under martial law. First published in 1958 in the magazine *Mito*, *No One Writes to the Colonel* hints at the dictatorship of Colombia's then chief of state, Gustavo Rojas Pinilla, and the brutality of the period of La violencia. (This topic is also discussed in Chapter 1.)

The colonel's departure from his hometown, Macondo, in 1906 provides another important historical development as it hints at the exploitation in Colombia by the United Fruit Company. The civil war known as the War of a Thousand Days had ended in 1902. The old colonel waited patiently for his pension, but after four years, he had begun to despair. His despair was intensified by the arrival of the United Fruit Company, finally forcing him to leave Macondo. The arrival of this so-called banana company, and the large wave of newcomers that the company attracted, is known as "banana fever." *No One Writes to the Colonel* mentions the banana fever with which *Leaf Storm* begins. *One Hundred Years of Solitude* culminates with the banana strike of 1928, the year when Gabriel García Márquez was born. The strike came as a result of workers receiving only poor wages, no medical benefits, and no rights to organize. When the workers struck in December 1928, at the Ciénaga train station, a massacre took place. The death count may or may not have been exaggerated, for most accounts vary from a handful to 3,000 casualties. These newcomers to Macondo, so highly despised in *Leaf Storm*, are just a memory in the old colonel's mind in *No One Writes to the Colonel*, but the tone with which he refers to the event surrounding the banana fever remains one of outrage: "The odor of the banana is eating at my insides" (161).

ALTERNATIVE READING: HISTORICISM

Historicism, as a school of literary criticism, expands on the idea of history, to which most readers can relate. As it is generally understood, history is a chronological account of events considered significant by a social group at a certain time after pursuing the cause and effect of such events. Thus, a historical reading focuses on verisimilitude, on factual events traced in time, either present or past. In historical readings the proper names of the protagonists are kept intact and the geographical places are exact. The reader normally gets the feeling, because he or she is led to feel this way, that what he or she is reading is the truth, with no room for the subjectivity involved in any given point of view. Biographies, historical novels, and journalism are three easily identifiable types of writings that follow the traditional historical approach. A *historicist* reading, however, does not focus on the points outlined previously but rather emphasizes the way, or mode, in which such information is *presented*. The story of the old colonel is about the old colonel, not about the exactness of the historical events that surround him. The War of a Thousand Days is documented in historical accounts interested in the historical basis that caused the war. Such a reading will include the exact names of the people, places, and governments involved. All this potential information can be found outside *No One Writes to the Colonel*, but the novella is interested in narrating it from a fictional point of view.

A historicist critic is interested in knowing why such work or works get published at the particular time of their publication. For a historicist, the author's point of view becomes less relevant as compared to the social, economic, cultural, and political conditions that shaped it. A historicist critic favors knowing what type of reader the author is aiming at. Therefore, a historicist reading examines the forms of prose in which the work is written. It also concentrates on how the plot and point of view are presented, and much less on what they say. In the case of Gabriel García Márquez's *No One Writes to the Colonel*, the historicist aspect is so clear that the reader runs the risk of not being able to go beyond the metaphorical level of the writing. The rhetoric used in the novella, in other words, may bury any subsequent meanings to the plot of the old colonel and his circumstances, as they appear at the literal level.

As a novelist, Gabriel García Márquez, in *No One Writes to the Colonel*, favors a selective point of view that brings to the reader's attention a state of violence, poverty, despair, death, solitude, and corruption, all at the imaginative level. The reader easily grasps this narrative prose, but the historical facts, which have determined the literal level of the narrative, are not as easily grasped. However, García Márquez's discourse in *No One Writes to the Colonel* does, in fact, combine the two levels—the literal and the imaginative. Although carefully disguised, the reader who is asked to assume a certain attitude toward both the plot and the point of view can identify the latent meaning of the narrative. The plot of *No One Writes to the Colonel* is a microcosm used by García Márquez to

rework an earlier type of Latin American novel known as the dictatorship novel or novel of violence (as it was called in Colombia).

In the 1940s in Latin America, novels about dictatorship and its consequences were written to denounce the atrocities suffered by people
under such regimes. In these novels the common folk proved unable to
escape the system. One of the first novels of this genre in Latin America
was Miguel Angel Asturias's novel *The President* (1946), an overt denunciation of the Guatemalan dictator Manuel Estrada Cabrera. In *No One
Writes to the Colonel*, García Márquez denounces the problems of the present, the 1950s, which are recurring as in the past, which was marked by
the violence of the civil wars of the end of the nineteenth century. The
situation of Colombia during the 1950s was very similar to that of the
turn of the century, when the colonel was a young man. The struggle in
both periods was over power between the Conservative and Liberal Parties. The same can be said of both periods about the prevalence of corruption, violence, injustice suffered by the poor, and the disparity of
wealth. *No One Writes to the Colonel* depicts the problems stemming from
the corruption of the 1950s but traces them back to the end of the 1800s.
In a historicist view, the indirect mode that García Márquez uses in the
novel speaks to various types of readers, including both those who are
politically oriented and those who are not. While the civil wars and La
violencia of the 1940s and 1950s are present and do affect the characters,
they do not take center stage. Rather, the focus is on the fictional work.
However, in doing so, the fiction is critical of both the present-day situation and the past. It is, indeed, a denunciation of the administration
of Colombian head of state Gustavo Rojas Pinilla. The death of the colonel's son is a symbol of the guerrilla struggles that Colombia was undergoing, starting with the killing of the populist leader of the Liberal
Party, Jorge Eliécer Gaitán, on April 9, 1948, in Bogotá. This violent act
was felt throughout the country, and similar events recurred for nearly
two decades. The rural violence, persecution, corruption, and disposses-
sion of land from small and large owners that Colombia was undergoing
in its history is what García Márquez depicts in a fictional mode.

Going back to the historicist principle that social, economic, cultural,
and political factors influence the production of literary works, it is important to note that *No One Writes to the Colonel* was written in Paris,
France, in 1956 (although not published until 1958 in the magazine *Mito*
and 1961 in book form). Gabriel García Márquez's cultural views were,
as they appear in the text, critical of how Europeans look at Latin America. Europeans, the novella complains, do not understand Latin American problems. Although the narrative is camouflaged, García Márquez

was concerned that readers who were aware of modern-day Colombia and had strong opinions about it might recognize the leaders and situations described in *No One Writes to the Colonel* and that unpleasant repercussions might result. García Márquez had already lost his post as a reporter for *El Espectador* when Gustavo Rojas Pinilla closed the newspaper. His unemployment led him to an economic depression. He had a similar concern with respect to the publication of *In Evil Hour*. Also set in a rural town that is plagued with violence, corruption, persecution, and death, the novel was written in 1955 but not published until 1966.

A historicist reading of *No One Writes to the Colonel* makes the novella an object of interpretation. The novella is a story about an old colonel and his rooster, but the significance of the novella is determined by the social, cultural, political, and historical implications of the times when Gabriel García Márquez first published it. Thereafter, the meaning and complexity of the novella become a denunciation of a corrupt political system that fails to take care of its citizens.

NOTE

The translation of the novella *No One Writes to the Colonel* was first published in English in 1968 in a volume titled *No One Writes to the Colonel and Other Stories*. The translation used in this chapter, however, is from the book *Collected Novellas*, which also includes *Leaf Storm* (1955) and *Chronicle of a Death Foretold* (1984).

5

The Short Stories

If Gabriel García Márquez had never put any of his novels to paper, wrote literary critic Gene H. Bell-Villada, his shorter fiction would have still gained him some niche in literary history. Bell-Villada puts García Márquez in the company of such acknowledged masters of short fiction as Anton Chekhov, Thomas Mann, James Joyce, John Cheever, and Grace Paley (Bell-Villada 119). However, the list of short story masters seems incomplete without the names of Edgar Allan Poe and Latin American short story writers such as Horacio Quiroga, Jorge Luis Borges, Julio Cortázar, Carlos Fuentes, and Juan Rulfo, among many others.

Gabriel García Márquez's short stories that are most often read in high schools and colleges in the United States come from his first three books in this genre. It was precisely as a short story writer that García Márquez began to publish, starting in 1947. His early short stories, such as "The Third Resignation" (1947), were published in local newspapers (see Chapter 1). While he continues to publish books of short stories, some of the stories contained in his first three books in this genre are nowadays considered classics.

Of these classics, five stories have been selected for discussion here. The five stories are presented in chronological order of publication: they are "Monologue of Isabel Watching It Rain in Macondo" (1955; from *Eyes of a Blue Dog*); "Big Mama's Funeral," "Balthazar's Marvelous Afternoon," and "Tuesday Siesta" (1962; from *Big Mama's Funeral*); and "A

Very Old Man with Enormous Wings" (1968; from *The Incredible and Sad Tale of Innocent Eréndira and Her Heartless Grandmother*).

PLOT DEVELOPMENT

The plot of a short story, such as the five in this chapter, will arouse the reader's interest over the duration of the narrative but cannot control the reader's emotional responses. For example, among a class of students, there will likely be many different responses to stories such as "A Very Old Man with Enormous Wings."

All five of the short stories discussed in this chapter begin with a character or scene, which precipitously initiates the plot. However, the plot in García Márquez's short stories appears ambiguous, not only in its creation of mood (the creation of a state of mind based on the narrative's information), but also in the way in which the story is told. Although the plot is seen as the plan of the short story, representing the order in which events are told, the reader must also pay close attention to causality (what incites the characters to do what they do).

Although the main characters play a unifying role, the omniscient narrator and the reader are the ones who must put the plot together. Certainly García Márquez's writing seems to challenge the reader with puzzle-like plots where the pieces do not fit together easily, or at all.

In each of the stories the setting is similar: a small, rural town, which is geographically far enough removed from other villages so as to seem to constitute an entire isolated world. Readers may think of the towns as being near or around the Atlantic Colombian coast on the Caribbean Sea. Frequently, the climate is oppressive: tropical, windy, hot and humid, and plagued by frequent and heavy rainfalls. Macondo, the fictional Colombian village of many of Gabriel García Márquez's works, is identified specifically in two of the short stories examined in this chapter: "Monologue of Isabel Watching It Rain in Macondo" (hereafter "Isabel's Monologue"), and "Big Mama's Funeral." In the other three stories, the town where the narration takes place, the reader may assume, is also Macondo or a town like it, but the place name is never mentioned.

Without exception the short stories all have an omniscient narrator, located outside the story, who narrates in the third person singular. This narrator knows everything there is to know about the characters.

As many critics have observed, García Márquez's short stories often depict a narrative structure where there are at least two forces in opposition, as is the case in "Isabel's Monologue." Isabel tells her story as she recalls matters, but her own husband denies the accuracy, and even the reality, of some of her observations. In another example, in "Balthazar's Marvelous Afternoon," there are two forces represented by social and economic class, the rich and the poor. In "Big Mama's Funeral," Big Mama is placed in opposition to the townsfolk. In "Tuesday Siesta" as well as in "A Very Old Man with Enormous Wings," an outsider disturbs the peace of the town.

All five stories are also characterized by the pervasive presence of the irrational and the supernatural. In "A Very Old Man with Enormous Wings," for example, the old man not only has wings, but also uses them to fly.

Another characteristic is that each short story depicts, in some detail, the daily life of a Hispanic rural town, with its sacred rituals and secular celebrations, including Sunday-morning church attendance and the almost spontaneous appearance of a small fair or carnival as a way to mark the unusual.

The following is a brief synopsis of the five stories based on their narrative structure.

"Monologue of Isabel Watching It Rain in Macondo"

In "Isabel's Monologue" the reader is again introduced to the character of Isabel, who is one of the main characters in *Leaf Storm* (see Chapter 3).

"Isabel's Monologue" can be read as a story that was intentionally not included in *Leaf Storm* or that was deleted from it. In "Isabel's Monologue," she does not mention the doctor, whose corpse is a focal point for the other characters' mediations and actions in *Leaf Storm*. The strained relationship between Isabel and her husband, Martín, a relationship alluded to in *Leaf Storm*, is dramatized in "Isabel's Monologue." Her father the colonel, who was a dominant character in *Leaf Storm*, appears in this story without his military title. Isabel also never refers to the major role he played in marrying her to Martín. Unlike *Leaf Storm*, where she is the mother of a precocious ten-year-old, in the short story she is five months pregnant with the child.

The time frame of the narrative can be measured by four consecutive days and nights of torrential rain. The persistence of the rain is central to the narrative.

As in *Leaf Storm*, time in "Isabel's Monologue" is marked by the sounding of the train's whistle at exactly the same time every day: two-thirty in the afternoon. In "Isabel's Monologue" it starts to rain Sunday morning after Mass and does not stop until Wednesday night. The storm, the reader is told by the omniscient narrator, carries away the train tracks and opens up the tombs in the cemetery. Isabel notices the smell of "the dead people floating along the streets" (134) and seems terrified by the idea. However, the reader cannot be sure if there are such floating dead people or if Isabel is imagining it all, as her husband insinuates. He says, regarding the floating dead people, "that's something you made up. Pregnant women are always imagining things" (134).

"Tuesday Siesta"

The opening of the short story sparks no particular interest in a reader of García Márquez, who generally uses more startling beginnings. Instead, as if in slow motion, "Tuesday Siesta" starts with a train coming out of a tunnel and passing by towns surrounded by banana plantations. Nevertheless, as if it were a still photo, it immediately awakens in the reader a quest for understanding that remains unsatisfied even after the story ends. The sudden dialogue in reported speech (someone else is quoting what the characters say) makes the reader wonder who is talking. Who is this old woman dressed in black, and to whom is she talking when she says: "you'd better close the window. The girl tried to, but the shade wouldn't move because of the rust" (99)?

The reader soon feels the solitude expressed by the description: there are only two people traveling in this third-class car, and they are going to a destination that is never disclosed. The narrator's ambiguity in speaking contributes to the reader's sense of intrigue. The twelve-year-old girl is the woman's daughter, but the woman, readers are told, "seemed too old to be her mother, because of the blue veins on her eyelids" (100). An hour later, at twelve noon, on a "bright August Tuesday," the two women are approaching "a town larger but sadder than the earlier ones" (101). Although, on the one hand, a specific time frame is insistently confirmed, on the other, neither the town nor the main characters are completely identified. The characters are known by their roles: the traveling mother, her daughter, and the priest. A recurring symbol used to mark time in *Leaf Storm* and "Isabel's Monologue," the train whistle is important once again in "Tuesday Siesta." The train, in fact, works as a narrative thread to help the reader understand the otherwise confusing plot. When the travelers get off the train, around two o'clock (three hours since the story has begun), the townspeople are taking a siesta. The old woman and her daughter "went directly to the parish house" (102). Here the reader finally starts putting the puzzle together, and the story starts to make sense. The mother and her daughter are making a trip to bring flowers to her son's tomb. The town's priest has the keys to the cemetery, and the old woman wants them. Nowhere is the woman's pride and dignity more obvious than at the priest's home. Examples of her pride and dignified bearing are noted previously, as, for example, in the way she sits in the train, although nobody but her daughter is watching. At the parish house she never loses her composure, and she succeeds in getting what she needs: the keys to the cemetery. The priest, who happens to be taking a siesta, wants her "to come back after three" (102); the woman responds that she is taking the train back at three-thirty. So determined is she that the priest gives in. When he asks whom she is coming to see, she gives the name Carlos Centeno: "he's the thief who was killed here last week . . . I am his mother" (103).

The omniscient narrator relates that a lonely widow named Rebeca, an old woman living alone for the past twenty-eight years, killed the thief at three in the morning. Rebeca, readers are told, killed the thief with an old revolver "that no one had fired since the days of Colonel Aureliano Buendía" (104).

The reference to Colonel Aureliano Buendía might pass unnoticed by someone who has not read *Leaf Storm*, "Big Mama's Funeral," or *One Hundred Years of Solitude*. However, although only fleetingly mentioned in several of the stories, his name seems to connect all the short stories. Each story, then, although able to stand alone, appears as a part of a layered world.

The end of the story, as is typical of Gabriel García Márquez's writing, is open to multiple interpretations. Although the townspeople were supposed to be taking a siesta, everybody, instead, was at their windows or on the streets, while the old woman, with the keys to the cemetery in her hand, "took the girl by the hand and went into the street" (106). That is how the story ends. Any climax or further conclusion is left to the reader's imagination.

"Balthazar's Marvelous Afternoon"

The narrative structure of "Balthazar's Marvelous Afternoon," of the five stories considered in this chapter, is perhaps the least confusing for nonexperienced readers of García Márquez. Time passes chronologically and the use of flashbacks is minimal. "The cage was finished" (138) announces the omniscient narrator from the start; the same voice reports that it took Balthazar two weeks to accomplish the work. The duration of time in the narrative, as the title announces, is less than one day in the life of Balthazar, a thirty-year-old carpenter. There appears to be less subjectivity in the telling of this story than in the other four. Not only are actions recounted chronologically, the dialogue itself is overheard by witnesses and reported in a straightforward manner. To the crowd that comes to the carpenter's shop, this is "the most beautiful cage in the world" (138). Nobody in the town appreciates the cage more than the doctor, Octavio Giraldo. To him, the cage is "a flight of the imagination" (140). A corresponding absence of interior monologue diminishes the reader's feeling of subjectivity. To Ursula, Balthazar's companion, the cage is simply the biggest she has ever seen, but she fails to comment on the beauty of it.

When the time comes to put a price on the cage, its creator hopes to get twenty pesos but Ursula hopes to get three times as much. Ironically, at the end of story, Balthazar gives it away for free. When Balthazar started making the cage, he had had one goal in mind: to give it to Pepe (a nickname for José), a twelve-year-old child and the son of the richest family in town. José Montiel, the child's miserly father, is a violent and heartless man who decides to pay nothing to Balthazar because he believes an adult should not contract with a child.

"Big Mama's Funeral"

"Big Mama's Funeral," like most of García Márquez's stories, is complex. After the initial reading, a first reaction might be that one is reading the simple story of a woman, Big Mama, who is getting ready to die, surrounded by relatives, a priest, and a notary. Thereafter, however, one realizes that the story is more complex, going back 200 years in the life of Macondo, and particularly its institutions of state and Church.

"Big Mama's Funeral," which is partly humorous, partly satirical, partly ironic, and most definitely full of hyperbole (extravagant exaggerations on the part of the narrator to emphasize the verbal account), describes the exercise of a limitless power by a matriarch who has been christened with the name of María del Rosario Castañeda y Montero. María del Rosario, after attending her father's funeral mass at age twenty-two, comes back to her house in Macondo as Big Mama. This is the name with which she will be recognized the world over, until the day of her death, at the age of ninety-two. Her life, explains the narrative voice, is the center of gravity of Macondo. Her death, like her actions while she lived, affects everyone. "She seemed, in truth, infinitely rich and powerful, the richest and most powerful matron in the world" (186). She was indeed powerful, but she was also corrupt, like her maternal grandmother, who fought in the War of 1885 against none other than the legendary (fictitious) Colonel Aureliano Buendía of *One Hundred Years of Solitude*, "Tuesday Siesta," and *Leaf Storm*.

If the reader moves from the textual level to an interpretative one, the difference between myth and history may become even more apparent. Seen in this way, "Big Mama's Funeral" portrays both history as fiction (the myth of Big Mama and her family) and fiction as history. The War of 1885 is a documented fact, but the legendary colonel and Big Mama's grandmother do not exist outside fiction.

The funeral in "Big Mama's Funeral" announces both the end of an era and the beginning of another, without taking a position as to whether the next era will be a better one. Instead, the significance of the death is left to literature, to future storytellers of the world. While the story can be seen as the awakening of Macondo from "an oppressive social system" (Foster 1979, 57), it is also about telling a story—about the art of storytelling.

"A Very Old Man with Enormous Wings"

The setting of "A Very Old Man with Enormous Wings" is reminiscent of the setting in "Isabel's Monologue." The narration opens with an omniscient narrator and a torrential rain: "On the third day of rain they had killed so many crabs inside the house . . ." (203). Where the heavy rains of "Isabel's Monologue" disinter the dead, in "A Very Old Man with Enormous Wings," the rains bring with them "an old man, a very old man, lying face down in the mud, who, in spite of his tremendous efforts, couldn't get up, impeded by his enormous wings" (203). To Pelayo and his wife, Elisenda, the first townspeople to see the man (who is in their own backyard), he is just an old man who speaks in an incomprehensible dialect. To their neighbor, he is "an angel" who is coming for Pelayo's sick child but has been knocked down by the rain (204). Just as the angel becomes immobilized the child seems to recover, and so the neighbor woman's words seem to confirm the supernatural: a visible angel really has come to protect the souls of dying children.

As in most of García Márquez's stories, the ordinary folk of the town provides one of the central focuses, thus taking center stage. In "A Very Old Man with Enormous Wings," the literal stage is that of two carnivals, the first centering on the activity surrounding the reputed presence of an angel and the second, a more traditional, but no less mercenary affair, with sideshows and feats of strength. Like Pelayo and his wife, the townspeople do not really consider the very old man an angel, yet their curiosity leads them to come and gawk as if he were a rare circus animal. The contradiction is that the townsfolk wish the old man were an angel, a superior being, which, among other possibilities, "could be put to stud in order to implant on earth a race of winged wise men that could take charge of the universe" (205). This dual attitude of skepticism and hope continues, even after the town's priest, Father Gonzaga, assures them that the old man is an impostor. The priest, as did the townspeople before him, notices that the angel does not conform to their idea of what an angel should be; "nothing about him measured up to the proud dignity of angels" (205). Despite the priest's observations and his insistence that the old man might be an evil figure, the news of a "captive angel" spreads throughout the town and surrounding communities, and the people come to see it. Taking advantage of the fact, Elisenda fences her backyard and starts charging admission to see the angel. Unlike Ursula's doomed ambition to make money in "Balthazar's Afternoon," Elisenda and Pelayo "crammed their rooms with money" (206). The couple continue to make money by exploiting the people's curiosity and "faith" until the arrival of another out-of-the-ordinary being: "the woman who had been changed into a spider for having disobeyed her parents" (207). The crowd's appetite for supernatural or grotesque spectacles is now met by the spider woman rather than by the angel. However, the crowd's shift in interest does not interfere with the fact that Pelayo's family has already improved their economic status by exploiting the angel.

The angel, meanwhile, becomes the pet of Pelayo's son. Just as a human would, the angel contracts chicken pox, suffers from high temperatures, and makes both Pelayo and Elisenda fear that he might die. One morning, as Elisenda is cutting onions in preparation for lunch, the old man truly flies away, like a "senile vulture" would, to her relief and that of the old man himself (210).

There are few indications of time in the story. One comes when the narrative voice announces, "at the beginning of December some large, stiff feathers began to grow on [the old man's] wings" (210). Readers will also note that some time has passed as the newborn son, in the course of the story, becomes old enough to go to school.

GENRE AND NARRATIVE STRUCTURE

In Western literature, the short story has its roots in ancient Greek fables, in tales like those of *The Thousand and One Nights*, and in the collections of stories of the English poet Geoffrey Chaucer and the Italian poet and scholar Giovanni Boccaccio. The short story, as we know it today in Spanish American literature, emerged in the nineteenth century.

The short story as genre can be differentiated from the novel and the novella because it is normally shorter. In fact, the short story encourages concise narration and economy of words. Often the main focus of the short story is the telling of the story, as opposed to character development. The number of characters can be few, and frequently they are not fully developed. At times, the number of characters can be reduced to one or two.

Of the five short stories chosen for this chapter, "A Very Old Man with Enormous Wings" is the one that best connects the mundane details of everyday life with what many critics agree to call magic realism. *Magic realism* is a term not fully defined nor always understood; yet it is often used to describe unique Latin American narratives that mix magic and myths with reality, predominantly the myths of the indigenous and the black communities of the Americas. All five stories, however, are representative of García Márquez's short-story writing, and they all depict three salient characteristics associated with modern short-story writing:

- Fragmentation of narrative time; the emphasis on the uses of time is such that time becomes a theme;
- Subjectivity of plot, normally determined by the difference of the character's viewpoint;
- Ambiguity of plot, mainly because the main theme is left open-ended.

The action of all five stories takes place in a small, rural town. In two stories it is named Macondo, and in the other stories it remains unnamed. This does not mean the stories are limited in meaning by being placed in a rural town. Instead, these short stories may be distinguished from works labeled *regionalist*, which emphasize the description of a local area and suggest that the problems of the characters are only peculiar to the people of that area. In the short stories of García Márquez, the physical settings are identifiably Latin American in general and Colombian in particular; however, the themes of violence, economic disparity, and the absence of social justice are universal.

In all five stories the reader finds a character—an individual—dealing either with reality, dreams, or illusions, but always operating within a society and affected by its demands. All five stories show a strife-ridden society, but the focus is on the characters and the way they deal with the problems that face them, for instance, the role of women in a patriarchal society in "Isabel's Monologue"; an individual's pride and dignity in "Tuesday Siesta"; the role of the artist in "Balthazar's Marvelous Afternoon"; the role of power in a corrupt oligarchic society in "Big Mama's Funeral"; and the exploitation of the individual in "A Very Old Man with Enormous Wings."

Many of Gabriel García Márquez's short stories open in media res, apparently in the middle of a series of actions, and use leaps of time, either forward or backward, to inform the reader of the complete story. This use of time is typical of a narrative technique that measures time in at least two ways. The first way corresponds to the way in which the events are narrated; it disrupts chronological order in presenting events to the reader. The second corresponds to the sequence in which the events actually occur. Until a story has been read through to the end, only the omniscient narrator knows the actual sequence of events. The reader, little by little, is able to fit together the pieces of the "time puzzle."

The element that is central to the short story is present at the very beginning. In "Isabel's Monologue," a pregnant woman, Isabel, seems to be talking to herself. In "Balthazar's Marvelous Afternoon" a carpenter has just finished his masterpiece, a birdcage. An outside narrator interested in reporting to the "world's unbelievers" that Big Mama has died is introduced in "Big Mama's Funeral." "A Very Old Man with Enormous Wings" commences with the arrival in town of a flesh-and-blood old man with wings. However, as is typical of García Marquez's technique, as the story unfolds it demands the reader's active participation. The narrative text presents a labyrinthine structure that pays little or no attention to the chronological sequence of events.

The stories, at first impression, seem to make no sense at all. It is often unclear whose voice the readers hear or whose viewpoint they are reading. Many of the stories incorporate the absurd, the unreal, the supernatural, elements of the underworld, and magic realism, combining the fantastic and the mythic with the ordinary activities of daily life. (The Cuban novelist Alejo Carpentier first applied the term *magic realism* to literature in the late 1940s.)

The following is a brief synopsis of the five stories based on their narrative technique.

"Monologue of Isabel Watching It Rain in Macondo"

In "Isabel's Monologue," events do not unfold in chronological order; instead, the story follows Isabel's thoughts using a technique known as stream of consciousness, which describes the flow, in any given order, of actions, thoughts, and feelings as they come to mind. Although she frequently narrates in the first person singular and the title says this is a "monologue," implying a single person speaking alone, the narration leaves room for ambiguity. In Macondo, the weather is hot, but three days of consecutive rain have made a change in the temperature. To Isabel it is the temperature of a fever chill. She says, "feet sweated inside the shoes" (92). It is unclear whose feet and whose shoes were sweating. If they were Isabel's feet, she would say, "my feet, inside my shoes." However, ambiguity is a technique frequently used in García Márquez's narrative, even in a monologue. The ambiguity, however, intentionally interferes with the understanding of the story, which seems to consist of juxtaposed thoughts that come and go as Isabel quotes the words of her stepmother, her father, and her husband.

Concerning the use of time as a narrative technique, "Isabel's Monologue" depends on the stream of consciousness, a technique that places great importance on time and often makes time a theme in itself. In this short story, time is fragmented and most definitely ambiguous. The reader must decide whether the events actually occur or whether the reader is reading about a dream. The main character, Isabel, is not sure whether she is actually dreaming. As she says, she is "confused by the mix-up in time." She then adds, "Good Lord, . . . it wouldn't surprise me now if they were coming to call me to go to last Sunday's Mass" (96). The sentence construction of the ending confirms the ambiguity of the story: it starts in the present tense, then moves to a subjunctive form in the past, and then goes back to the present, only to mention an event that obviously has already taken place.

"Tuesday Siesta"

According to Harley D. Oberhelman, García Márquez has been quoted saying that "Tuesday Siesta" is his best short story, and he (García Márquez) recognizes it as one containing "purely technical tricks" (Oberhel-man 1991, 20). "Tuesday Siesta," indeed, will surprise readers with its narrative technique. The opening seems to follow a chronological order that soon is broken by a flashback (an earlier event brought up in the middle of the narration, interrupting the time sequence of the story). The use of the flashback allows the reader to start putting together the pieces of the puzzle-like story. The reader learns, through the flash-back, that the poor woman and her daughter, both dressed in black, are coming to this nameless town to bring flowers to her son's tomb. Only then do readers learn that the son was killed in an attempted robbery. The flashback, however, does not answer the ambiguity created by the use of language, and above all, by the way the story ends. The omnis-cient narrator delivers a story known fully but revealed only in frag-ments; the narrator thus creates confusion, anguish, and intrigue in the readers.

The story seems to follow a technique in which the opening of the narrative presents the reader with numerous possibilities of what the story may be about; most of those possibilities appear to be eliminated after a reading of the flashback; but then the end of the story leaves the reader, as the opening did, with numerous possibilities of interpretation.

How are the townspeople going to react to the two women? Oberhel-man, for example, sees an unfriendly town. He sees a mother that "boldly faces the ominous challenge of a hot Tuesday afternoon in the streets of an unfriendly town" (Oberhelman 1991, 22). Are the townsfolk so unfriendly as to interfere with her intent to see her son's tomb? Will they stone her for daring to break the peace of the town, first, by asso-ciation, by her son's intentions to rob an old woman's house, and second, by her stoic, proud, dignified attitude?

"Balthazar's Marvelous Afternoon"

The opening of the story, by an omniscient narrator, is in medias res. However, the order of events related to the finished cage and the selling of it evolve in a rather easy-to-follow format. The time frame reveals that Balthazar has been working on the cage for two consecutive weeks; he turned thirty in February; and Ursula has been living with him, unmar-ried, for four years. This is what the omniscient narrator knows, but time in the story is marked differently: "it was the first week of April and the heat seemed bearable because of the chirping of the cicadas" (189). The plot itself, that of selling the cage to José Montiel, follows a chronological order. The time frame of these events begins one April afternoon when Balthazar finishes the cage and ends the morning after, at five o'clock.

"Big Mama's Funeral"

In "Big Mama's Funeral" the narrative technique is similar to that of "Isabel's Monologue" in the use of a juxtaposition of events that do not follow a linear and logical story. From the funeral at the opening of the story, an omniscient narrator takes the reader through 200 years in the life of Macondo, the same town where "Isabel's Monologue" takes place.

"Big Mama's Funeral" alludes to an oral tradition. At the start of the story and at its end, the narrative technique makes it clear that the reader is reading a piece of folklore, a folktale that has been transmitted by word of mouth—the essence of what is known as folk literature. The narrative voice tells the reader that before Big Mama, her father ruled Macondo, and before her parents, her grandparents. This form of oligarchic government (a type of government by a few people, who are often related to one another) is a system that, in this story, comes to an end with the death of Big Mama.

The narrative technique in "Big Mama's Funeral" is rich in humor, irony, satire, and the use of hyperbole. The humor in "Big Mama's Funeral" can be found throughout the story, as in the following instance. As the crowds gathered for Big Mama's funeral, a large parade of beauty queens march, in single file, behind a "universal queen." There are queens for everything—a banana queen, a soybean queen, and, as the narrator says, a queen for "all the others that are omitted" (199).

Humor in García Márquez is often satirical, as in the previous quotation. A satire, in literature, often focuses on the character's vices or shortcomings, with an intent to call for change or improvement. Through humor, the narrator attacks, with wit, human folly. In the quotation about the queens, the criticism of beauty pageants is obvious.

In "Big Mama's Funeral," irony, like humor and satire, is present throughout the story. For example, the reader knows that the words of admiration and awe expressed for Big Mama indicate precisely the opposite. Certainly neither a president nor the Pope would come to the funeral of a matron who dies in a remote, unknown, little rural town. "Big Mama's Funeral" is filled with humor and satire; it cleverly censures a feudal society, where the individual is absolutely powerless.

The narrative voice uses the stream of consciousness technique, as in "Isabel's Monologue." This gives the reader the illusion that many years have gone by within the story, but in reality there are only fourteen days of narrative discourse. This is itself is a kind of hyperbole, an exaggeration of a funeral, as is the size of Big Mama. In this short story, exaggeration is a narrative technique. It becomes so matter-of-fact that the reader will laugh, while acknowledging that the narration implicitly denounces what it narrates. The story is in the form of a folktale, no doubt, but it seems to covertly underline the social and historical disgust of peoples who are tired of both omnipotence and omnipresence. Tired of everything: and Big Mama was indeed everything.

"A Very Old Man with Enormous Wings"

The narrative technique of this story is similar to the previous four yet offers two differences worth mentioning. First, the locale (the setting where the narrative takes place) is geographically different. Unlike the previous stories, this one takes place in a seashore town. Second, the time frame moves in linear form (in chronological order), from the angel's arrival to his departure, several years later.

Written in 1968, a year after the publication of *One Hundred Years of Solitude*, as Oberhelman points out, this story represents a transition from the fiction of Macondo. By this he means that the book from which this short story was taken, *The Incredible and Sad Tale of Innocent Eréndira and Her Heartless Grandmother*, differs thematically from the first two volumes of short stories, *Eyes of a Blue Dog*, and *Big Mama's Funeral*. He writes:

> The transition is to central themes later seen in his most recent fiction: exploitation on both a personal and a national scale, the extraordinary power of the human imagination, and the use of the sea as an enduring metaphor. (Oberhelman 1991, 36)

"A Very Old Man with Enormous Wings" is most definitely a story of powerful imagination and of exploitation. The reader of this short story must accept that it indeed depicts an imaginary world where angels can be old, unattractive, sickly, and yet have wings and fly. The narrative structure of this story, viewed through the treatment of both plot and character development, clearly exemplifies magic realism.

CHARACTER DEVELOPMENT

The short story, as a genre, does not have time for the extensive character development typically found in the novel. For the reader, the time of the reading is, by definition, short, even if much time passes within the short story itself, as is the case in both "Big Mama's Funeral" and "A Very Old Man with Enormous Wings."

The short story often focuses on a single component. It is a brief close-up, but not always of character. It may depict a town or an existential situation, as in "A Very Old Man with Enormous Wings," for example. In this story, Elisenda and Pelayo are types that represent the town. Rather than regarding the old man as a supernatural or heavenly creature, they keep him in their chicken coop and use him to make money. The town, unsure whether the old man represents something miraculous, comes to examine and admire the old man as a novelty but returns finally to provoke and taunt him. Later, just as Elisenda and Pelayo's interest shifts away from the old man, whom they now regard as a nuisance, the town's interest shifts in wonderment to the spider woman.

Nevertheless, there are certain important observations to be made about character development in Gabriel García Márquez's short stories. Often the depiction of a character appears as a portrait or a sketch rather than a full-blown painting, painstakingly completed over the length of a work. Even though the reader appears to witness the transformation of María del Rosario Castañeda y Montero to Big Mama on the day of her father's funeral, it is witnessed from outside the character and the story does not reveal how she developed.

Many characters appear in more than one story; a short story may sometimes provide a close-up of a single character the reader has met in a different story. Of the five short stories considered here, "Isabel's Monologue" best exemplifies this technique, which is common in the writing of Gabriel García Márquez. The continuity of character in novels, novellas, and short stories contributes to the construction of a coherent, credible world. Many of the same characters alternately play larger and then smaller roles. Apart from his pivotal role in *One Hundred Years of Solitude*, many characters in the novellas and short stories also know Colonel Aureliano Buendía. Among these short stories, he is mentioned with admiration in "Big Mama's Funeral" and "Tuesday Siesta."

An additional observation about character development regards the types of characters in the short stories: with the exception of Isabel in "Isabel's Monologue," the main female characters represent strong women. These include the strong-willed mother in "Tuesday Siesta," the ambitious and domineering Ursula in "Balthazar's Afternoon," the equally domineering Elisenda in "A Very Old Man with Enormous Wings," and, most definitely, the unlimited power of Big Mama in "Big Mama's Funeral." The model for the female character in García Márquez's writing is, without a doubt, a strong, iron-willed woman who never succumbs. She faces and fights the adversities brought on her, either through societal codes or through her own marital status. From Ursula Iguarán, the matriarch in *One Hundred Years of Solitude*, to Fermina Daza, in *Love in the Time of Cholera*, García Márquez seems to pay tribute to female characters in his fictional works. The same can be said of his portrayal of nonfictional female characters, as in his journalistic work, *News of a Kidnapping*.

There is one additional characteristic of García Márquez's short stories that appears seemingly obvious, that is, the less than spiritual role of the Church. The Church as an institution, through the character development of its leaders, appears more as a bureaucratic organism than as a spiritual leader. The Church hierarchy is too busy, for example, to pay attention to the needs of the smalltown clergyman who writes asking for advice regarding the angel. The knowledge of Father Gonzaga in "A Very Old Man with Enormous Wings" is as limited as that of a woodcutter—the job Father Gonzaga held before becoming a priest. Another example is the priest in "Tuesday Siesta." He seems skeptical of the things he says and not interested in the pain of a mother whose son was killed. While these two clerical figures are depicted as rather indifferent, the lay members of the congregation do not fare much better. The churchgoers in "Balthazar's Marvelous Afternoon" do not seem to remember the commandment to love thy neighbor as thyself. They walk by Balthazar, who is lying in the street, and they ignore him because he is drunk. In García Márquez's fiction, the clergy are not men equipped with theological training or answering a calling or vocation, but simply men doing a job.

What follows is a more detailed description of character development in each of the five short stories examined in this chapter.

"Monologue of Isabel Watching It Rain in Macondo"

The characters in "Isabel's Monologue" are taken from García Márquez's first novella, *Leaf Storm*. As is the case in the novella, Isabel is married to Martín. In the short story, Isabel is the main character as would be expected from the title. Ironically, however, Isabel differs in character development from the women typically depicted by García Márquez. Indeed, Isabel is their opposite. She is weak in character, subservient to her husband and her situation, inactive, and bereft of free will. The story depicts her as motionless. While everyone around her seems to be in motion, she sits and ponders. As she watches the torrential rains fall, she loses her sense of time and of reality.

"Tuesday Siesta"

Character development in "Tuesday Siesta" is of particular interest to the reader because the story centers on a dead man outside the narrative time. He was a thief named Carlos Centeno Ayala, and he is the only character with a name. His mother, the main character, comes to town to pay homage to him at the cemetery. Her twelve-year-old daughter accompanies her. On the one hand, she is an outsider, who is rejected by the community. On the other hand, she is a strong individual who defies the community. As is often the case with García Márquez's female characters, she is the embodiment of a strong, solid, decisive, goal-oriented woman, who will remind readers of Ursula Iguarán in *One Hundred Years of Solitude* and Fermina Daza in *Love in the Time of Cholera*. As might be expected of her character, she manages to get the key for the cemetery from the town's priest, walks to the cemetery, leaves flowers on her son's grave, and leaves town as quietly as she entered. Although she is the mother of a thief, she leaves behind an image of dignity and pride.

"Balthazar's Marvelous Afternoon"

This story is named for Balthazar, but once again a female character, Ursula, truly plays center stage. Ursula, who is a strong character, usually makes the economic decisions for herself and Balthazar. Although not married, Ursula and Balthazar live as husband and wife. The character development of this couple is reminiscent of the character development used in *No One Writes to the Colonel*. They are developed as the antithesis of one another. He is a dreamer, who builds a birdcage for a child without worrying about price. She is a pragmatist (a practical person) who views his work in monetary terms. As is the case with the old couple in *No One Writes to the Colonel*, Ursula and Balthazar complement each other. However, like the old colonel in *No One Writes to the Colonel*, Balthazar makes the final decision for the couple when he decides to give away the birdcage.

"Big Mama's Funeral"

The number of characters in "Big Mama's Funeral" is large and varied. There is one, nevertheless, who outshines all the rest: María del Rosario Castañeda y Morales.

Possessing the characteristics of a rigid matriarch, this woman's Christian name means little or nothing to the townsfolk, who think of her as Big Mama. Her mighty power has been passed down to her and her predecessors, from generation to generation, for a total of 200 years. Her power is omnipresent (is present everywhere at all times). It permeates all aspects of life in Macondo: the social, political, economic, and moral systems all obey her rule. Nothing escapes her power, supervision, influence, and right to approve; above her is only God, and beneath her is everybody else. Her power is absolute: she has power over people, places, and both material and immaterial things. To the people of Macondo, her rule is untouchable, undeniable, and indivisible. Her power over them is second nature, and they cannot think of her as a mortal being.

However, as is the case in Greek mythology, where heroes often have a fatal flaw, this tropical goddess suffers from a lack of love and from infertility. Her kingdom is one of abundance, but her personal life is one of solitude and she dies a childless virgin. As a consequence, her ancestral line comes to an end. There will be no more Big Mamas to inherit the absolute power her family had enjoyed for 200 years. Ironically, after her death, no one remembers her rule. On the contrary, everyone—the Pope, the president, the beauty queens, the crowds—now feels free to exercise free will. The only one who might have objected is gone.

Beyond the literal meaning of the story, there is a clear analogy between Big Mama and the Spanish rule in the Spanish Americas. It is not difficult to see the parallels between what goes on in the short story and the feudal authorities, the loss of the Spanish prestige in Europe, and the decline of the Spanish power in Latin America. A feeling of emancipation is reflected in the collective character of the townsfolk.

"A Very Old Man with Enormous Wings"

All the characters in this story, with the exception of the angel, share a common characteristic: they all believe in winged angels, but in a pre-conceived fashion. Angels cannot be old, ugly, or sickly. Everyone—from the priest, Elisenda, Pelayo, and the neighbor to the town in general—seems to react in the same way, within the same parameters. The townspeople, as character, can, therefore, be viewed equally well through Elisenda, Pelayo, and Father Gonzaga.

Elisenda and Pelayo are simple people. They live under very poor economic circumstances and their only child is sick. When Pelayo comes upon the winged old man he does not know what to think of him. Neither does his wife. Their frame of reference has no concept for such a reality. Their first response to it is awe, but after a short while they start to find the winged old man familiar, even human-like. Their neighbor, an elderly woman who supposedly understands all matters of life and death, calls the winged old man an angel. The townspeople, however, crowd into Elisenda and Pelayo's house. Their curiosity brings them to see this winged old man, whom they treat like a circus animal. Although the narrative voice never describes the winged old man as an angel, the characters do, and decide to put it to a test. Elisenda and Pelayo capitalize on the townspeople's doubt and start to charge everyone who wants to see him. Indirectly, the angel does perform the miracles he is supposed to. The sick child of Elisenda and Pelayo gets well, and their poor economic status changes. The angel, nonetheless, does not get any better treatment. He continues, until the end, to be treated as a circus animal.

Elisenda and Pelayo do not behave any differently than the rest of the townspeople. They, like the people who come from afar to see the winged old man, seem conditioned by their ignorance and superstition. They all want the old man to perform miracles as proof of his supernatural powers. They want to use the winged old man as a civil, military, and cultural figure. Some people even think of him as a stud for a new super-race. In the end, the entire furor over the angel shifts to a newer arrival—another freak-like spectacle, the spider woman. The townspeople move on to another object of amusement, and the angel is left behind. Only then, when no one is paying attention, does the very old man with enormous wings fly away.

Father Gonzaga, as a clerical figure, is called upon by the townspeople to clarify whether the old man is indeed an angel. However, Father Gonzaga is only a simple and ordinary man who was a lumberjack before he was ordained. He consults a catechism book but finds no answers. Father Gonzaga then turns to the Church's bureaucracy: the bishop and the Pope. However, instead of an answer, Father Gonzaga receives more questions from the Church authorities. The problem, however, solves itself when the townspeople's fascination with the angel shifts to the spider woman. Since the Vatican does not respond any further to Father Gonzaga, he loses interest as well.

Thus, the town as character is portrayed as indifferent, not firm in its beliefs, frivolous, superstitious, and superficial. This is a town that moves back and forth, lacking firm convictions.

THEMATIC ISSUES

The interpretation of thematic issues may vary from reader to reader. For example, the role of the Church, a rather stable and influential power in Latin America, seems to pass unnoticed. The role played by the priest in "Tuesday Siesta" is irrelevant, and therefore it goes unnoticed. In "A Very Old Man with Enormous Wings," the priest not only has a minor role in the story, but the townsfolk seem to ignore him. The five short stories discussed in this chapter are individual portraits that can be better seen by thematic issues that tie them together. These are themes that can be perceived throughout García Márquez's works because they are either personal or universal themes. These are themes that appeal to everyone and that stand the test of time. The themes examined here are: the stranger in town, greed versus generosity, lack of love between a couple, and solitude.

The theme of a stranger in town, an outsider who does not fit into the community, is an important one in both "Tuesday Siesta" and "A Very Old Man with Enormous Wings." In both short stories the outsider fails to fit into the social structure of the town. In "Tuesday Siesta," the outsider is an older woman who may be known to the community. She walks the streets as someone who knows exactly where she is going. Everyone in town watches her arrival and departure, but no one talks to her, perhaps out of fear. The woman has come to visit her son's grave. The townsfolk, as if to watch a parade, come out to see her. There appears to be no pity for her loss. She comes and leaves without human contact, except for the priest. The reader feels the tension building and wonders whether she and her twelve-year-old daughter may be stoned to death. The tension experienced by the reader is similar to the tension in *Leaf Storm* (Chapter 3), and for the same reason—a stranger who has been rejected by the community. In "A Very Old Man with Enormous Wings," the old man plays the same role. The townsfolk do not interact with him; instead, they treat him as a circus animal whose only value is entertainment.

The theme of greed versus generosity is clearly seen in "Balthazar's Marvelous Afternoon." Balthazar, a poor carpenter who seems to play a messianic (savior) role, is represented as having a heart of gold and a love for children. His concubine, however, can be viewed as the human representation of greed. While Balthazar is content to give his work, a masterfully built birdcage, to José Montiel's boy for free, Ursula incites Balthazar to charge a large amount. It is due to her greed that Balthazar ends up having to give the birdcage away. She wants sixty pesos for the birdcage, which José Montiel, the boy's father, refuses to pay. José Montiel argues that adults should not negotiate with children (143). José Montiel plays the role of the heartless rich man in town, like that played by Sabas in the novella *No One Writes to the Colonel*.

Another theme that seems to appear in several of the short stories of this chapter is the lack of love between a couple. In "Isabel's Monologue," Martín, Isabel's husband, does not love her, even though she is pregnant with his child. In the story, he speaks badly of her. In *Leaf Storm*, where the pair is more fully developed, Martín abandons Isabel and their ten-year-old son. In "Balthazar's Marvelous Afternoon," Ursula and Balthazar are not married but have lived together for four years. In a small town such as theirs, Ursula can thus be seen as a woman unworthy of marriage. Likewise, in "A Very Old Man with Enormous Wings," Elisenda and Pelayo do not seem to enjoy a loving relationship. They seem more interested in benefiting from the old winged man than even in taking care of their sick son.

The one theme that envelopes all five stories, as might be expected by readers of García Márquez, is the theme of solitude. One of the most prominent themes in Gabriel García Márquez's work, it interests many readers perhaps because it is a natural condition for humankind. Ironically, to be alone, in solitude, the individual needs the presence of others. Only when the individual is aware of others can he or she experience solitude.

The setting in all five stories is an isolated town that seems to have been forgotten by civilization. The main characters in each story also suffer from physical isolation, another form of solitude. In "Tuesday Siesta," the entire town rejects the thief's mother. No one seems to know where she came from or to care about her. In fact, there is a mutual hatred, as reflected in the woman's words and the attitude of the town. Do not even drink their water, she tells her daughter, and above all, no matter what, do not cry (101).

In "A Very Old Man with Enormous Wings," the winged old man is viewed as an object, not a human being. He is isolated in a cage as if he were, indeed, an animal. His isolation is total. He does not speak the same language, ignores the town's social and cultural codes, and is the only one of his kind in the town.

At the end of "Balthazar's Marvelous Afternoon," Balthazar lies drunk in the street as if he were dead yet no one offers him assistance, not even the Christian women who are seen walking to church that very morning.

In "Isabel's Monologue," the solitude suffered by Isabel is perhaps the most poignant variety that a person may bear. She seems to suffer so severely that she talks to herself as if she has lost her mind.

In "Big Mama's Funeral," the solitude of Big Mama, ironically, is the greatest of all. Everything about her is big, including her solitude. Although she is as rich as King Midas, Big Mama lacks what humans need most, love and sexual companionship. She dies a virgin, with no family to mourn her passing or continue her bloodline. She is indeed the epitome of solitude, alone in the forgotten town of Macondo, where, according to the narrative voice in *One Hundred Years of Solitude*, none of its inhabitants will have a second opportunity on earth.

ALTERNATIVE READING: RECEPTION THEORY

Reception theory focuses on the reader's role in literature, as opposed to analytical criticism, a literary theory that pays particular attention to the text as a self-contained work (see Chapter 3). As such, reception theory is interested in the act of reading—that is, the mechanics and use of language, as interpreted by the reader. It focuses on how the reader responds to the facts found in the narrative, the inferences a reader makes when reading a given text, and methods that help to bring the reader into a form of consciousness that allows for the criticism of his or her own identity and beliefs. Thus, the reader is an active entity in the creation of meaning. The text has meanings that are activated only when the reader reads them. Thus, it is up to the reader to activate the potential viewpoints present in the text through which García Márquez interprets the world. In the latter half of the 1970s, literary critic Wolfgang Iser was among the theoreticians who paid special attention to reception theory. According to Iser, all texts have certain gaps, which the reader must fill to derive his or her own understanding of the text. The text itself, however, demands that the reader react on the basis of what the text contains.

Reception theory critics generally group the readers into two categories: the *real reader* and the *hypothetical reader*. The real reader is defined by a specific reading public such as the one in literature classes or those whose responses are recorded by critics in relation to a given literary work; this reader is also identified as the implied reader. Thus, the real reader and the implied reader are the same.

The hypothetical reader is a category often identified as the so-called ideal reader (Iser 27). The hypothetical reader can be constructed or reconstructed from a social and historical knowledge of the times. The hypothetical reader (also identified by theoreticians as the ideal reader), of all possible readers is the one, Iser notes, born from the brain of the philologist (someone who studies languages from linguistic and historical backgrounds), the critic, or the author him- or herself (Iser 28). The hypothetical reader is the one capable of understanding exactly what the author meant when writing the text; as this is an impossibility, this reader is purely fictional and has no basis in reality (Iser 29).

Reception theory is seemingly prescriptive. This literary theory assumes that the real reader may be able to activate, or interpret, the gaps that the author intentionally leaves for the reader to fill. Reception theory allows for different possible ways of reading the same text. The real reader is capable of, and willing to, understand the text individually but sees the role of the text to be stronger. It is through the text that the implied reader makes inferences, elaborates illusions, and arrives at conclusions, in accordance with his or her historical, cultural, and individual circumstances.

The five short stories selected for this chapter are all challenging. Being able to interpret them successfully puts great demands on the reader. By examining "Tuesday Siesta" in detail in terms of a reception theory model, readers should better understand how the theory works in practice.

How does the reader react to the use of language in the opening sentence of "Tuesday Siesta"? What are the reader's inferences when the following is read: "the train emerged from the quivering tunnel of sandy rocks, began to cross the symmetrical, interminable banana plantations, and the air became humid and they couldn't feel the sea breeze any more" (99).

The reader may ask: who are *they*? Are there two people or more? Are *they* all of the same gender and age group? Are *they* a couple, and if so, are they married or unmarried? Are *they* a father and son or daughter? Are *they* just friends? The possibilities for interpreting the *facts* of the opening sentence are numerous and may vary from reader to reader.

A reader may also ask: where is this story taking place? Any attentive reader may imagine a tropical place where banana trees grow near the sea, but the question remains as to exactly where.

The fact that so many speculations and inquiries may be drawn from the opening sentence proves, on the one hand, that most readers bring to the text their own active participation, whether knowingly or not. On the other hand, as the reader continues, the text answers many of the inquiries. According to British literary critic Terry Eagleton, the reader makes implicit connections, fills in gaps, draws inferences, and tests out hunches. The reader, in the terminology of reception theory, as Eagleton notes, *concretizes* the literary work: without his or her continuous active participation there would be no literary work at all (Eagleton 66).

"Tuesday Siesta," as well as the other short stories reviewed in this chapter, is filled with *indeterminacies* (elements within a narrative text that depend for their effect or result on the reader's interpretation). However, due to ambiguity in the use of language, the interpretations may vary in a number of different ways.

The reader's response to the indeterminacies (questions) of *they* and *where* in "Tuesday Siesta" might be influenced by his or her own interests and viewpoints. The reader eventually knows that the indeterminate *they* means an old woman and her young daughter, both dressed in black and traveling by train. However, the more the reader learns in response to his or her inquiries, the more complex the text becomes.

At the end of the short story the reader may not necessarily have answers to all the indeterminacies (questions) that the narrative may have provoked. Was the old woman once a citizen living in this town? Is the town so typical that we need not know its name? Why is there so much pride and dignity in the old woman's behavior? The reader has to end the story on his or her own terms, for the ending is an indeterminacy.

In reception theory, the act of reading is always a dynamic one, moving both in time and space. The reader, whether successful or not, strives to make sense from what he or she reads. The reader organizes the material as it is being read, selecting what he or she considers relevant and concretizing certain information. In concretizing, the reader attempts to see in the text not what he or she is already prepared to see and understand, but what "Tuesday Siesta" suggests. This in turn allows the reader to elaborate one or more perspectives that culminate in an *integrated illusion*. An integrated illusion may be temporary in the sense that what the reader holds to be a fact on one page may prove to be altogether different after he or she turns the page. Illusion may also operate in the sense that what the reader comes to understand might be what he or she wanted to read into the story. The reader brings into the story his or her own education and upbringing, including religious beliefs, race, gender, and age.

As the title of "Tuesday Siesta" implies: "at that hour [when the two women got off the train], weighted down by drowsiness, the town was taking a siesta" (101). The reader concretizes the information and elaborates an image, which, in reception theory, is referred to as an illusion of the townsfolk. This illusion is almost immediately contradicted by the text. What comes next in the story contradicts both the short story's title and the illusion that the reader was concretizing: the townsfolk, at that hour, are not asleep and instead carefully observe the two female characters in their progress through the town.

The reader's efforts—of trying to reconcile the indeterminacies (gaps or questions) of the text with his or her own illusions—continue throughout the text, for García Márquez's short stories do not necessarily move through time in a linear fashion. He employs *backgrounds* and *foregrounds* (the use of devices and techniques such as the flashback or the interior monologue so that language calls attention to itself). He also creates different layers of meaning, which the reader continually attempts to understand, either consciously or not.

García Márquez deliberately leaves elements of his short stories in a rather vague and often ambiguous fashion. This is, indeed, his writing style. To be able to read García Márquez's short stories according to reception theory, the reader must be willing to read the text with a critical awareness that allows for a viewpoint different from his or her customary expectations. This is not necessarily because of García Márquez's use of magic realism, the absurd, the supernatural, or the elements of the underworld, but because the main premise of reception theory is a belief that the act of reading should open the reader to new viewpoints. Through the act of reading the reader must be willing to question his or her values and allow them to be transformed.

6

One Hundred Years of Solitude
(1967)

Gabriel García Márquez's *One Hundred Years of Solitude* was first published on May 30, 1967, in Buenos Aires, Argentina. The cover of the
first edition, which was never repeated, depicted the silhouette of a galleon floating amid trees against a blue background, which contrasts with
three geometric yellow flowers on the lower part of the cover in the
foreground (Cobo Borda 101). The novel was an immediate best-seller in
Spanish: "not since *Madame Bovary* [by the French author Gustave Flau-
bert] has a book been received with the simultaneous popular success
and critical acclaim that greeted *One Hundred Years of Solitude*" (Janes
1991, 13). In three and a half years, the book sold almost a half million
copies. As a result, previous books by García Márquez were reprinted
in large numbers in the Spanish-speaking world (Vargas Llosa 78). When
translations of *One Hundred Years of Solitude* were published, the novel
achieved additional acclaim and honors: in 1969, in Italy, the book won
the Premio Chianchiano (Chianchiano Award); the same year, in France,
it won the Prix du meilleur livre étranger (Award for best Foreign Book);
in 1970, in the United States, it was selected as one of the best twelve
books of the year by *Time* magazine. Although it is difficult to read because of its literary technique, its appeal is that of a classic, which bridges
the worlds of academia and popular culture. According to Jorge Luis
Borges, the Argentine poet, essayist, and short-story writer, *One Hundred
Years of Solitude* is a book as "profound as the cosmos and capable of
endless interpretations" (quoted in Cobo Borda 106).

The Buendía Family Tree
(According to José Miguel Oviedo)

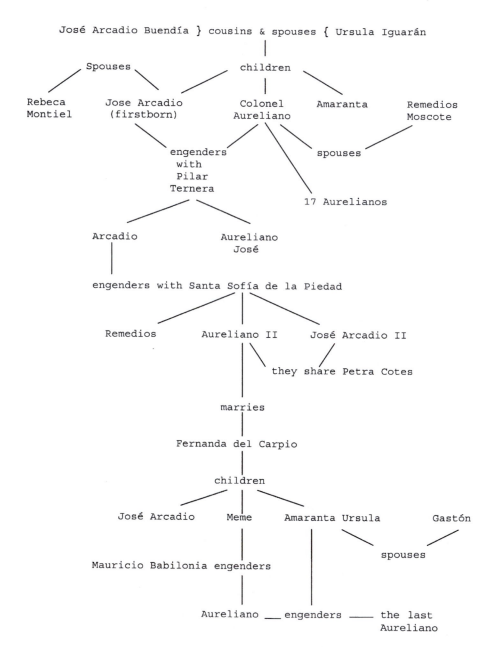

José Arcadio Buendía } cousins & spouses { Ursula Iguarán

Spouses — children

Rebeca
Montiel

Jose Arcadio
(firstborn)

Colonel
Aureliano

Amaranta

Remedios
Moscote

engenders
with
Pilar
Ternera

spouses

17 Aurelianos

Arcadio

Aureliano
José

engenders with Santa Sofía de la Piedad

Remedios

Aureliano II

José Arcadio II

they share Petra Cotes

marries

Fernanda del Carpio

children

José Arcadio

Meme

Amaranta Ursula

Gastón

spouses

Mauricio Babilonia engenders

Aureliano ___ engenders ____ the last
Aureliano

As many critics have noted, *One Hundred Years of Solitude* was written in eighteen months, following a period in which García Márquez suffered from a writer's block. However, *One Hundred Years of Solitude* was indeed in gestation since the late 1940s, when García Márquez was in his early twenties (see Chapters 3 and 5). *One Hundred Years of Solitude* had been appearing as if in segments, with the invention of mythical Macondo and Colonel Aureliano Buendía; the use of a cyclical form of time; and the repetitiveness of events, images of magic realism, and elements of the underworld and the absurd; but suddenly, like pieces of a puzzle, everything was brought together and seemed to fit perfectly. Although *Leaf Storm* chronologically first introduces the saga of Macondo, *One Hundred Years of Solitude* encompasses the beginning and the end, the *alpha* and the *omega*, the genesis and the apocalypse, of Macondo and its people. The landscape of mythical Macondo and several of the main characters of *Leaf Storm* (1955), *No One Writes to the Colonel* (1961), *Big Mama's Funeral* (1962), and *In Evil Hour* (1962) announce the birth of this masterpiece.

PLOT DEVELOPMENT

Different plot developments may become apparent depending on where the reader focuses his or her attention. The reader may focus on the discovery and Spanish colonization of the Americas; on the wars and fights between the Liberal and Conservative Parties; on American neo-colonialism; on the effects of a dictatorship; on love, the lack of love, eroticism, or incest; or on the solitude and isolation of a town and its people. Any plot the reader chooses has such a plethora of information that he or she would be hard-pressed to organize and recall everything that is taking place.

The lineage and events of the Buendía family, however, can be seen as the main story in the narrative, regardless of interpretation. However, this still does not make it an easy story to follow. The difficulty in understanding the story can be attributed to the enormous amount of information given in each chapter, and indeed on each page. Literary critic Harold Bloom wrote that his first impression, on reading *One Hundred Years of Solitude*, was that of an aesthetic battle fatigue, since every page is so full of life that it is beyond the capacity of any single reader to absorb (Bloom 1). Mexican author and literary critic Carlos Fuentes, before Bloom, affirmed that *One Hundred Years of Solitude* should be read at least twice to begin to understand it. Most readers find themselves overwhelmed by the number of events and characters involved and become unable to maintain the plot's thread. This often leads readers to put the book down unfinished. However, diligent readers will be left with the empowering feeling of having read about a universe filled with strong women and men who dare to dream. *One Hundred Years of Solitude* is nowadays seen as a classic of contemporary literature, a tour de force of great virtuosity and strength.

One Hundred Years of Solitude begins in medias res (in the middle of events) and covers a wide focus. The omniscient narrative voice introduces great suspense at the very opening of the novel when the reader is faced with a violent image: one of the main characters, Colonel Aureliano Buendía, is about to be killed by a firing squad. The omniscient narrative voice knows everything that happens to the characters and understands why they behave as they do. The chapter ends and the execution fails to take place. Although the reader is given enough information to imagine the founding of Macondo and the major roles of Ursula and the gypsy Melquíades, the opening chapter does not provide enough information to find out why Colonel Aureliano Buendía is to be killed. In fact, the colonel never is killed. As readers learn several chapters later, José Arcadio saves his younger brother, the colonel, from the firing squad. Within the opening chapter the reader goes back in time and witnesses the "memory" that opens the novel. It concerns the time when the founding father, José Arcadio Buendía, paid for a chance to see, along with his two sons, a block of ice. The contemporary reader may fail to see a block of ice as a great invention, but for a rural Colombian man at the end of the nineteenth century, it was an invention beyond measure. José Arcadio Buendía is not naive, he is simply unaware of what is happening outside Macondo. This is a man who does not know about the magnet and sees dentures as a form of magic.

Succeeding chapters introduce José Arcadio and give more background on his brother, Aureliano, who grows up to become a colonel. Aureliano marries Remedios Moscote, with whom he has no children; however, he does engender seventeen sons, all named Aureliano, each with different mothers. Amaranta, the only daughter of Ursula and José Arcadio Buendía, never marries, preferring to stay home and help around the house. Amaranta's name reappears at the end of the novel, in that of Amaranta Ursula. Amaranta Ursula gives birth to a son out of wedlock. It is this son, named Aureliano Babilonia, who will be the last of the dynasty of Buendías. He will fulfill the prophecy that one of the Buendías would be born with a pig's tail as a result of incest.

The repetition of names causes confusion to the reader, although the author is simply reflecting the Spanish tradition of passing the father's name on to his firstborn, a tradition also found in Europe and the United States. José Arcadio, by contrast, is recognized by his monumental size and is referred to by the author as José Arcadio, while his father is referred to as José Arcadio Buendía. José Arcadio, before leaving Macondo to join a group of gypsies, leaves Pilar Ternera pregnant with his son. When the baby is born, he is also named Arcadio, honoring both the father and the grandfather. This chaotic and circular way of repeating the names *Arcadio* and *Aureliano* is discussed in depth later in this chapter under the section on character development.

Pilar Ternera is the daughter of one of the founding families, but her social status is beneath the Buendías. She lives a life of no restrictions, unattached and carefree. She initiates young Aureliano (the legendary colonel) into sexual matters and ends up having a son by him named Aureliano José. These two grandchildren of the Buendías, born to Pilar Ternera, confirm the family's downfall initiated by the incestuous marriage of their grandparents, founders of Macondo. Both grandchildren are the first Buendía bastards in a town where illegitimacy is far from the exception. Although Colonel Aureliano Buendía fathers seventeen sons, plus Aureliano José, these eighteen grandchildren's lives contribute minimally to the way in which the plot of *One Hundred Years of Solitude* unfolds.

For over half of *One Hundred Years of Solitude*, the life of Colonel Aureliano Buendía functions as the leading thread to the plot. Some readers may choose him as the central protagonist of the novel, although he dies—of old age, defeated, without any honors, ignored by the crowds and in complete solitude—while the novel continues. His own family is not aware that he is dead until the next day at eleven in the morning. His whole life seems like one big failure. He loses all the wars he fights, and none of his eighteen sons continues his bloodline. It is through Arcadio, the Buendías' grandson, that the lineage and the plot continue. With his lover, Santa Sofía de la Piedad, Arcadio fathers three children: Remedios the Beauty, Aureliano Segundo, and José Arcadio Segundo. These great-grandchildren of the original Buendías continue the emphasis on the circular aspect of the plot. Remedios the Beauty is named after Remedios Moscote, the child-wife of Colonel Aureliano Buendía. Remedios the Beauty is free of small-town conventionalisms. Unaware of her eroticism and her beauty, she prefers the solitude of the house, where she goes around nude. However, her beauty is tinged with tragedy, which leads those who become attracted to her to their death.

Like their grandfather (José Arcadio) and their grand-uncle (Colonel

Aureliano Buendía) before them, Aureliano Segundo and José Arcadio Segundo also share the same woman (Petra Cotes), but no children are born of her. However, Aureliano Segundo marries Fernanda del Carpio and does have three children with her to carry forward the Buendía name. Fernanda del Carpio brings to the Buendías the refinement they lack but also the prejudices they had lacked as well. Although Ursula, the founding mother, accepts the first two bastards (Arcadio and Aureliano José) as members of the family, Fernanda del Carpio, who was educated "to be a queen" (222), feels compelled by social and moral prejudices to hide the pregnancy of her daughter, Meme. When the child of the love between Meme and Mauricio Babilonia is born, Fernanda del Carpio hides the identity of her grandson. This child, also named Aureliano (Aureliano Babilonia), best describes the confinement and solitude of the Buendía descendents. By way of his solitude and confinement, he manages to translate the parchments written by Melquíades in Sanskrit. As Aureliano begins to decipher the parchments, he (the fictional reader) and we (the real readers—those with the book in their hands) somehow come to understand why the plot development is so difficult to follow. He decodes: "Melquíades had not put events in the order of man's conventional time, but had concentrated a century of daily episodes in such a way that they coexisted in one instant" (446). As Aureliano Babilonia reads the parchments, he begins to read of his own life. He learns that the object of his love is his aunt, Amaranta Ursula, and that the baby boy they have was supposed to be born with a pig's tail and eaten by ants. Aureliano Babilonia is thus deciphering the instant he is living.

The labyrinthine plot, viewed through the Buendías' lineage, comes to an end as the novel ends. As Aureliano Babilonia deciphers the parchments, he and the reader both come to understand that the end is apocalyptical. He knows he will never leave the room of what is left of the Buendías' house. He knows his death is imminent. He reads that the town of Macondo will be wiped out by the twirling wind and erased from the map "when Aureliano Babilonia would finish deciphering the parchments" (448). However, Aureliano Babilonia continues to decipher the parchments. Why would anybody continue to read in the knowledge that it would speed up his own death? This is left up to the reader to decide. There are those who say that Aureliano Babilonia continues to read and others who believe that he stops as if in a freeze-frame.

The end of *One Hundred Years of Solitude* is indeed puzzling. Aureliano, the last of the Buendía dynasty, is decoding Melquíades' parchments. He comes to understand that he will not be able to leave the room in the house where he is reading because Macondo will be erased from the surface of the earth. This is written in Melquíades' parchments. Would he then stop reading and thus stop the destruction of Macondo—and his own destruction? Literary critic Emir Rodríguez-Monegal thinks that is exactly what Aureliano does. "He, Aureliano, is petrified forever in the last line in the act of reading" (Rodríguez-Monegal 152).

GENRE AND NARRATIVE STRUCTURE

One Hundred Years of Solitude can be considered the magic realist novel par excellence, but only at the expense of simplifying it. In an effort to be *objective*, some literary critics began referring to novels such as *One Hundred Years of Solitude* as "Novela Total." The term probably needs no translation—and a translation would probably fail to describe anything. In the late 1960s most critics in Spanish were satisfied with the term *Novela Total* and Anglo critics with the term *New Latin American Novel*.

Although stating that the New Latin American Novel could not yet be baptized under a given name, the Mexican novelist Carlos Fuentes was ready to group the writings of García Márquez, Vargas Llosa, José Donoso, and Manuel Puig with writers such as William Faulkner, Malcolm Lowry, Herman Brock, and William Golding. The last four, wrote Fuentes, went back to the poetic roots of literature. Through the use of language and the self-conscious structuring of the novel, rather than through psychology and intrigue, these writers created a form of reality that attempts to be *totalizing* inasmuch as it invents a second reality, which is parallel to the one outside the text. Through this totalizing second reality within the text, the reader of *One Hundred Years of Solitude* may or may not recognize the hidden part of the truth that the novel unfolds, but it exists regardless.

The broad scope of Carlos Fuentes's analysis encompasses American and European influences or similarities in the way *One Hundred Years of Solitude* deals with language, time, and space in order to unfold the story of the text.

One Hundred Years of Solitude opens in medias res, but unlike *Leaf Storm* (see Chapter 3), where the beginning is also the end, in *One Hundred Years of Solitude* this is not the case. Discretely divided into twenty chapters (which are not numbered), the time span of the novel is roughly between 1820 and 1927 (hence the title, *One Hundred Years of Solitude*). However, there are occasional references back to the sixteenth century, as if to suggest the beginning of the colonization of Spanish America.

(One example is the episode where José Arcadio Buendía finds a galleon.) While the geographic space seems to be limited to the Buendías' home and the town of Macondo, if the reader thinks of it as an allegory (a story with a double or multiple meaning: a primary meaning, that of the story itself, plus other meanings), *One Hundred Years of Solitude* can be seen as taking place wherever the reader imagines.

Unlike *Leaf Storm* or the short stories "Monologue of Isabel Watching It Rain in Macondo" and "Tuesday Siesta" (see Chapter 5), where García Márquez strives to make use of experimental modern techniques such as stream of consciousness or interior monologue, and the flashback, *One Hundred Years of Solitude* employs what can be referred to as traditional writing: the dominance of make-believe over realism (the representation of life and nature without idealization) and the dominance of an omniscient narrative.

Most critics see *One Hundred Years of Solitude* as a novel that can be read in a myriad of ways, allowing multiple interpretations including the mythological and historical. Three decades after its publication, the interpretations are countless. Without being exhaustive, the narrative structure of *One Hundred Years of Solitude* contains the following examples of literary constructs: popular culture through scenes of the daily life of a Hispanic rural town, with sacred rituals and secular celebrations; repetitiveness; hyperbole; a chaotic time frame due to a circular narration; religious elements; eroticism; social and political conflict; and myth.

The narrative voice is that of an omniscient narrator. Through this voice the reader comes to know the life of six generations of the Buendía family, whose members are founders of Macondo, and both witnesses and participants in the rise, fall, and total destruction of the community through its civil wars, foreign exploitation, plagues, incestuous and non-incestuous love, isolation, death, and solitude. The omniscient narrator can be seen both inside or outside the text and sometimes even as a character witness, knowing everything that happens to the characters but remaining apart from them. The narrator is outside the text when telling the readers, for example, that Colonel Aureliano Buendía is about to be killed by a firing squad at the start of the novel. Shortly thereafter, the omniscient narrator appears as witness when we read the descriptions of the genesis of Macondo and the yearly visits of a family of gypsies lead by Melquíades. Much later in the novel, the omniscient narrator again appears as witness when noting that the shooting of Colonel Aureliano Buendía by the firing squad never took place.

The omniscient narration seems to be inhabited by the pervasive presence of the irrational and the supernatural. Melquíades, leader of the gypsies and fictional author of the Buendías' story, survives leprosy, beriberi, and the bubonic plague; he eventually dies but then is resurrected. José Arcadio Buendía, the founding father, is said to have had an imagination bigger than miracles and magic put together. From the start of the novel, the villagers of Macondo are convinced, as is his wife, Ursula, that José Arcadio Buendía "had lost his reason" (5).

The story told in *One Hundred Years of Solitude* is believable, but the facts that unfold are exaggerated, blown out of proportion, and even irrational, as if to mock the act of storytelling by mocking what is told, the way it is told, and why it is told. The exaggeration becomes comical, and as a result, the reader ceases to see it as irrational and perceives it instead as something possible. The excesses of gluttony, cruelty, virility, sexual potency, violence, death, longevity, and solitude are all treated in an obviously illogical fashion. The fact that the narrative voice recounts such irrational events in a most natural way makes the reader overlook the irrational and therefore agree with what he or she reads, while still accepting its irrationality at some level. Remedios the Beauty, for example, rises to heaven as effortlessly as if she were simply taking the elevator to the top of the Empire State Building. The narrative structure looks at the irrational as daily routine, as matter-of-fact. This, in short, is one way of explaining the rather open-ended concept of magic realism.

Another visible construct of the narrative structure is the concept of two forces in opposition: examples include love and death, the fight between liberals and conservatives, and the juxtaposition of the brothers José Arcadio and Aureliano. José Arcadio is the first to be born to the Buendía family and Aureliano is the legendary Colonel Aureliano Buendía. They can be seen as the antithesis of each other.

CHARACTER DEVELOPMENT

Character development in *One Hundred Years of Solitude* is as complex as the novel itself. This complexity can be observed in the large number of characters inhabiting the novel and the tradition of passing on the first name of the father to his firstborn. The repetition of names creates chaos and confuses the reader. The worlds of Aurelianos and Arcadios (for males), of Ursulas and Amarantas (for females) seem to weave a kind of tapestry where the threads are not as important as the whole picture. García Márquez does with character development what artist Maurits Cornelis (M. C.) Escher did with optical illusions, creating repeated patterns, impossible constructions, and infinite space. The reader is not always sure of who is being referred to, for these names may carry either a symbolic or an allegoric meaning, depending on the reader's interpretation (see the section in Chapter 5 on Reception Theory).

Trying to describe each character individually would be too time-consuming and complex to be useful. However, the main characters can be grouped by the characteristics they share. Female characters, for example, are developed as emotional beings who experience both love and hate. The female characters are drawn between the love and passion they feel for their men and the sad destiny that surrounds each couple. All female characters in the Buendía family, with the exception of Ursula and Amaranta Ursula, lead their suitors to either death or defeat. José Arcadio, Rebeca's husband, is mysteriously killed in his own house; the Italian-born Pietro Crespi commits suicide after being rejected by Amaranta; all the suitors of Remedios the Beauty tragically die in an effort to admire her beauty; and Mauricio Babilonia is shot in the back while secretly visiting Meme and left unable to walk.

Ursula (the matriarch), Amaranta (Ursula's daughter, sister of Colonel Aureliano Buendía), and Amaranta Ursula (the last female of the Buendía's dynasty) are among the female characters deserving special attention. Ursula is first cousin and wife of José Arcadio Buendía, the patriarch of Macondo. She represents perseverance in life, and the cyclical time of the novel revolves around her. She witnesses the founding of Macondo, gives birth to the first José Arcadio (the legendary Colonel Aureliano Buendía) and the never-married Amaranta, she sees her two sons marry, and she lives to see six generations of Buendías die, making the one hundred years of the novel her own experience. Ursula is the centerpiece of the Buendía family. She is, on the one hand, the submissive wife who generally follows her husband's decisions and wishes, but on the other hand, she manages to leave Macondo for five months in search of her firstborn, José Arcadio. She fails to find him, but when she returns to Macondo she seems to be rejuvenated. She comes back bringing a different lifestyle, ready to introduce progress to Macondo. Ursula is conscious of her matriarchal responsibility and exercises it at all levels. She behaves as the patient and faithful wife to her aged and mad husband, who must be tied to a tree to restrain him. She is a loving mother who defies an army to visit her son in jail. She is also the one who, without remorse, throws Pilar Ternera out of the house for her extravagant sexual behavior. She is the loving grandmother who takes care of the illegitimate grandchildren of her two sons. She is self-assured and decisive when others are not, and she always seems to have the last word without sounding like a tyrant. Ursula reminds readers of the power of Big Mama, the central character in "Big Mama's Funeral" (see Chapter 5).

Compared with the rest of the female characters in *One Hundred Years of Solitude*, Ursula stands out because of her strength, both physical and emotional. Fearless in her convictions, she manages to stop a firing squad that, under the corrupt and absurd decision of her son José Arcadio, was ready to execute an innocent man. Compared to the egotism of her daughter, Amaranta, she is a generous mother who tirelessly feeds, not only her own large family, but also all those who happen to stop by her house for whatever reason. Compared to Remedios the Beauty, whose scent turns men insane, Ursula is poised and sensible. Compared to Pilar Ternera, whose fertility and sex drive are such that she mothers a child with both of Ursula's two sons, Ursula is serene and unyieldingly fights to keep her family together. Gabriel García Márquez himself described Ursula as the ideal woman (Joset 89).

Amaranta, daughter of the founders of Macondo, is a particularly interesting character due to the complexity of her personality. As is common practice with García Márquez's characters, her name, Amaranta, foreshadows her personality. Phonetically (relating to sound), Amaranta in Spanish closely resembles the sound of *amargura* (bitterness). It may also refer, as Jacques Joset points out in a footnote to *One Hundred Years of Solitude* in Spanish (Joset 121), to a plant from India, *amaranto* (amaranth). The plant, in Indian antiquity, was a symbol for immortality, and as such, the Indians consecrated it to the dead.

Amaranta is tall and slim, with an air of distinction. She is portrayed as a jealous woman. She hates Rebeca (who has grown up in the Buendía household as a member of the family) because they both have fallen in love with the same man, Pietro Crespi. Feeling humiliated by Crespi's indifference, Amaranta promises him she will never let him marry Rebeca. Ironically, Rebeca marries Amaranta's brother (her own half-brother), José Arcadio, and Pietro Crespi commits suicide. Amaranta's extreme temperament forces her into self-imposed isolation. She dies lonely and a virgin.

Amaranta fully shares the solitude of the Buendía family. She grows old rejecting Colonel Gerineldo Márquez, who has proposed marriage to her. Like the Buendías, Amaranta also seems to have a special relationship with death. She works on weaving her own shroud for four years, believing correctly that she will die at the moment when she completes it. She also orders the measurements for her own casket and announces that she will die on February 4. In a most carnivalesque way, she offers herself as a messenger for anyone who wishes to send news to the dead. On the day of her death, she bathes, refuses to take confession from Father Antonio Isabel, and forces her mother to give public testimony that she died a virgin.

Another important female character in *One Hundred Years of Solitude* is Amaranta Ursula. As her name indicates, her great-grandmother, Ursula Iguarán, and her great-grandaunt, Amaranta Buendía, influence her character. Indeed, Amaranta Ursula is a synthesis of all the female characters in *One Hundred Years of Solitude*. Amaranta Ursula is identical to her great-grandmother, the founding matriarch of Macondo. She is dynamic, indomitable, vigorous, and has no prejudices. Also like her great-grandmother, she is happy and centered. The beauty of Remedios the Beauty was also passed on to her. Like Meme, her own sister, Amaranta Ursula uses good judgment and shows great interest in her studies. Amaranta Ursula is the daughter of Aureliano Segundo and Fernanda del Carpio. Like her mother, Amaranta Ursula receives a strong religious training in Brussels, Belgium. She returns from Belgium married to Gastón, an older, Flemish man. Foreshadowing yet another character, Fermina Daza in *Love in the Time of Cholera*, she dresses fashionably, wears expensive jewelry, and shows herself to be a free spirit, liberated of prejudices.

Although Amaranta Ursula dreams of returning to Macondo with a faithful husband, she also wants to change the age-old traditions of the Buendías. For example, she wants to have two sons named Rodrigo and Gonzalo, not Aureliano and José Arcadio. (In real life, Mercedes Barcha, wife of Gabriel García Márquez, got Amaranta Ursula's wish—she has two sons, named Rodrigo and Gonzalo.) Amaranta Ursula's European training, however, does not change her. Like her great-grandfather, José Arcadio Buendía (the founding patriarch of Macondo), she does things one day only to undo them the next. Like many of her ancestors, she also loves with abandon. When her husband, Gastón, leaves her, she falls in love with her own nephew, Aureliano Babilonia, the son of her sister, Meme. Aureliano Babilonia and Amaranta Ursula are the only couple in *One Hundred Years of Solitude* to find true love. This love, however, brings destruction on them, as Amaranta Ursula dies giving birth to the last of the Buendías, the one with a pig's tail as feared by the matriarch Ursula Iguarán in the beginning of *One Hundred Years of Solitude*.

The male characters can also be described by common, salient traits. The male names are repeated unceasingly through the six generations of Buendías. The names are not picked at random; they relate to the function that each character plays in the plot. The omniscient narrator suggests the meaning of the names by attributing marked characteristics to those bearing a given name. The Arcadios, for example, are large in stature, whereas the Aurelianos are smaller. The Arcadios are fond of loudness, whereas the Aurelianos are introspective. The Arcadios are corpulent, monumental in size; the Aurelianos are bony, thin, and parsimonious. The Arcadios are active, strong-willed, independent, and dictatorial, even to the point of being tyrants. The Aurelianos are solitary, shy, and interested in reading. (One of them deciphers Melquiades' parchments.) The only instance when this name classification becomes confused is with Aureliano Segundo and his twin brother, José Arcadio Segundo, who are so much alike that even they would call each other by the wrong name. However, like a trick of magic realism, the games they play end up confusing them and they are changed for life. The names they use in the game begin to determine their physical characteristics, changing even their biological heritage. Thus, Aureliano Segundo, like all the Arcadios in the family tree, grows to be tall and strong, and José Arcadio Segundo, who otherwise would have been tall and strong, is short and bony. José Arcadio Segundo shows interest in public affairs and tries to decipher Melquíades' parchments, whereas Aureliano Segundo ends up leading a frivolous life. However, the twins die on the same day.

The male characters, more than the female characters, embody the myth of solitude, which permeates the novel. In his solitude, José Arcadio Buendía (the founder) initiates a long meditation about the passage of time. His son, Colonel Aureliano Buendía, the father of seventeen Aurelianos with seventeen different women and who "survived fourteen attempts on his life, seventy-three ambushes, and a firing squad" (113), dies of old age, in miserable solitude, next to the same tree where his father had died years before him.

THEMATIC ISSUES

One Hundred Years of Solitude opens with an allusion to war (Colonel Aureliano Buendía is about to be shot by a firing squad), but the theme of war is not a primary issue. The solitude shared by every member of the Buendía family, combined with incest, comprises the central themes of *One Hundred Years of Solitude*.

The solitude endured by the Buendías is a kind of curse, which they brought on themselves for their inability to fall in love, their strongly held superstitious beliefs, and the foundation of the family from an incestuous marriage. When José Arcadio Buendía marries Ursula Iguarán, they both know they are first cousins. Although the husband thinks nothing of it, the wife is filled with irrational fears and the fatal superstition that those who marry their own family may give birth to a deformed child with a pig's tail. She dies of old age without confirming her fear, but it is realized at the end of the novel, when Amaranta Ursula, not knowing she is related to him, falls in love with her nephew, Aureliano Babilonia. They give birth to the last of the Buendías, who is born with a pig's tail.

The solitude shared by the Buendías can be easily observed by the isolation of the town, which appears to have been forgotten by civilization and the outside world. The paths the main characters follow in life also emphasize solitude. Ursula talks to the dead, a form of solitude as nobody but herself can hear them; she also suffers from blindness, thus enduring a life in the dark. Her husband dies in solitude tied to a tree, left to the elements, and ignored as if he were indeed a part of the tree and not her husband, founder of Macondo, father, grandfather, and admired patriarch. Their three children all live and die in solitude, as well. Amaranta, their only daughter, never marries by choice. She rejects the marriage proposals of Pietro Crespi and Gerineldo Márquez and dies a virgin. The two sons also choose a life of solitude. José Arcadio, the firstborn, leaves Macondo to travel around the world as a gypsy. When he returns, although he is not in love, he marries Rebeca, but Rebeca, who brings to Macondo as a child the insomnia plague, a form of solitude that leads to the loss of memory and a state of idiocy that has no past (48), is an adopted daughter to the Buendías. The illusion of incest is obvious to those outside the Buendía family. Pietro Crespi, for one, cannot understand how siblings can get married, for he is in love with Rebeca, but she rejects him to marry her own half-brother. The extreme solitude of Pietro Crespi is such that, after being rejected by both Rebeca and Amaranta, he finds refuge in suicide.

Aureliano Buendía, the second son but the first to be born in Macondo, marries the child Remedios Moscote. Like his brother, he fathers no legitimate children. His decision to marry Remedios Moscote is capricious, not one arrived at out of love. Remedios, who is more interested in playing with dolls, does not feel love for him either. She still wets her bed at the time of the wedding. A silent and solitary man by nature, Aureliano Buendía lives and dies in solitude. Ursula, his mother, says he is incapable of loving. The two brothers, José Arcadio and Aureliano, each have a son with Pilar Ternera but neither one of the babies is born out of love. Pilar Ternera has sex with them for sheer pleasure. In the same vein, the marriage of Fernanda del Carpio and Aureliano Segundo is one of convenience, as are the relationships of Petra Cotes, who is shared as a lover by Aureliano Segundo and José Arcadio Segundo.

The solitude of the characters can be brought on by a lack of love between a couple, whether in marriage or otherwise, but solitude can also arise merely as part of the human condition. Indeed, in order to understand life, a person has to think of birth and death as, by their very nature, forms of solitude. However, to experience solitude, the characters in the novel—and the readers outside of it—have to be aware of the other: other people, other societies, and other languages. This confirms, for example, the fact that in the novel, readers witness *the discovery* of theories that elsewhere have already been discovered and the amazement of the townspeople when they first see an astrolabe, a map, a magnet, a magnifying glass, ice, and dentures. Such solitude, in fact, is one of the themes that can easily distinguish the literary works of García Márquez.

Returning to the theme of war, which is not the primary issue in *One Hundred Years of Solitude*, it is nonetheless intimately related to the political turmoil depicted in the novel. The wars between liberals and conservatives lasted nearly twenty years. During this time, the liberals fought thirty-two wars against the government (the Conservative Party) and lost them all. According to the narrative voice, the conservatives come to Macondo to disrupt the harmony and peace in which the town and its inhabitants lived. The discontent starts with the arrival of Don Apolinar Moscote. He comes as a representative of the government to exercise the law, but to José Arcadio Buendía, founder of the town, he only brings chaos. Soon after the arrival of Apolinar Moscote and his family, the ordered universe of Macondo is threatened by confusion, disorder, abuse, and finally war. The wars in the novel end, but the solitude of the Buendías does not.

SOCIAL AND HISTORICAL CONTEXT

One Hundred Years of Solitude portrays a period of time that stretches from the early 1800s to the early 1900s. These years encompass Colombian civil wars, neocolonialism, political violence, corruption, sexuality, death, and solitude, in the midst of other dominant themes. These concerns, however, are treated through myth and fantasy with a magic-realist format that leaves many readers unaware of the historical, political, and ideological content of the novel's background.

Most critics have pointed out that the social and political turmoil of

One Hundred Years of Solitude seems to transcribe the Colombian violence of countless civil wars and particularly the violence of the late 1940s, an epoch noted for its violent tendencies (see Chapter 1). The foundation of the fictional town of Macondo in *One Hundred Years of Solitude*, as literary critic Joaquín Marco pointed out, is, in fact, a violent act that finds its roots in the Spanish tradition of "honor," with clear sexual connotations of "machismo" (Marco 48). Honor and machismo also appear in *Chronicle of a Death Foretold* (1981), where both are central themes. The violence of *One Hundred Years of Solitude* focuses on the historical fight between a pair of opposing political parties, the Liberals and the Conservatives, which had the greatest rivalry Colombia had ever known. Although all the Buendía family figures prominently in the narrative, it is through Colonel Aureliano Buendía that the reader gets to read of fictionalized events in the wars between the two political parties. It is interesting to note that Colonel Aureliano Buendía, a liberal, as governor of Macondo, grows to be as cruel, despotic, and abusive as the conservatives he fights in the novel. In fact, *One Hundred Years of Solitude*, in its depiction of the Buendía family, favors the liberals, yet the omniscient narrator is quick to point out their flaws. The Buendías are seen as liberal leaders, but they are also portrayed as the town's ruling oligarchy (a type of government where power is exercised by few members, often of the same social class).

Just as interesting to note, in the patriarchal world of the novel, is the fact that a woman—the colonel's mother, Ursula—is the only one capable of changing his corrupt behavior. Ursula is indeed one of the pillars that sustains the novel. The fictionalized wars of Colonel Aureliano Buendía mirror the many civil wars Colombia fought during the nineteenth century and the first three decades of the twentieth century.

The novel's account of how Colonel Aureliano Buendía fought thirty-two wars and lost them all seems to capture the exaggeration of magic realism, but the history of Colombia records countless major uprisings between 1821 and 1930. During those years, some historians have documented between seventy and eighty wars. Reality, then, is sometimes as difficult to believe as fantasy itself. If the character of Colonel Aureliano Buendía was modeled after General Rafael Uribe Uribe, as some scholars have suggested, then reality once again surpasses fiction. As Regina Janes wrote,

> Uribe Uribe outdid Aureliano Buendía in the length if not the intensity of his military career, since he lasted almost thirty years from his participation at the age of seventeen in the war

of 1876–1877 through the other conflicts to 1902. (Janes 1989, 135)

In the same vain, the narrative makes references to American colonialism as expressed through the exploitation of banana plantations. To this effect, the narrative describes the banana strike of 1928, once again mixing fact and fiction.

When reading *One Hundred Years of Solitude*, the reader misses something if he or she thinks that it re-creates only the past of Latin America and ignores the current time when the novel was published—the late 1960s. The violence that Colombia was undergoing in the 1960s is not dealt with in the same way that the "Novel of the Violence" deals with it. From 1948 to 1964, Colombia underwent a number of assassinations that were referred to as La violencia (the Violence). A good number of novels written about such events were published and are often called "Novels of the Violence." *One Hundred Years of Solitude* picks up on the events of La violencia but mixes García Márquez's experiences with the civil wars of the nineteenth century and the banana strike of 1928, the three most important historical events according to critics and scholars of *One Hundred Years of Solitude*.

Having mixed these events with a strong emphasis on myth, fantasy, humor, and magic realism, *One Hundred Years of Solitude* might be attacked for not being politically involved. What readers have to consider, however, is that politics in *One Hundred Years of Solitude* are in the background and disguised through magic realism while the art of storytelling takes the foreground.

ALTERNATIVE READING: INTERTEXTUALITY

In literary theory, intertextuality, in a broad sense, can be understood as the text's quality of interdependence on other written works. Julia Kristeva, a Bulgarian-born psychoanalyst and feminist critic living in France, introduced the term in the 1960s. According to Kristeva, every literary text is an intersection of texts. Although the term can be applied differently, most critics agree on the basis that any given work seems to assimilate and reflect a literary tradition that antecedes it. Thus, intertextuality stresses the active role of the reader in making the connections the author may have thought of at the time of the writing of the text. As such, an intertextual reading of *One Hundred Years of Solitude* allows the reader to connect García Márquez's novel with previous literary works.

For example, critics have often connected *One Hundred Years of Solitude* with the works of William Faulkner (see Chapter 2).

However, readers can also connect *One Hundred Years of Solitude* with works that emerged around the time of its publication and later texts that have been influenced by it. Although seemingly hypothetical, there are critics who view intertextuality in an even broader sense, suggesting even that the text can be connected with future discourse—with books that are yet to be published.

For most Anglo-American critics the intertextuality of *One Hundred Years of Solitude* can be traced back to the Bible and, also to the work of such diverse authors as Franz Kafka, François Rabelais, William Faulkner, and Virginia Woolf, among others. The Kafkaesque influence can be seen in the nightmarish atmosphere surrounding the "absurd" logic of the characters and the absurdity of power. The Rabelaisian influence is obvious in the use of humor and hyperbole (a form of exaggeration that is used to emphasize a particular quality, for example, a physical trait such as strength or size). In English we use the word *gargantuan* to mean huge. In fact the word is derived from a character in a work of the early French writer François Rabelais, *Gargantua et Pantagruel*. Regarding the influences of Faulkner and Woolf, Gene H. Bell-Villada noted that the integration of geography, history, climate, family life, and narrative experiment is reminiscent of Faulkner, while García Márquez's sense of perfectionism is due to his readings of Virginia Woolf (Bell-Villada 1990, 86).

In an interview given by García Márquez two years after the publication of *One Hundred Years of Solitude* he explained the concept of intertextuality when he said, "literature is a science one has to learn, and there are 10,000 years standing behind [everything] that gets written" (Bell-Villada 70). Although in this instance García Márquez was referring to the short story as opposed to the novel, the quote can apply to most forms of writing.

The following is a detailed intertextual reading of *One Hundred Years of Solitude* using the Bible as a model. The similarities are numerous; therefore, it is convenient to group them in themes.

One of the main themes is the power of creation, which Chapters 1 and 2 of the Book of Genesis attribute to God. It is through God's power that all things were created and on which they depend. Contrary to the biblical narrative, in *One Hundred Years of Solitude* we find an American banana company taking the place of God by assuming the power of creation. In an attempt to improve the yield on its business, the United Fruit Company sped up the growth cycle of the banana crop with a resulting change in the climate and the flow of the river. There are other characters in *One Hundred Years of Solitude* that exercise divine or supernatural powers. There is the gypsy Melquíades, for example, who, with his inventions, becomes the creator for the people of Macondo. Putting to use the properties of the magnet, he affirms that all things have a life of their own. He uses the magnet to make the townsfolk believe that pots and pans have a life of their own. The magnet Melquíades uses is large enough to pull metal objects out of the house. This image is also confirmed when we read that a strong force lifts up four children who were trying to destroy the parchments written by Melquíades.

Melquíades, like God, enjoys immortality. He dies from a fever "on the beach at Singapore" (18) and his body is thrown into the Java Sea, yet he returns to life and can be seen within the novel interacting with characters of several different generations. It is also Melquíades who brings to Macondo the novelty of ice, making José Arcadio Buendía say, "this is the great invention of our time" (19). Through acts like this, God's power of creation is replaced by human acts. In general, most of the acts related to Melquíades are impregnated with the supernatural power that the Book of Genesis attributes only to God.

Melquíades is not the only character that exercises such divine powers. Ursula can also be seen to possess a certain kind of power when she claims that, like her daughter, Amaranta, she has control over her death. She anticipates that she will die on a clear day. (Her only daughter, Amaranta, knows that she will die the same day she finishes her shroud.) In this novel, humankind is the lord of life and death, not God, as the Book of Genesis firmly declares.

Another theme is that of an earthly paradise, which is mentioned in Genesis 2:8–20. The biblical earthly paradise is a pleasant place located near several rivers; a new and fertile place recently created; a happy place where humans are immortal and meant to be lord and master, exercising power over everything that was created, naming every living and nonliving thing. The description of the founding of Macondo is similar to that of the biblical paradise: José Arcadio Buendía wants his family and those who follow him to settle on the bank of a river, as most great civilizations have done in the past. Thus, Macondo is a village by the river. The fiction is inspired by the Colombian towns built on the banks of the Magdalena River. The descriptions are also similar: in *One Hundred Years of Solitude* the world is indeed new and recent for the Buendías and the few families that arrive in Macondo with them. They come to Macondo from a place where things were different. Thus, they have to point to some of them for the lack of a name. Some literary critics have said that Gabriel García Márquez was mocking *Christopher Columbus' Diary*. How could the Italian-born navigator have communicated, asks García Márquez, if not by pointing? Macondo, reads the novel, was a truly happy village where no one was over thirty years of age and no one had died (10). Thirty years can be considered the perfect age because it was the age of Christ at the beginning of his ministry. The reference seems to refer to that fact inasmuch as people were living in a state of happiness and enjoyed privileged qualities not common to normal beings. Furthermore, many years after the founding of Macondo, the characters still talk about the earthly paradisiacal privileges.

The third biblical theme that can clearly be seen in *One Hundred Years of Solitude* is that of the flood. In Chapters 6 through 8 of Genesis, one reads of the moral corruption into which the descendants of the first couple fell. One also reads that the flood was a form of punishment from God in order to cleanse the world of sin, offering, in this manner, the opportunity of a new beginning to those who were faithful to Him. There is a parallel in *One Hundred Years of Solitude* when Macondo succumbs to moral corruption, marked essentially by incest, and therefore suffers the consequences of a flood. In the same fashion that the Bible indicates, with precision, that the flood lasted "forty days and forty nights" (Genesis 7:12), *One Hundred Years of Solitude* says, just as specifically, that "it rained for four years, eleven months, and two days" (339). The precision can also be found in the last phase of the flood. Whereas in Genesis one learns that at the end of the forty days Noah opened the window and released a bird to check whether the waters had receded (Genesis 8:6–12), *One Hundred Years of Solitude* states, "one Friday at two in the afternoon the world lighted up with a crazy crimson sun . . . and it did not rain again for ten years" (355). Even the end of *One Hundred Years of Solitude* reminds readers of the comparison of Macondo to Paradise, which comes to its destruction when "the uncertainty of the future made [the inhabitants] turn their heads toward the past. They saw themselves lost in the lost paradise of the deluge" (439).

A fourth theme that is strongly marked in *One Hundred Years of Solitude* and makes it analogous to the Bible is that of Macondo as a special, chosen town. The theme of a chosen town is one of the keys to interpreting the Bible. The second part of Genesis, Chapters 12 through 50, tells the stories of the great ancestors, men and women called patriarchs and matriarchs, who were the founders and members of the tribe of Israel. The story begins with Abraham and Sara and continues with Isaac and Rebeca and their children, Esau and Jacob. Jacob fathers twelve children, who are the beginning of the twelve tribes of Israel. The number twelve comes to be a significant number in reference to this chosen tribe, whose story continues in many of the books that make up the Bible and comes to its climax with the Twelve Apostles, in the New Testament, who will be the ones that will guide "the new tribe of God" to the Church.

In Genesis 12:1, God tells Abraham: "go from your country and your kindred and your father's house to the land that I will show you." When the Buendías move from their town, however, they "headed toward the land that no one had promised them" (25). Although the Buendías feel that nobody has promised them a land, they take the initiative to start a new town and *One Hundred Years of Solitude* repeatedly refers to the founding couple as "a patriarch" and "a matriarch." In Genesis 24:50–62 one reads the story of Rebeca, who was welcomed into the house of Patriarch Abraham to marry his son, Isaac. Analogously, the Buendías welcome into their home a child and decide to call her Rebeca. On the other hand, when Ursula restores her home she decides to build a diningroom with a table with twelve places, recalling the biblical number that refers to the chosen tribe of Israel, which originated with the twelve children of Jacob and the twelve places that Jesus assigned to his apostles at the Last Supper. If one counts the four generations of children that live in the Buendía home in Macondo, the descendants of the Buendías also number twelve.

The fifth and last intertextual reference to the Bible is the apocalyptic end of *One Hundred Years of Solitude* and the usage of the apocalyptic genre. In the Bible, apocalyptic literature is characterized by the use of codified symbols, which meant that not every reader can understand it— only those for whom it was meant. This genre developed in Israel around 200 B.C. when the tribe had to go through great suffering and persecution, and it was used in the book of the Prophet Daniel. In the New Testament the Apostle John uses it in his book of Apocalypse to criticize the Roman Empire and the emperor without putting the readers at risk of persecution or death during the harsh beginnings of Christianity. The Book of John contains a message full of hope for a persecuted tribe, expressing the victory of divine justice over evil. To this message, John adds in Chapter 21 of Apocalypse the belief that Christ will return victorious at the end of the world, initiating a new era in a new land, where suffering and death are nonexistent.

In *One Hundred Years of Solitude*, however, readers find the manuscripts of Melquíades to be indecipherable. Four generations of Buendías try to interpret them and fail because they cannot understand the code in which they were written. The last of the Buendías finally manages to decipher them and understands their prediction that his family lineage will end with him; then he dies and the novel ends. In Apocalypse 7:3–4, one reads that the chosen ones for the final salvation will be those who remain faithful to God and that they will be identified by a sign on their forehead. The seventeen children of Colonel Aureliano Buendía also carry a sign on their forehead, ashen crosses that "inspired a sacred respect, as if they were caste marks" (252). However, the significance of the sign in the novel is opposite to that in the Bible because its bearers are marked for destruction rather than salvation: "they were hunted like rabbits by invisible criminals who aimed at the center of their crosses of ash" (256). Extraordinary phenomena in nature are evident signs of the end in apocalyptic literature. Ursula sees "luminous disks" in the sky and attributes to them a sign of death and destruction. The disks that Ursula sees may be the same celestial comet that the Aztec emperor Montezuma saw in the sixteenth century, which he too believed was an omen of death and destruction. When Ursula dies, the novel notes that Santa Sofía de la Piedad sees "a row of luminous orange disks pass across the sky" (369). However, the most evident signs occur at the end of the novel. Contrary to Apocalypse 8:5, where natural phenomena such as thunder, lightening, rumbling, and earthquakes indicate the end of this world but the definite beginning of the New Jerusalem, the novel presents natural phenomena, such as unending rain followed by a wind with the strength of a cyclone, as signs of the end. However, this is an end of sure destruction, "because races condemned to one hundred years of solitude did not have a second opportunity on earth" (448).

7

Chronicle of a Death Foretold
(1981)

The publication of *Chronicle of a Death Foretold* broke Gabriel García Márquez's self-imposed "publication strike." (He had pledged to not publish anything for as long as Chilean dictator Augusto Pinochet remained in power.) García Márquez's period of silence started in 1976 and ended in a spectacular way in 1981 with the publication of *Chronicle of a Death Foretold*, which was written, according to some critics, at the urging of other Chilean authors. While it is common for countries such as Mexico, Argentina, and Colombia to have their own publication run of 5,000 to 30,000 copies, 30,000 being the exception, *Chronicle of a Death Foretold* was, without doubt, an exception beyond that. García Márquez's publishing house, located in Spain, Argentina, Colombia, and Mexico, published 1 million copies of the book. Immediately after, as might be expected, García Márquez gave private interviews and newspaper reviews appeared the world over. One year after the publication of *Chronicle of a Death Foretold*, in 1982, newspapers around the world announced that García Márquez was that year's winner of the Nobel Prize in literature. The glory days that had followed the publication of *One Hundred Years of Solitude* in 1967 had returned.

Chronicle of a Death Foretold reconstructs an actual murder that took place in Sucre, Colombia, in 1951. In an interview for the Argentine newspaper *La Nación* (The Nation), García Márquez declared that Cayetano Gentile Chimento—Santiago Nasar in the novel—had been one of his childhood friends. On January 22, 1951, two brothers of the Chica family (Vicario in the novel) killed Cayetano because their sister was taken back to her family by her husband, Miguel Reyes Palencia, on their wedding night when he discovered that she was not a virgin. Similarly to the way the murder takes place in the novel, in broad daylight, the two brothers knifed Cayetano to death in the town's plaza. In spite of the parallels, *Chronicle of a Death Foretold*, uses an anonymous town and fictional names for the characters. In this sense, the narrative is not a chronicle. García Márquez did not talk to any of the witnesses, nor did he use the real names and places as a chronicle would when recounting past events. Nevertheless, García Márquez insists that the circumstances and the events of *Chronicle of a Death Foretold* are absolutely truthful.

The incident was highly publicized in Colombia and elsewhere. García Márquez's reconstruction of the story is now a classic in Latin American literature. Six years after its publication in Spanish, in 1987, Italian movie director Francesco Rossi released it as a film. To date, the public can also enjoy *Chronicle of a Death Foretold* on the stage, where it continues to be performed for Spanish-speaking audiences.

PLOT DEVELOPMENT

The first chapter opens with a sentence announcing that on that day, the main character, Santiago Nasar, is going to be killed. While this event is the focus of the narrative, there is at least one subplot: the wedding of Angela Vicario and Bayardo San Román. There is also a secondary event that distracts the characters in the novel while the killers go about their business: the visit of a bishop. At the last minute, the bishop decides not to get off the boat in which he is traveling. The omniscient narrator, functioning like a murder detective, reconstructs the crime bit by bit. In the process, he describes a classic coastal town where religion and law as institutions are inefficient in protecting the townsfolk. Santiago Nasar and his friends are all members of the ruling class. The narrator's family, for instance, is best friends with the Nasar family and so has reasonable expectations that the bishop will pay them a personal visit during his stay in town (199). The town's economic makeup presents a background of contrasting wealth and poverty. Santiago Nasar, an only child, lives in one of the best houses in town, has two mulattas as maids, and is the owner of a farm, named the Divine Face. His death gives the novel its title. With few exceptions, nearly everybody in the town, the mayor and the priest included, know that the identical twins, Pedro and Pablo Vicario, are looking for Santiago Nasar in order to kill him. What makes the plot intriguing are the pieces of information that are left for the reader to put together. Santiago Nasar, for example, is not aware that he is the target of the Vicario brothers until right before the time he is attacked. However, the threads that weave together the murder are all present in the first chapter. As is the case with *Leaf Storm* and *Love in the Time of Cholera*, the plot of *Chronicle of a Death Foretold* unfolds in an inverted fashion. Instead of moving forward, the plot moves backward. This provides the reader with the pleasure of decoding, as a detective would, all possible reasons, circumstances, and motivations for the crime that takes place. By the end of the first chapter, readers have been told who killed Santiago Nasar, how he was killed, and why. These facts, however, are the guideposts that allow García Márquez an opportunity to take readers through an intricate and detailed labyrinth of surprises.

The second and subsequent chapters flesh out the plot, so to speak. Bayardo San Román is the man who marries Angela Vicario, only to return her to her parents five hours after the wedding ceremony. Angela is not a virgin, which has significant and potentially dangerous consequences, of which Angela is amply aware. She knows that there is no love between her and Bayardo, and she wants to stop the marriage. The Vicarios, however, are impressed by his wealth and oppose her decision. The comedy of errors, which turns into a tragedy, builds up bit by bit and minute by minute. Angela does not love Bayardo and neither does he love her. Rather, he is enamored with the concept of being married to a beautiful woman. The wedding celebration is an excuse for Bayardo San Román to show off his wealth and power. The narrator comments that Bayardo could marry any woman he chose. He is the son of a decorated hero who had defeated Colonel Aureliano Buendía in one of the civil wars of the nineteenth century. (This is the same Buendía who features prominently in *One Hundred Years of Solitude*.)

If lack of love is not a good enough reason to stop Bayardo San Román and Angela Vicario from getting married, Angela's loss of her virginity to someone other than Bayardo is enough to cause her return. Bayardo does not beat Angela for her indiscretion, but her mother does, for hours. Questioned and pressured to name the perpetrator, Angela names Santiago Nasar. Pedro and Pablo, her twin brothers, know what to do next. In fact, the whole community knows that to restore the Vicarios' honor, which resides in Angela's virginity, Santiago must be killed: one only washes one's honor clean with blood. Pig butchers by trade, the twins set out to kill Santiago and carve him up like a pig (186). However, readers do not witness this event until the last chapter. Before that, the plot reconstructs the psychological reaction of the twins, who believe they are innocent, "before God and before men" (220). After three years in jail awaiting trial, the twins are acquitted by the court because their action is considered a legitimate defense of their family's honor. Before the murder, the twins tell everybody of their intent but people do not believe them. When the town's mayor is told, he treats them like children, confiscates the butcher knives, and sends them home to sleep. They come back with a second set of knives but look for Santiago in places where they know he will not be. They are hoping not to find him; they plan to kill him yet hope someone will stop them. However, no one takes responsibility to see that the killing does not occur. In fact, there are those, like Santiago's maid, Victoria Guzmán, who want Santiago dead. She does not tell Santiago, although she is aware of it, that the Vicario brothers are looking for him to kill him.

The reader comes to the end of the third chapter and reads, "they've killed Santiago Nasar!" (237). However, the plot has not yet entirely unfolded. The reader is still not a firsthand witness; he or she continues to be led, and the narrator still holds the reader in suspense. Almost tormentingly, the narrative voice continues leisurely to piece the story together. Indeed, no stone is left unturned. The narrator recounts the story of the life of both Angela Vicario and Bayardo San Román. Foreshadowing *Love in the Time of Cholera*, Angela Vicario starts an epistolary (a continuous series of letters) that continues for seventeen years. After she has written Bayardo San Román nearly 2,000 letters, he shows up with two suitcases. In one of them he has all the letters Angela has written, all unopened. In the other is clothing in order to stay. Bayardo San Román is no longer trim, handsome, and elegant. He needs glasses to read, he is fat, and he is losing his hair. "She knew he was seeing her just as diminished as she saw him" (255). Have they reconciled their understanding about love? It seems like another error in a comedy that is meant to be a tragedy. Angela does not love Bayardo; he takes her back for not being a virgin; her brothers kill Santiago Nasar to regain her honor and that of her family; she realizes, seventeen years later, that she really loves him. The plot, unfortunately, affords no time or interest for this second chance.

Finally, in the last chapter, the reader witnesses the brutal and horrid crime. Now there is no escape: neither Santiago Nasar nor the reader can escape their fate. The murder is gruesome, but the story is wonderfully told. Before the curtain falls, the narrator brings to the reader's attention the fact that in this tropical tragedy there is also a comedy of errors. Cristo Bedoya, Santiago's friend, can stop the crime but does not. He has a gun that he does not know how to use—he cannot even tell if it is loaded. Those who want to come forward to prevent the killing of Santiago are uncertain and are put off by his apparent carefree attitude. Once Santiago is told of the Vicarios' plan to kill him, he decides to go home. However, rather than using the back door to his home, which always is left unlocked, he decides to use the front door, which faces the plaza. His mother, thinking that he is inside the house, locks the front door seconds before Santiago gets to it. The attack begins, and nobody does anything to stop it. Indeed, Santiago's screams go unheard as they are confused with the sounds of the bishop's festival.

GENRE AND NARRATIVE STRUCTURE

Chronicle of a Death Foretold reads like a fictional work. The reader of García Márquez, however, should be interested in knowing that the account the novel relates is based on a factual event. However, as Latin American literary critic Gonzalo Díaz-Migoyo put it, "it is an account no less imaginary for being faithful to the facts and, conversely, no less historical for being a work of the imagination" (Díaz-Migoyo 75). The faithful facts to which Díaz-Migoyo refers took place in Sucre, Colombia in 1951, thirty years before *Chronicle of a Death Foretold* was published. On January 22, 1951, Miguel Reyes Palencia returned his wife, Margarita Chica Salas, to her family on the morning after the nuptial night because she had not been a virgin. A short while later, Margarita's brother, Victor Chica Salas, killed Cayetano Gentile Chimento for stealing his sister's honor without an intention to marry her.

Chronicle of a Death Foretold is a combination of journalism, realism, and detective story, and therefore a hybrid genre. Its journalistic orientation, announced in the title of the novel with the use of the word *chronicle*, is seen in the novel's precise detailing of the time of each event and the matter-of-fact usage of language that marks the plot and presents the events of an atrocious and horrid crime. Journalism, however, attempts to report on the basis of fidelity to the facts. As such, *Chronicle of a Death Foretold* is a deceiving chronicle, for the facts are altered by the fictitious additions made by García Márquez. In real life, the returned bride continued to live alone after her return, while the embarrassed husband left the country, got married in Costa Rica, and went on to have twelve children with his new wife. In the novel, Angela stays with her mother and Bayardo goes off and is not heard of until seventeen years after the date of the wedding, when he and Angela reunite.

The story is told in a journalistic style of reporting. García Márquez freely admits that he is the narrator who is reconstructing the story. Luisa Santiaga, the narrator's mother in the novel, is the name of García Márquez's own mother, and Luis Enrique, the narrator's younger brother, is also the name of García Márquez's own younger brother. Luisa Santiaga has a daughter who in the novel is a nun; García Márquez, in real life, has a sister who used to be a nun. As if that were not enough, the narrator recounts that on the night of Angela and Bayardo's wedding, he proposed marriage to Mercedes Barcha, only to marry her fourteen years later because at the time she was just finishing primary school. García Márquez married a woman of the same name, Mercedes Barcha, to whom he proposed on the exact day of the wedding in 1951 and whom he wed fourteen years later because she, too, was just finishing primary school. Most of the story has a factual/journalistic base with a few exceptions, such as the fact that García Márquez was not in town at the time of the crime, nor were the lovers ever reunited. Both instances are fictitious. The realism of *Chronicle of a Death Foretold* is seen in its intent to faithfully portray life in a coastal town. The novel accurately describes the routine of everyday life: the ways in which the town's people prepare for the visit of the bishop, and celebrate at Angela's wedding; the habit of the single young men to spend time at the bordello; and even the fact that, as a result, one of the Vicario twins is suffering from a venereal disease.

Chronicle of a Death Foretold, as is typical in realistic fiction, is interested in ordinary people, whom it faithfully depicts at both the social and the psychological levels. The reader of *Chronicle of a Death Foretold* is exposed to the inner workings of the minds of the twin brothers and the nature of the personality of other characters. As a detective story, *Chronicle of a Death Foretold* seems to fit the pattern almost perfectly. The murder is being pieced together by the nameless narrator, a friend of the victim, in the same manner that a detective might approach the case. However, *Chronicle of a Death Foretold* is intentionally deceiving—moreover, it can be read as if inverted or backward. From the start the reader knows the culprits, so there is no unsolved crime. Instead, the reader looks to find out whether the victim or the culprits is actually in the wrong. The absurdity of the crime, however, calls for a reader who might question who really killed Santiago Nasar. The physical evidence indicates that the killers are the Vicario brothers, but is there any responsibility on the part of the townsfolk or the legal or religious authorities? This is a question for the reader to decide. In that sense, then, the novel can indeed be read as a detective story.

The narrative structure of *Chronicle of a Death Foretold* will seem familiar to the García Márquez reader. It starts in medias res (in the middle of things). At the start of the novel, an omniscient narrator (a character within the novel who knows everything there is to know) is describing the last hours in the life of Santiago Nasar. The time line of the events is very precise and linear, faithfully following the clock. However, the reading is not so linear. Even the events of the main plot do not unfold in a straightforward manner, but rather move back and forth in time. Besides dealing with the genesis of the main plot, *Chronicle of a Death Foretold* also has a subplot describing the short-lived idyll of Bayardo San Román and Angela Vicario. This subplot, contained in Chapters 2 and 4, plus the intrusions by the omniscient narrator discussing the origin of the characters, makes the narrative structure a bit complex, although not impossible to follow. In the end, the focus remains on the killing of Santiago Nasar.

The narrative structure, like the genre, is rather deceiving. The story of Santiago Nasar's murder is described with rigid adherence to the exact hour and minute of each event because of the insistence by the narrator to be exact. However, the time line presented to the reader is arbitrarily jumbled and replayed haphazardly, moving forward and backward in time with equal ease. While Chapter 1 stars at 5:30 and has Santiago killed by 7:05, an hour and thirty-five minutes later, the narrator eventually takes the reader all the way back to the end of the nineteenth century and its civil wars.

CHARACTER DEVELOPMENT

As is the case with most of Gabriel García Márquez's fictional work, the number of characters in this novel is large. In *Chronicle of a Death Foretold*, this is due to the fact that the entire coastal town where the murder takes place is an active participant. In *Chronicle of a Death Foretold*, as in *Leaf Storm* and *No One Writes to the Colonel*, the community is charged with a moral responsibility for its indirect participation. As a result, the community can be viewed as a character. There is an abundance of names that come in and out of the plot, comprising nearly eighty characters. The main characters, however—those most involved with the plot of the murder—are relatively few: Santiago Nasar, Bayardo San Román, Angela Vicario, and the Vicario twins, Pedro and Pablo. The secondary characters are much more numerous, however. As is typical of García Márquez's writing, female characters densely populate this novel. There are women who do everything they can to stop the murder, particularly Clotilde Armenta and Luisa Santiaga; and there are also women who, each in some fashion, contribute to Santiago's death, including Flora Miguel, Plácida Linero, Victoria Guzmán, and Divina Flor. The secondary male characters are also numerous. Cristo Bedoya is instrumental in the plot, as are Father Carmen Amador, the mayor, Lázaro Aponte, and General Petronio San Román.

The description of the main character, Santiago Nasar, is both detailed and exquisite. Santiago is handsome, young, and well-mannered and has an enviable fortune at the tender age of twenty-one. He is a lover of horses, a fan of falconry, and, from his father, he is supposed to have learned both courage and prudence. Santiago is portrayed as a happy young man. He is described as pale, curly-haired, and, like his father, with Arabian eyes and long, dark eyelashes. He is the only child of a marriage of convenience. From his father he has inherited a cattle ranch, the "Divine Face." He is known as a peaceful man, although he is also a lover of guns. However, he is never armed unless he is dressed to tend his ranch. Being a first-generation Colombian of Arabic descent, the reader might expect that Santiago practices the Islamic religion, but instead he is deeply Catholic. On the day he is killed, he was hoping to kiss the bishop's ring. His social life, although he is a rich and rather aristocratic young man, is as simple as that of the rest of the townsfolk. A lover of parties, Santiago Nasar has an intimate group of friends. His friends include the narrator, the narrator's brother, Luis Enrique, and Cristo Bedoya. The four friends grew up together, went to school together, and vacationed together. Their friendship lasted right up to the day Santiago was killed.

When Santiago was fifteen, he fell completely in love with María Alejandrina Cervantes, a local prostitute. The love affair lasted fourteen months. It was so strong that his own father stepped in to end it, entering the brothel and dragging Santiago out after delivering a beating with his belt. To complete the punishment, the father isolated his son at the ranch. At the time of Santiago's death, he was formally engaged to Flora Miguel, a loveless arrangement favored by both families. The marriage was to be held within the year.

Fate plays an important role in the character development of Santiago. He is accused by Angela Vicario of being responsible for the loss of her virginity. This is the reason why he is killed at the hands of Angela's brothers. Everyone in town, including his best friends and his maids, knows that he has been sentenced to die—except Santiago himself. According to the police report, he died from seven stab wounds. What seems ironic is that there is never any proof that Santiago is, in fact, responsible, as Angela claimed. Among the many facts supporting Santiago's innocence are the facts that he and Angela were never seen together in public, he considered her a "fool," (251) and they belong to separate social classes in a town where social class determined identity. Supporting a case for Santiago's guilt is Santiago's fame as a "sparrow hawk," (251) who liked young girls, especially those beneath his social class (like his father before him). The narrative voice, however, suggests that Angela Vicario was probably protecting someone she really loved and picked Santiago's name because she thought that her brothers would never dare to kill such an important man as Santiago. However, one way or another, Santiago dies. As the narrative voice explains, never was a death more foretold. Despite all the efforts, no one is able to stop it, not even Father Carmen Amador or the mayor, Colonel Lázaro Aponte.

The husband of the bride, Bayardo San Román, is a thirty-year-old man whose personality evokes opposing remarks. "He looked like a fairy," but "I could have buttered him and eaten him alive," (202) says one of the female characters. He is known for his honesty; good heart; religious inclinations; knowledge of Morse code, trains, and medicine; ability as a swimmer; and love of a good party. On top of all this, he is immensely rich: the townspeople gossip that "he's swimming in gold" (203). However, he is not a man whom someone gets to know when they first meet him, and his golden eyes, says the narrator's mother, "reminded me of the devil" (204). He is heartless when he literally browbeats Xius into selling him his house in order to please Angela's caprice and to demonstrate his own power. Although Bayardo San Román is a member of a distinguished family, he shows up in town alone. Nobody knows where he came from or what he stands for. Before he even meets Angela Vicario, and after seeing her only once, he decides that he is going to marry her, and six months later, he does. He never tries to court her, but instead seduces her family, showering them with presents and his charming personality. Angela and Bayardo's wedding is both extravagant and costly, perhaps to hide the fact that their marriage is a loveless one. In fact, their fated marriage only lasts five hours. Bayardo San Román takes his wife back to her parents when he discovers that Angela is not a virgin. After the tremendously emotional embarrassment of being held up to ridicule, Bayardo locks himself in his new home and is found intoxicated a week later. Finally his family comes to his rescue and takes him away.

Bayardo continues to surprise the reader with his strange personality up to the end of the novel. Seventeen years after that fateful Monday when he returned his wife to her mother, he seeks out Angela. He is now fat, balding, old, wearing glasses and, as if he has lost all his pride, returns to the woman who had caused him such embarrassment.

Angela Vicario's role is twofold. She is the cause of the death of one main character, Santiago Nasar, and the reason for the destruction of another, Bayardo San Román. She is a member of a poor and simple family. Her father, Poncio Vicario, has gone blind from the eyestrain of his work as a goldsmith. He is a man without a will of his own, who is dominated by his wife. His wife and Angela's mother, Purísima del Carmen Vicario, was a schoolteacher until she married Poncio. She rules the house with an iron fist. Angela has two older sisters, both married, and twin brothers, Pedro and Pablo, who are pig butchers by trade. Angela is a beautiful twenty-year-old who, like her father, lacks character and determination and does not enjoy the moral support of her mother. She lives in fear of her mother's demanding character, a fear that is emphasized on the night when her parents, her sisters, her husband's sisters, and her twin brothers decide that she must marry a man she has hardly seen and does not love. Although she makes explicit her lack of love for her husband-to-be, her mother flatly responds, "Love can be learned too" (209). Angela tries to commit suicide but does not have the strength to do so, so she realizes that she has no other alternative but to marry Bayardo San Román. She arrives at this decision with the hope that she will manage to fool Bayardo into believing that she is a virgin on the night of their wedding. On the day of the wedding, she continues the charade by wearing the traditional dress of a virgin. This is later interpreted as a profanity against the sacred symbols of purity. In truth, however, she is horrified in the knowledge that she has to face her husband that night. Her husband does not have to think twice about what to do once he becomes aware that his wife is not a virgin. He decides to denounce his marriage and return Angela to her parents. Although humiliated and full of shame, her feeling of horror changes into one of liberation when Bayardo takes her back to her parents. Angela not only knows that he does not love her, she also considers herself inferior to him and says that he is too much of a man for her.

After the death of Santiago, Angela and her family are asked by the town's mayor to leave the town forever. Angela then undergoes a positive change. She spends her time embroidering and regains her zest for life. Inexplicitly, she cries after Bayardo and nearly goes insane over him, so much so that she starts to write frequent, desperate love letters. This absurd obsession continues for seventeen years, during which she writes nearly 2,000 letters but gets not a single response. She takes consolation in the fact that her letters are not returned to her. This is a clear foretelling of *Love in the Time of Cholera*, except that the roles are reversed. In *Chronicle of a Death Foretold*, it is the woman who writes in order to achieve a goal, whereas in *Love in the Time of Cholera*, it is the male who writes with the same intent. In both instances, the writers attain their goal, and in both, ironically, the two letter writers are first rejected yet, over time and with persistence, gain the loved one.

Pedro and Pablo, the twin brothers of Angela, are twenty-four years old and known in town by their good looks. They have the innocent demeanor of a child, and their reputation is that of good young men. Their fate, however, is to kill Santiago to restore Angela's honor and reputation. Pedro is six minutes older than his brother. He seems to be more imaginative, decisive, sentimental, and authoritarian. When they both show up to enlist in the military at the age of twenty-one, Pablo is exempted so that he can help take care of his family. During his time in the military, Pedro's character develops as one willing to give orders and to decide for his own brother. It is Pedro who decides that they must kill Santiago Nasar.

Throughout the novel the reader becomes aware that the twins do not really want to kill Santiago yet must do so to save the family's honor. The narrator states that the twins did more than could be imagined to get someone to stop them, yet no one did so. From the very start of the ordeal, they publicly announce that they are going to kill Santiago Nasar. They tell the priest, the police, and every passerby. When the news reaches the mayor, he half-heartedly tries to stop the crime by taking away their knives, but they get others. As if to confirm their child-like innocence, they bless themselves when they see the town's priest and bless themselves again right before killing Santiago. On the day when they are taken into custody and put in jail, they suffer mental and emotional torment. Pedro affirms that he can smell Santiago on him regardless of how much he washes himself. He adds that he cannot sleep, an insomnia that continues for eleven consecutive months. Pablo suffers from diarrhea, which leads Pedro to think that his brother had been poisoned. Although the brothers suffer the psychological fallout of having killed a man, they do not view themselves as sinners and refuse to confess themselves to a priest when they have the opportunity to do so. When they leave jail, they decide to do so in broad daylight so that everyone can see their faces and judge their innocence and lack of shame. The mission of the Vicario brothers in the novel is odious. The twins especially fear that the Arab community in town will react against them; but the Arabs in town, surprisingly, hold no grudge against the killers.

Clotilde Armenta is a strong woman, valiant and decisive, who tries wholeheartedly to stop the killing of Santiago. She and her husband, Rogelio de la Flor, own a shop where they sell milk in the morning and goods during the day; they also operate a bar in the evenings. Therefore, their shop is almost always open. Their business is located in the plaza, which Santiago's house faces. It is in their shop that the Vicario twins wait for Santiago in order to kill him. Clotilde sells the twins a bottle of liquor for no other reason than, hopefully, to get them too drunk to act. At first she thinks that the brothers do not have the heart to kill any man. However, as they continue to drink, she starts to realize that they are indeed serious. She also senses that the twins are looking for someone to stop them. She insists that the town's mayor, Lázaro Aponte, do something, and she is disillusioned when she realizes that he will not arrest the twins but simply takes the first set of knives away from them. Worried about the consequences that this might provoke, Clotilde sends people out to warn Santiago. She also sends a young girl to tell Father Amador. In addition, she sends a warning note to Santiago's maid, Victoria Guzmán. However, all her efforts are futile.

Luisa Santiaga is the mother of several characters in the novel. Her children include the narrator and Luis Enrique, both intimate friends of Santiago. Her youngest son is Jaime. She has a daughter who is a nun and another daughter, Margot, who is also a good friend of Santiago. Luisa Santiaga is strong in character. She is the godmother of Santiago and the person for whom he was named. Luisa Santiaga is the one who takes to the streets in an attempt to warn Plácida Linero, Santiago's mother, that the Vicario brothers are looking for her son to kill him. She rushed to the Nasars' house to prevent the crime, but her efforts are also in vain—she does not arrive in time.

Among the female characters close to Santiago Nasar who actually may have contributed to his death in various ways, the four most salient are Flora Miguel, Plácida Linero, Victoria Guzmán, and Divina Flor.

Flora Miguel is a woman who lacks grace and judgment. She is the conventional fiancée of Santiago Nasar. Her character is frivolous and selfish. Although she has been Santiago's betrothed since her teenage years, she demonstrates her immaturity at several opportune moments. Early on the day when Santiago dies, somebody tells Flora that the Vicario brothers are looking for her fiancé to kill him. She feels humiliated and hurt because of the rumor concerning why the Vicario brothers want to kill him and decides to end the relationship with Santiago instead of asking him for an explanation. When Santiago arrives at her home, Flora Miguel is so upset that she throws Santiago's "loveless" letters at him and bitterly screams, "I hope they kill you!" (270). Santiago stands there speechless, not knowing what to do. She runs to her room and locks the door.

Plácida Linero is Santiago's mother. She is one of the last people in town to hear about the Vicario brothers' intent. She is described as a beautiful woman who has lived in solitude since her husband, Ibrahim Nasar, died. As a solitary woman, she spends time interpreting dreams, yet she fails to interpret her son's dream as an omen of his death. Ironically, it is she who, in trying to stop the crime, closes the front door of her home to her son as he approaches to escape the Vicario brothers.

Victoria Guzmán deliberately abets the crime although she could have helped to stop it. Her decision to remain silent and thus allow the killing to proceed dates back to her youth, when Ibrahim Nasar, Santiago's father, seduced her and made love to her in secret for several years in the stables of his cattle ranch. As Victoria grew older and Ibrahim fell out of love with her, he brought her into his house as a maid. Victoria fears that Santiago is contemplating doing the same thing with her daughter, Divina Flor. Therefore, she despises Santiago. Knowing what it is to be a sexual object of a man who seems to have it all, Victoria Guzmán withholds the warning message that Clotilde Armenta sent with a beggar earlier on, which would have been early enough to prevent the crime. Victoria does this knowingly, as if to take revenge. She may have fallen as a young woman, but she is determined to prevent the same from happening to her daughter. The name *Victoria* is reminiscent of victory, as if to emphasize Victoria's triumph over an age-old tradition in which the landlord abuses the rights of women, whether maid, slave or otherwise.

Among the male secondary characters, there are two worthy of special mention: Cristo Bedoya and General Petronio San Román. Cristo Bedoya is one of Santiago's intimate friends. He is a young medical student who accompanies Santiago during the last minutes of his life. Of the circle of friends who grew up together in school, it is he who suffers the frustration and anguish of knowing Santiago's fate without being able to change it. He partakes, with Santiago and their other friends, in the celebration of Angela and Bayardo's wedding. He is so close to Santiago that he loves him like a brother. He and Santiago walk along the dock together while waiting for the bishop to arrive. The townsfolk look at them in bewilderment, knowing what is about to happen but not realizing that Santiago and Cristo are unaware. After Cristo and Santiago separate, an Arab friend of Santiago's father tells Cristo that the Vicario brothers are going to kill his son. Cristo races around, trying to find

Santiago and warn him. However, his efforts, too, are fruitless, and he witnesses Santiago's fatal stabbing just a few steps away.

General Petronio San Román is Bayardo's father. He is a hero of the civil wars of the nineteenth century and a member of the Conservative Party. His role in the novel, although small, is sufficient to demonstrate the glory and power that he gratuitously parades in public. The first time he arrives in town, he does so in a Ford Model T convertible with official license plates, in the company of his wife, Alberta Simonds, a tall, large mulatta from Curacao, and his two daughters. For Bayardo's wedding, he arrives with his family and his illustrious friends on the official vessel of the National Congress, loaded with wedding presents. At first glance, everybody in town knows that his son can marry any woman he wants. Petronio San Román, as a character, represents a recurring theme in García Márquez's writings, that of the two opposing Colombian parties, the Conservatives and the Liberals.

THEMATIC ISSUES

The reader, depending on the choice of focus, can recognize several different themes in this novel. For example, a reader may focus on the theme of machismo, a theme that, in turn, can be related to the theme of moral responsibility.

The theme of machismo in *Chronicle of a Death Foretold* can be observed as a form of emphasis on male pride and on the characters' sexual behavior. Upon his arrival to town, Bayardo San Román attracts the attention of the female characters by his looks and the way he dresses. His looks, however, make some female characters say that he looks like a *marica* ("a fairy"). This reaction by the female characters denotes an expected code of male behavior. This societal code is perhaps the justification for the bordello in town. It is male behavior to frequent this place, where women can be used as objects of desire. The males are proud to go there and feel no shame to show the results, not even when sexually transmitted diseases appear, as is the case with Pedro Vicario. Bayardo San Román shows his male pride when he returns Angela Vicario. The Vicario brothers flaunt their machismo in the abusive way they drink and also by defending an age-old tradition of placing the family's honor in the women's virginity.

The sexual behavior of the male characters shows an attitude passed on through the generations. Santiago Nasar, like his father before him, is a "sparrow hawk" (251). Both father and son have made a sport of having their young female servants for their own sexual satisfaction. The pun on *sparrow hawk* by the narrator is intended, both literally and sexually. Santiago's father, Ibrahim Nasar, teaches him the art of domesticating high-flying birds of prey. In addition, fidelity, to Santiago and his father, is not a part of the sexual or moral code. Males in this community can express their sexuality in any way they want because theirs is a patriarchal society (ruled by men according to men's needs). It may seem contradictory for the reader to realize that Bayardo San Román returns his wife because she is not a virgin when the same society glorifies men who go after women only to take away their virginity. The female characters succumb to this patriarchal society where women are educated to be stoic wives, passive beings capable of giving and expected to ask for nothing in return.

The incident motivating the killing of Santiago Nasar in *Chronicle of a Death Foretold* is the loss of honor by Angela Vicario. The blood of virginity, when lost outside the sanctity of marriage, can only be washed off with the blood of the perpetrator, cries an age-old Spanish folk tradition. In the town where the novel takes place, this tradition is morally acceptable. Therefore, the Vicario twins must kill Santiago Nasar to restore the family's honor. The townsfolk go along with this and see the twins' deed as morally acceptable; hence, they do nothing to stop the killing. There is only a small minority within the novel that objects to the killing. The majority views the Vicario brothers' deed as a socially and morally acceptable response. Within the moral parameters of Colombian rural society of the 1950s and 1960s, the loss of a woman's virginity without the balm of marriage destroyed not only the honor of the woman, but also that of the family. Such an act could only be absolved with the death of the perpetrator. This is why, without a legal trial or a simple conversation to clarify the innocence or the guilt of Santiago Nasar, the Vicario twins are convinced of their moral duty. Since Angela's father is blind, and thus unable to carry out this duty, the burden falls to the brothers. Ironically, the twins, who are now in charge of guarding the moral values of the family, were seen the night before drinking and carousing at a house of ill repute, in the company of Santiago Nasar, their ultimate victim. Moreover, one of the twins, Pedro Vicario, is suffering from a venereal disease that the town's doctor cannot cure. Pedro's blennorrhagia (gonorrhea) demonstrates a moral life that is, indeed, hardly praiseworthy.

On the surface, the Vicario family professes a strong moral value system. However, regarding Angela, they are a family that pays no attention to such essential values as love, respect for others, and free will. They know, because Angela tells them, that she does not love Bayardo San Román and does not want to marry him. However, they ignore her and decide to marry her even without her consent. Their morality takes a back seat when it comes to this marriage of convenience because Bayardo San Román is rich beyond imagination.

The moral value system of Bayardo San Román, the offended husband who returns his wife, is also ambiguous, if not ironic. He is the one who decides to marry Angela at first sight, before even being introduced to her. He is the one who, instead of courting her, pays more attention to seducing her family with his money and his charm. It is he who marries Angela, as if to purchase his happiness with his immeasurable fortune. It is Bayardo who, showing no scruples, forces Xius, a widower who married and lived in love in his house for many years, to sell that house to him because he wants it. Bayardo, as a character, shows no moral value system greater than his monetary system.

The moral and legal institutions of Church and state pay little attention to the Vicarios' thirst for revenge. Father Carmen Amador, who presumably is in charge of the town's religious values, refuses to get involved although he is clearly capable of putting a stop to the planned murder. He justifies his action by saying that he was concentrating his attention on the imminent arrival of his bishop. Ironically, the bishop arrives but does not disembark to greet the people who so anxiously await his visit. The civil authorities could stop the killing, but also choose to ignore it. The mayor of the town, Lázaro Aponte, could incarcerate the twins for carrying the knives and threatening to kill Santiago, but he chooses not to. It is his nonchalant way of enforcing the law that permits the twins to commit their crime.

Relating to the theme of moral responsibility, the town at large also bears its share of responsibility for the crime. The narrator insists that everybody in town knows the intention of the twins, but few make an honest attempt to stop it. There seems to be a kind of secret complicity among the townsfolk. Their silence can be viewed as a form of acceptance, a belief that the crime against Angela had to be avenged. Santiago, according to the town's code of moral responsibility, has done something wrong. The town's moral value of virginity is superior to a man's death. Only the blood of the perpetrator can wash off the blood of stolen virginity. The Vicario brothers believe that, but the townsfolk seem to enforce it. Early in the morning of the day of the killing, a crowd of women, men, children, and young people congregates on the dock to receive the visiting bishop. This type of behavior is consistent with what would be expected of a Christian town. Therefore, one would also expect to find a solid moral value system. However, when it comes time to stop the killing, the townspeople assume a passive role and act as mere observers of the spectacle. Their inaction seems to imply that redeeming a family's lost honor by the killing of the perpetrator is consistent with their collective sense of moral values.

All the town's individuals, from the civil and religious authorities to the simple folks, demonstrate an ambiguous sense of morality that challenges the presumed values of the town and the fundamental beliefs of society.

SOCIAL AND HISTORICAL CONTEXT

Chronicle of a Death Foretold is one of García Márquez's works that is least concerned with the political context, which permeates many of his other writings. Whether in *Leaf Storm, No One Writes to the Colonel, In Evil Hour, One Hundred Years of Solitude*, or *Love in the Time of Cholera*, the reader is faced with descriptions of the Colombian civil wars of the end of the nineteenth century. In *Chronicle of a Death Foretold*, however, this historical fact is dealt with in a single reference. The reference, however, should not pass unnoticed. General Petronio San Román, father of the groom, Bayardo San Román, is a member of the Conservative Party regime. Although the narrator describes him with admiration (he routed Colonel Aureliano Buendía of the Liberal Party), the narrator's mother, when she recognizes the general, will not even shake his hand. Luisa Santiaga remembers him as a traitor who ordered his troops to shoot Gerineldo Márquez in the back (208).

Although the historical context of the novel can be inferred from what has already been noted, the novel is not at all clear about the exact time of the events. What is clear is the time when García Márquez, working as a journalist, first heard of the incident, 1951; and the time when he published the book, 1981. In the early 1950s, Colombia was experiencing terrible shootouts between conservatives and liberals. This social and historical moment, recognized in Colombian history as La violencia (the Violence), is neither the background nor the focus of the novel. What are the background and focus, instead, are the disparity and even hatred between the rich and the poor. The marriage of Bayardo San Román and Angela Vicario provides a striking example of opposing social and economic forces. No one in town is as rich as Bayardo San Román. It is his wealth, along with his charm, that wins people over to him. This includes everyone—the priest, the mayor, and the town's aristocracy. Because of his wealth, Angela Vicario's mother says, in response to Angela's statement that she does not love Bayardo, "Love can be learned too" (209). The attacks on the wealthy found in *No One Writes to the Colonel* are well camouflaged in *Chronicle of a Death Foretold*, due, perhaps, to an effort to fully focus on the main plot. Another such attack, for example, occurs when Faustino Santos, an obscure character, asks the Vicario brothers why they must kill Santiago Nasar when there are plenty of other rich men who deserve to die first (223). The narrator, however, adds that Faustino Santos says this jokingly.

By 1981, when *Chronicle of a Death Foretold* was published, Colombia was facing many of the guerilla factions still fighting today. The guerilla groups of Colombia have been at war with the government's army since the 1950s. The Colombian guerillas, as reported by the world news, continue to resist to the present day. In 1981, García Márquez and his wife, Mercedes, were linked by rumor to a guerilla group, M-19, which specialized in urban violence. Although just a rumor, the government forces wanted to arrest García Márquez and his wife. The couple sought asylum in the Mexican embassy and then left the country. Later that year, Colombian President Belisario Betancur invited the couple to return (Anderson 70).

ALTERNATIVE READING: NEW TESTAMENT (INTERTEXUALITY)

In intertextuality the reader acknowledges that there is no orphan book. That is, no book is totally independent; every book can, in one way or another, be related to another book or books. Thus, critics often talk about influences of one writer over other writers and connections of one book to other books. (Intertextuality in its theoretical form was first introduced in Chapter 6.) The biblical reading in this chapter assumes the same concepts. A biblical reading of any text, in this case *Chronicle of a Death Foretold*, looks for ways in which the Bible as text has influenced the structure of another literary work. The Bible, as is also the case with Greek classics such as *Antigone, Oedipus Rex*, and *The Iliad*, has often been connected with modern works. Intertextuality allows the reader not only to find connections, but also to make interpretations. These interpretations may vary according to time and place, from generation to generation, and from reader to reader. Not all readers react in the same way to the same connection. This biblical reading of *Chronicle of a Death*

Foretold, for instance, is one that favors irony. Thus, this interpretation offers an ironic intertextual reading of some Christian elements found in *Chronicle of a Death Foretold*.

Irony is a way or mode of seeing things, a way of viewing existence. There is irony when one says something to express exactly the opposite (verbal irony). One often says, for example, "Aren't you sweet" to express dislike about someone else's poor manners. Irony in literature is a mode of representation that seems to negate that which it describes. Therefore, when García Márquez tells a story as he does, the reader is expected not to take the literal meaning of the text. Instead, the irony presented in his works should be "appropriated" by the reader (the reader should make it his or her own). When the reader is faced with irony, he or she must give to it an individual interpretation or "tone." When García Márquez uses irony, he knows that he can use humor, for example magic realism, to tell something serious. Unlike satire, irony does not pretend to censor or ridicule the faults and vices of the society that it depicts. Instead, it simply presents the absurdity of life. One of the greatest examples of irony in literature is the work *Don Quixote* by the Spanish author Miguel de Cervantes Saavedra.

The Vicario family is the protagonist in *Chronicle of a Death Foretold*. The word *vicarious* (*vicario* in Spanish) has a highly relevant and meaningful Catholic connotation. *Vicarious* denotes something done or endured by one person substituting for another. Therefore, the mission of someone acting vicariously is of great importance. For example, the Pope, according to Catholic theology, is Christ's substitute on earth and acts vicariously for Him.

The Vicario brothers are named Pedro and Pablo. Ironically, Pedro (Peter) and Pablo (Paul) are the names of two of the principal apostles of the Catholic Church. Both are considered pillars of the Church. Peter was the first Pope, appointed by Jesus himself to take his place (vicariously) to lead his flock, the Church (Matthew 16:18). The Apostle Peter, a fisherman by trade and a rather ignorant and simple man, showed great leadership in the books of the Gospel. It is he, among the twelve original apostles, who took the initiative and made decisions on matters of importance. Although he denied knowing his master three times, Peter was the first to enter the empty tomb of Jesus and give testimony to his resurrection. Like Peter the Apostle, Pedro Vicario in the novel is a simple and ignorant man but the leader of the two brothers. It is he who generally makes the important decisions, it is he who establishes the family's pig business and who decides to kill Santiago Nasar to redeem his sister's honor. Pedro is the one who convinces his brother Pablo that they have done nothing wrong and therefore need not confess their action to the priest.

The Apostle Paul was not one of the original twelve, nor was he ever Pope, but his mission, which was an important one, was to carry Christianity to pagan communities. Without his efforts, Christianity might not have spread beyond Israel. In *Chronicle of a Death Foretold*, Pablo Vicario assumes leadership, after the mayor of the town takes away the brothers' first set of knives. He seeks out a second set of knives and practically drags Pedro forward to complete their task. Pablo is the first to run to kill Santiago when the brothers see him approach his house. Without Pablo's obstinacy, Santiago might not have died.

Angela Vicario is another character who can be interpreted as substituting for someone else. The irony is in her name, Angela. The reader of *Chronicle of a Death Foretold* will think of an angel. In Catholic doctrine, an angel is a spiritual being endowed with both intelligence and free will. An angel is a messenger of God and an advisor of humans. The word *angel* also denotes qualities of beauty, innocence, truth, and purity. Angela Vicario is certainly beautiful, but unlike an angel, she is not pure. She not only loses her virginity before she is married but also hides the truth from her husband-to-be. She is, like her twin brothers, a vicarious being. She assumes the role of an angel but performs it poorly. She condemns the innocent Santiago Nasar to death and her husband, Bayardo San Román, to shame. The reader of García Márquez may remember that angels in his work do not generally seem to enjoy the biblical qualities that angels traditionally hold. In the short story "A Very Old Man with Enormous Wings," for example, the angel is treated like a circus animal (see Chapter 5).

Angela's mother is Purísima del Carmen Vicario. Ironically, she, too, plays a vicarious role. Her name, Purísima, leads the reader familiar with Catholic theology to think of the purest (*purísima*) figure, the Virgin Mary. As if to honor Mary's name, Purísima pays particular attention to the upbringing and the education of her daughters. She looks like a nun, recalls the narrator. Purísima Vicario is unrelenting in the education of her daughters as dutiful wives. To Purísima Vicario, there are no better daughters in the entire town. They are perfect, she would say; but they are not. Purísima (the purest) fails to see the lack of purity in her youngest, Angela.

To complete the irony of the Vicario family, the narrative includes the father, Poncio (in English, Pontius). Pontius Pilate is remembered for washing his hands during the trial of Jesus. He did not want to be held responsible for the death of an innocent man. Poncio Vicario, like Pontius Pilate, also washes his hands when the time comes to decide the future of his daughter Angela. When the Vicario family gets together to consider the marriage proposal of Bayardo San Román, it is the wife and Angela's siblings who decide in favor of the marriage. As the head of the family, Poncio Vicario should make the decision, but instead he remains silent, saying nothing. Poncio symbolically washes his hands on two other occasions: the killing of an innocent man, Santiago, and the public shame of Bayardo San Román. The religious irony is clear to the reader. The family's name is Vicario and Vicario translates as *vicariously*, which in turn means to play the role of someone else. This family is intentionally named Vicario because its members are playing a role they wish not to lead.

The irony of this biblical intertextual reading is most obvious when the reader examines the character of Santiago Nasar. Santiago incarnates, even in small details, the persona of Jesus. Jesus was born in the Middle East (Bethlehem). The Nasar family comes from the Middle East and speaks Arabic, a language spoken today in the birthplace of Jesus. Nasar, Santiago's family name, reminds the reader of the word *Nazareth*, Jesus' hometown. Santiago Nasar's cattle ranch is significantly called the "Divine Face"; it is a ranch that Nasar tends with meticulous care. The majority of the witnesses describe the day of the killing as ominous. They note that it started to rain by five in the afternoon. They also mention that at the time of the murder, there was a light rain falling. Ironically, however, Santiago comments to everyone he meets that it is a beautiful day. The day that Jesus died was also gloomy and foreboding. It was cloudy and started to rain late in the day. Catholics, however, celebrate that day as a beautiful day because, with Jesus' death, humanity achieved salvation.

Although there were many disciples who followed Him, Jesus selected a group of twelve to continue his mission. Among them were three apostles who were close friends of one another, Peter, James, and John. James and John were brothers. In *Chronicle of a Death Foretold*, Santiago Nasar also has three close friends, Cristo Bedoya, the narrator, and Luis Enrique. Two of the friends are also brothers, the narrator and Luis Enrique. Jesus shared three years of his life with the apostles, but his three closest friends participated in the most significant moments of his life: the Transfiguration, when Jesus allowed Peter, James, and John to look on his divinity; his most important miracles; and his agony on the Mount of Olives.

In the last days of his life, Jesus celebrated Passover in the company of his apostles, a most important celebration for Jews. This is a day of eating, singing, and dancing, a joyful celebration of the release of the Jews from their Egyptian captivity. Santiago Nasar also spends some of the last hours of his life in the company of his friends at a celebration. He and his friends take part in the wedding celebration of Angela Vicario and Bayardo San Román. The novel presents Santiago with his friends together at one table: eating, drinking, enjoying themselves, and even sharing a cup of wine with the groom, Bayardo San Román. Catholic theology presents Jesus as the groom and the Church as his mystical wife.

Immediately after the Passover dinner, Jesus retired with his apostles to the Garden of Gethsemane because he knew that the time had come for him to be turned over to the authorities for judgment. This was a special moment, and Jesus called for his closest three friends, Peter, James, and John, to console him and pray with him because he knew that he would soon die. After the wedding, Santiago also retires with his three closest friends, Cristo Bedoya, the narrator, and Luis Enrique. Ironically, the friends do just the opposite of praying. They go to a bordello run by María Alejandrina Cervantes. The Vicario brothers also stop at the bordello, where they sing and drink with Santiago Nasar and his friends five hours before they kill him. This scene reminds the reader of Judas Iscariot who, like the Vicario brothers, ate and drank with Jesus shortly before betraying him. When the Roman soldiers came to the Garden of Gethsemane and arrested Jesus, Peter drew his sword and cut off the ear of one of the soldiers. Jesus disapproved of this action and surrendered himself without resistance, an act that culminated in his own death. When Santiago Nasar is about to leave the house of his fiancée, Flora Miguel, and return to his own home minutes before he is killed, Nahir Miguel, Flora's father, offers him a rifle to defend himself from the Vicario brothers. However, Santiago Nasar does not accept the weapon.

When Santiago is killed, he is wearing a white linen suit that he chose to wear because he was expected to greet the visiting bishop. This is a small detail, but one that can be interpreted as having great significance. A tunic of white linen is the appropriate dress of priests in the Catholic Church. In both the Old and New Testaments, a white tunic was reserved for the priest who presided over the liturgy. This tradition continues in the present time. Jesus was dressed in a white tunic when he was taken prisoner by the Romans. At that moment, He was both priest and victim. In *Chronicle of a Death Foretold*, Santiago dresses in white when he is killed and, like Jesus, he is victim (although not priest).

Jesus was judged by both civil and religious authorities. Santiago is judged by the conscience of the townspeople at large, including both the civil and religious authorities. To some, Santiago is innocent; to others, he is guilty. Pontius Pilate realized that Jesus was innocent, and he did not want to bear the responsibility for His death. Therefore, Pilate let the townspeople decide. Although there were those who would have let Jesus go free, the majority decided that Jesus must die, and nothing changed their decision. The Vicario brothers do not want to kill Santiago, and they do everything possible to avoid doing so. However, in effect, the town at large insists that Santiago must die by doing nothing to stop the deed.

The townspeople play a significant role in *Chronicle of a Death Foretold*. The whole town prepares to witness the death of Santiago Nasar in the same way that they would prepare to watch a parade. Jesus died, having been nailed to a wooden cross. Similarly, the blows that kill Santiago are delivered against the wooden door of his home. After His hands and feet were nailed to the cross, Jesus' side was pierced with a spear and water and blood flowed from the cut. Santiago is stabbed in the hands and the side. The first time Santiago is stabbed the knife comes out clean, but thereafter, blood comes from the cut in the back. Just before Jesus died, He invoked the name of his mother. In *Chronicle of a Death Foretold*, Santiago cries, "Oh, mother of mine" (273) shortly before he dies. At the foot of the cross where Jesus died, Jesus' mother cried along with the Apostle John and a few women, among them Mary Magdalene, the sinner whom Jesus had saved from being stoned to death. As Santiago is bleeding to death, his mother cries for him, along with his friend Cristo and María Alejandrina Cervantes, the madam of the local bordello.

After his death, Jesus rose from the dead, according to Catholic doctrine. His resurrected body was totally different from His human body. Those who saw Him said that His clothes were brilliantly white and His face radiantly beautiful. In *Chronicle of a Death Foretold*, Divina Flor, Santiago's maid, has a vision after Santiago's death. In her vision, Divina Flor sees Santiago Nasar walking up the stairs dressed in white with a bouquet of flowers in his hand. Argénida Lanao, the oldest daughter of Santiago's neighbor says, minutes before Santiago dies, "His Saracen face with its dashing ringlets was handsomer than ever" (275).

Finally, as was the case with the life and death of Jesus, according to the Christian tradition, an innocent man, Santiago Nasar, is put to death to atone for the community at large.

8

Love in the Time of Cholera
(1985)

Carlos R. Rodríguez, a friend of García Márquez and well-known literary critic, wrote that if *One Hundred Years of Solitude* had not secured the road to Stockholm for García Márquez to receive the Nobel Prize in literature, *Love in the Time of Cholera* would have done so. Although with reservations, the critic considers *Love in the Time of Cholera* superior to *One Hundred Years of Solitude* (239–244). *Love in the Time of Cholera* may be seen as the product of a more experienced author, who no longer needs the resources of magic realism and ambiguity to surprise the reader. There are other critics, by contrast, who find strong similarities between *Love in the Time of Cholera* and *One Hundred Years of Solitude*. Kathleen McNerney, for instance, finds that Florentino's letter writing can be thought of as constituting the novel itself, just as Melquíades' parchments tell the story of *One Hundred Years of Solitude* (McNerney 79). McNerney also points out the obvious about the novel by saying that the story is framed around an unusual love triangle (McNerney 74). The love triangle can be called unusual because one of the lovers is not physically involved but instead waits more than fifty years for his turn. It is also an unusual novel because the greatest lovers of all time have always been depicted as young, not old. With García Márquez's novel, readers around the world are reminded that love is ageless, in the sense that lovers do not have to be young to fall in love. Although falling in love may indeed be a common practice among the elderly, societal and cultural etiquette views such love as inappropriate and even shameful, as the character of Ofelia, Fermina's daughter, expresses it in the novel. However, neither the aging of Florentino and Fermina, society, nor anything else can interfere with the sublime love the old couple shares.

Love in the Time of Cholera, like all Gabriel García Márquez's works, explores the solitude of the individual and of humankind. In this novel, the existential anguish of feeling alone is portrayed through the solitude of love and of being in love.

PLOT DEVELOPMENT

Curiosity and suspense are two key words in understanding the plot of *Love in the Time of Cholera*. The reader feels the curiosity of a private detective in trying to figure out who Jeremiah Saint-Amour is, why he committed suicide, and what he wrote in the eleven-page letter he left for Dr. Juvenal Urbino. Who is Jeremiah's lover, and who is this man named Florentino Ariza? The latter shows up at the doctor's funeral and tells the widow: "I have waited for this opportunity for more than half a century, to repeat to you once again my vow of eternal fidelity and everlasting love" (64).

The novel's opening chapter foreshadows the importance of Dr. Juvenal Urbino and his wife, Fermina Daza, but most readers would not expect this since Dr. Urbino dies before the end of the first chapter. Naively, the reader may expect to see Dr. Juvenal Urbino bury his friend, Jeremiah Saint-Amour, at five in the afternoon. Instead, in disbelief, the reader learns that the doctor dies, after lunch on the same day, for the absurd reason of trying to catch a parrot. The narrator continually contradicts any suppositions readers may have made regarding the plot. This type of narrative stimulates readers to continue with the long, and at times slow-moving, love story.

The plot of *Love in the Time of Cholera* is, among other possibilities, about learning to wait, about perseverance and endurance, and about never forsaking the object of one's love. However, it is also about eternal fidelity and everlasting love, as Florentino Ariza stated it in the previous quotation.

Subsequent chapters take readers back in time to a story of love at first sight. If the novel followed a traditional linear plot line, it would have started with the second chapter, when Florentino, at age eighteen, meets Fermina, who is thirteen. The background of the plot is that of a port city, Cartagena de Indias, in the coastal northeast of Colombia, which has suffered through cholera panic and countless civil wars. The different social spheres of the plot's background depict an impoverished and dying wealthy class; an emerging middle class, which includes foreigners; and the poor classes, which make up two-thirds of the total population. The poor classes include mulattos and blacks, plus a few Chinese who account for a small Chinatown of four streets.

Nothing seems impossible for the young lovers, Florentino Ariza and Fermina Daza. While the two seem determined to fight for one another against all odds, Fermina's father, Lorenzo Daza, an illiterate Spanish immigrant, is equally decided to marry Fermina well. He strongly believes in upward mobility, and his last resort is his daughter's wedding. Florentino, being poor, is not a choice of whom Fermina's father will approve, but Fermina persists in her relationship with Florentino despite her father's wishes. However, after receiving four years of love letters, poems, telegrams, and music written and played just for her, Fermina suddenly tells Florentino that what she feels is not love. It is all an illusion, a spell she no longer believes in and wants no part of. Her reaction seems as unexpected and childlike as her reaction when they first met.

What readers thought was a perfect example of a fairy tale is thus ended by a stubborn young protagonist. Is Fermina indeed out of love or is her statement a reaction to her father telling her they are ruined? She turns her back on Florentino but he does not give up. Instead, he waits for the opportunity to reassure her of his love when they meet once again: fifty-one years, nine months, and four days later, at the funeral of Fermina's husband, Dr. Juvenal Urbino.

During those years, with Florentino Ariza out of the picture, Dr. Juvenal Urbino's persistence triumphs over the indifference of the young and beautiful Fermina. They first meet as doctor and patient (140). Dr. Juvenal Urbino goes to the wrong house, looking for an eighteen year-old girl who is supposed to be suffering from symptoms of cholera. Perhaps because he pays no attention to Fermina's flowering beauty, she thinks he is a selfish man, unable to love anyone other than himself. Fermina's father, however, is very taken with the doctor's family name. Eventually, the beautiful young girl, who is scorned and ridiculed by the social group to which Dr. Urbino belongs, goes on to marry the town's most eligible bachelor. Her wedding is splendid and unforgettable. The ultimate glory of the wedding is that the three-term president of the country attends (188). Does Dr. Juvenal Urbino love her? According to the omniscient narrator, Juvenal Urbino is aware that he does not love Fermina. Although he marries her out of physical attraction and even vanity, on their honeymoon he realizes that he could, indeed, fall in love with her.

Their Paris honeymoon lasts sixteen months, and the small-town girl learns of fashion, art, and literature. In this city, where Dr. Juvenal Urbino went to medical school, the young couple wants to see Victor Hugo, the French romantic writer, for whom Dr. Juvenal Urbino has a special liking, but they have to be content with the shared memory of glancing at Oscar Wilde (the Irish writer, poet, and dramatist who died in Paris). By the time the young married couple comes back to Cartagena de Indias, Fermina is six months pregnant with her first child.

After seeing Fermina coming out of church, pregnant with her first child, Florentino Ariza makes the decision "to win fame and fortune in order to deserve her" (199). He decides to wait "even till the end of time" (199). However, in a prejudiced society, economic success is not enough for a man whose bloodlines are unknown. Florentino Ariza was baptized, although he is a bastard, "a child of the street" in Spanish vernacular. He is the son of an unwed mother and a father who died without leaving him anything. Florentino's mother is herself an illegitimate child. Despite this background, Florentino Ariza manages to work his way up to become president of the River Company of the Caribbean—the only such company existing for the past one hundred years. During the entire time while Florentino waits to talk to Fermina again (fifty-one years, nine months, and four days), he never stops thinking about her, but he has many affairs, which he refers to as noncommitted love. He keeps a diary (actually, twenty-five in all), where he records the affairs of 622 lovers all grouped under one title: *They* (the feminine plural form in Spanish is *Ellas*). Some of these affairs appear as subplots interconnected to the main plot. These female lovers, each with their own strong will and sexuality, contribute to the strengthening of character that Fermina would observe later on, and even admire. Most of the lovers are widows. However, there are also married women; single women such as Leona Cassiani, with whom his affair lasts, off-and-on, for thirty years; prostitutes; and an incestuous affair with América Vicuña, a fourteen-year-old blood relative, who is entrusted to him by her own parents. Most readers, whether male or female, would question Florentino's conduct in light of his vow of eternal fidelity and everlasting love to Fermina. What kind of man could be so callous as to mislead a fourteen-year-old relative (who ends up committing suicide)? Is this something only a bastard, a son of the streets, would do?

Florentino feels inferior to Dr. Juvenal Urbino. They are members of two very different social classes, which is also true of Dr. Juvenal Urbino and Fermina Daza. However, the two classes converge into one for Juvenal and Fermina. This is not the case for Florentino and Fermina, despite Florentino's accomplishments and contributions to society.

Fermina becomes a faithful and loving wife. She fulfills her obligations both as wife and mother, and she grows to be the perfect consort for an important public figure. They have a son, Marco Aurelio, who becomes a doctor, thus continuing the family tradition; and a daughter, Ofelia, who is as beautiful as Fermina Daza was when she was young. Fermina's father, Lorenzo Daza, was a successful outlaw who was asked to leave his country because the governor of the province knew he had ignored all human and divine laws (254). When Lorenzo Daza dies, Fermina does not wear mourning but cries for him secretly. Fermina's strong character hardly ever breaks. Among the few times she does break is when her husband is adulterous. At age fifty-eight, the specter of infidelity enters the heart of Dr. Juvenal Urbino. He has an affair with Miss Bárbara Lynch, "a tall, elegant, large-boned mulatta" (292), who is a doctor of theology. Fermina's anger, interestingly enough, is not so much because of her husband's infidelity but because her honor is the subject of gossip and, also, because Barbara Lynch is black. As a result of her husband's indiscretion, Fermina leaves the house for two years. She goes to live with her cousin Hildebranda in the countryside.

After reading about all these happenings, the reader is brought back again to the present time. It has been two weeks since the doctor died and two weeks since Florentino spoke to Fermina. It is at this point that the plot continues.

Fermina and Florentino's love story can be clearly seen in two parts. The first is when Florentino ingeniously, but unsuccessfully, tries to conquer Fermina's love. Although he is not experienced, he manages to win her attention and innocent teenage love until she comes to realize that she does not love him. The second part takes place at the end of their lives. She is now seventy-two years old and he is seventy-seven. He persists in his love for her, and Fermina, although still firm and strong of character, accepts him.

The abundance of literature that Florentino Ariza absorbed in his childhood and his extraordinary ability to write are two elements that contribute greatly to the novel's plot. Florentino wins Fermina over, both the first and the second times, with the letters he writes to her. The first time they are both teenagers. Their relationship, at that time, is exclusively based on Florentino's love letters, to which Fermina responds with equal passion. They hardly ever have a chance to talk, to interact, or to get to know each other. Their relationship during the first part, although strongly passionate, is rather precarious. The passion they both experience is such that Florentino proposes and she accepts. However, their childlike game has gone too far and the spell is broken for Fermina.

When they meet again nearly sixty years later, for most of which time Fermina was married, she rejects Florentino once more. It is at this time, nevertheless, that Florentino starts to write to Fermina again. His letters are formal in the beginning, in an effort to console her, but later he changes to a seductive mode. Florentino is not as graceful and handsome as Dr. Juvenal Urbino, but the power of his penmanship and his wholehearted insistence give him the edge that he needs to win her love. His tenacity—obsession, even—convinces Fermina that it is never too late to love. The novel ends on this upbeat note.

Although labyrinthine, the plot of *Love in the Time of Cholera* is rather accessible, even for first-time readers of Gabriel García Márquez. One can easily recognize the causality of events, even though they are not presented in strict chronological order—the novel begins in medias res (in the middle of things). The plot begins with the teenage love of Florentino and Fermina. The crux (the central or critical point) and longest part of *Love in the Time of Cholera* is what happens while Florentino and Fermina live separate lives. This time frame allows for personal growth and the maturation of the concept of love. The denouement coincides with the last chapter of the novel. Near the end, Fermina muses over how a person can be happy for so many years, through good times and bad, without even knowing if the emotion was really love (399). The novel culminates with the couple making love again and again. This is an elderly couple that is happy to be together and to be alive. Their relationship seemed hopeless except for Florentino's chronic romanticism and tireless desire to love Fermina. However, what unites this couple in love is the combination of Florentino's perseverance and Fermina's strong character. In the end, it is Fermina who faces the toughest battle in order to love. The battle that seems to summarize her will and determination is the one against her own daughter, Ofelia, who believes that love at her mother's age is revolting. Ofelia insists that Florentino's reputation, as everyone knows, is that of a pervert, and that Fermina's relationship with him will only do harm to the family's name. Fermina's response is a categorical, "they can all go to hell" (392).

GENRE AND NARRATIVE STRUCTURE

Love in the Time of Cholera is an intentional return to nineteenth-century realism and the outright fantasy we associate with García Márquez is absent, asserted critic Gene H. Bell-Villada (Bell-Villada 191). However, although there is plenty of realism in *Love in the Time of Cholera*, realism alone does not circumscribe the novel. Realism, in its purest form, rejects imaginative idealizations in favor of a detailed reality and sometimes focuses on triviality and the sordid aspects of life and nature. Realism is obvious in *Love in the Time of Cholera* in the portrayal of people's attitudes, physical settings, and material conditions. The descriptions of Florentino, Fermina, and Juvenal Urbino in the novel are so detailed and complete as to make them picture perfect, in the sense that the reader can almost see them as if in person; this technique is highly favored by realism. The same is true for the deplorable conditions in which the poor live, which is certainly emphasized in the decay of nature along the Magdalena River. The reality of the description discloses the exploitation of a dying nature. It is interesting to note the parallelism between the aging of Florentino and the decay of nature in the scenes where he takes the second trip down the Magdalena River, this time with Fermina. Furthermore, like a realist novel, *Love in the Time of Cholera* favors the lives of the middle and lower classes. The time frame of the novel, on the one hand, also calls for realism, for realism was most prominent in France between 1850 and 1880, around the time when Fermina and Juvenal Urbino lived in Paris for eighteen months. On the other hand, between 1880 and 1910 most Latin American writers began experimenting with realism as a literary form and the Latin American countries experienced social and cultural changes along with foreign investment. In Latin American literature this new reality adopted the French and Spanish tradition of realism, which tries to depict a faithful representation of life.

While this is indeed true for a realist novel, it is not necessarily the case for *Love in the Time of Cholera*. The detailed representation of both people and nature in *Love in the Time of Cholera* seems to come up short when it comes to the idealization of Fermina by Florentino. The concept of love itself loses its entire realist meaning and changes the novel into a *realist romantic* novel, which is a combination of the two. Unlike the objectivity of realism, the love of Florentino for Fermina is totally subjective. Like a true romantic, Florentino believes in the idea of dying for love. He dresses in black, the favorite color of romantics; he reads and writes poetry; and his face is pale like the descriptions of romantic poets.

While love as a theme does not necessarily call for romanticism (love in literature can be traced as far back as the Middle Ages), *Love in the Time of Cholera* depicts love both realistically and romantically.

Unlike many of García Márquez's works, including his first book, *Leaf Storm, Love in the Time of Cholera* does not reflect an experimental structure. There is no shift in viewpoint and no use of stream of consciousness, two rather typical examples of experimental structure in García Márquez's writing. However, the structure at the start of *Love in the Time of Cholera* will not seem strange to readers of García Márquez. As is the case with most of his writing, *Love in the Time of Cholera* starts with a technique most commonly used in motion pictures: in medias res, or in the middle (see Chapter 3). At the very start of the novel the reader is presented with a dead man that the reader knows nothing about. The omniscient narrator provides any and all information. The death of Jeremiah Saint-Amour, a secondary character, provides the opportunity the narrator needs to talk about love between socially and economically displaced blacks, in the same way that the death of Dr. Juvenal Urbino provides the opportunity to talk about love among the ruling class. The death of Dr. Juvenal Urbino also takes place in the first chapter when he is eighty-one years old. The first chapter, which opens in medias res, sets up the story, which is told thereafter in chronological format, which is easier to read but not often used by García Márquez. The events are narrated in a linear fashion, following the lives of Fermina Daza and Florentino Ariza. (The narrative structure of the novel could have started with Chapter 2 had it been a completely linear narrative.)

An interesting way of viewing the structure of *Love in the Time of Cholera* is suggested by the epigraph that appears at the start of the novel, which suggests that the structure be viewed as a song, a *vallenato*. The epigraph reads:

> The words I am about to express:
> They now have their own crowned goddess.
> Leandro Díaz.

To Florentino, Fermina is indeed the *diosa coronada*, the crowned goddess. Florentino repeats the verse verbatim at least five times throughout the novel. The first time is when Florentino sees Fermina dressed in what looks like a Greek tunic, with a garland of fresh gardenias in her hair that "made her look like a crowned goddess" (74).

Where does this epigraph come from and who is Leandro Díaz? The epigraph itself is part of a *vallenato*, a musical genre that normally talks about folk heroes, love affairs, and other quarrels and was influenced by a combination of African, European, and folkloric Indian sounds. Leandro Díaz is among the best-known singer/songwriters of such genre. However, *vallenato* music is an obscure genre hardly known outside Colombia. Why then would García Márquez select such a little-known musician? The epigraphs in *Leaf Storm* (1955), *Chronicle of a Death Foretold* (1981), *The General in His Labyrinth* (1989), and *Of Love and Other Demons* (1994) bear the names of people who are highly recognizable. The epigraph in *Leaf Storm* is by Sophocles, one of classical Athens's three great playwrights (the other two being Aeschylus and Euripides). The epigraph in *Chronicle of a Death Foretold* is by Gil Vicente, a Portuguese dramatist of the sixteenth century who wrote both in Spanish and Portuguese. *The General in His Labyrinth* contains an epigraph by Simón Bolívar, the South American liberator. In *Of Love and Other Demons* the epigraph is by Thomas Aquinas, the Italian religious philosopher of the Middle Ages turned saint who, to date, is still one of the most influential theologians of the Catholic Church.

García Márquez's choice of a relative unknown, Leandro Díaz, is consistent with his tendency to favor popular culture, which he views as the source of all culture, and it also signals the autobiographical nature of the story, which mirrors the love relationship between his own parents (see Chapter 1).

Another point regarding García Márquez's selection of this musician relates to the manner in which he sometimes thinks of his writings. The Colombian magazine *Cambio* (Change) quoted him as saying that *One Hundred Years of Solitude* is a 400-page *vallenato* and *Love in the Time of Cholera*, a 380-page *bolero*. *Bolero* is another form of Latin American music, whose dance is also known as *bolero*. While the *vallenato* talks about single folk heroes, such as Colonel Aureliano Buendía in *One Hundred Years of Solitude*, *boleros* normally depict love songs where the lovers go through penance, suffering, and often rejection, as in *Love in The Time of Cholera*.

CHARACTER DEVELOPMENT

Character development in *Love in the Time of Cholera* depends both on the consciousness of the omniscient narrator and on the consciousness of the characters as they interact in the novel's story line. *Love in the Time of Cholera* presents fewer characters than *One Hundred Years of Solitude*. The illusion in the former, however, is the same as in the latter. A reader envisions tumultuous crowds, large gatherings, parties, celebrations, and crowded neighborhoods with lots of people on the streets. They see a moviehouse with no empty seats, vibrant cities and towns, and people everywhere: at church, traveling, walking down the streets of Cartagena de Indias, the Colombian country side, and the streets of Paris. Most of the people in these crowds are only references without names. Some of them exist in the memory of the reader for what they were doing at the moment of the narrative, as if in a snapshot. The president of the republic is merely an enunciation, as is Dr. Adrien Proust, the father of the famous French writer Marcel Proust, and the twenty-eighth president of the United States, Woodrow Wilson. It is the same with other established literary figures, fashion designers, and generals who participated in the Colombian civil wars. They come in and out of the narrative as a sketch. Although this is true for most of the minor characters, the main characters are carefully and meticulously drawn.

Fermina Daza, Juvenal Urbino, and Florentino Ariza are developed from a social and psychological viewpoint. These viewpoints are strongly enriched by the moral and religious principles that the characters share. Whereas Fermina and Florentino appear as the two pillars on which the novel stands, Juvenal Urbino is strong enough to shake the structure and change the course of the narrative. Through the plot, which is seemingly simple yet abundant in detailed information, the reader gains extensive knowledge of who Fermina, Juvenal, and Florentino really are. The reader may end up judging them, but the author does not; without judgment, the narrative includes their likes and dislikes, preferences, shortcomings, reactions, and ambitions.

Fermina's character is developed in three clearly defined phases. These three phases are marked by significant details within the novel. The first phase can be observed when she is a teenage girl living in her father's house. At that time Fermina is described as long-boned, slim, with steel-blue hair and clear almond eyes, and an inborn haughtiness, diligent, and of strong character (41). She loves flowers, birds, and domestic animals. Fermina's haughtiness, stubbornness, and cleverness can be seen when her father sends her away, on a journey to forget (102). However, the plan does not work, as the two young lovers find a way to communicate by telegraph. When Fermina returns, a year and half later, her father thinks that his daughter has forgotten her young lover. However, when she opens the balcony window the morning after their arrival, "she no longer thought of him as the impossible sweetheart but as the certain husband to whom she belonged heart and soul" (121). Most readers are therefore astonished when she decides to end the relationship, which she now sees as a chimera. With her first sight of Florentino after their long separation, the spell is broken. She argues that their love is just an illusion (126). The reader may think that her reaction is immature (recall that she is only seventeen), but the author does not comment.

The second phase in Fermina's character development starts with the realization of her father's dream "to turn his daughter into a great lady" (100). Lorenzo Daza wants a propitious marriage for his daughter Fermina, which results in a marriage of convenience to the renowned doctor Juvenal Urbino. Throughout her marriage, she adapts to an upper social class but never fully embraces it. She turns into a serious, faithful, and responsible woman. Hers is a stable, perfect family: a hard-working husband and two children, a boy and a girl. Of the three phases of her life, this is the longest and most tedious.

The third phase in Fermina's character development comes when she reencounters Florentino at the death of her husband, after fifty-one years, nine months, and four days. Fermina behaves as a respectable widow, mature and self-controlled, but Florentino eventually manages to win her over. She then gives herself totally, generously sharing with him a kind of love perhaps neither had ever experienced before.

Dr. Juvenal Urbino de la Calle is meticulously developed. As readers we become aware of the smallest details of his personality and of his roles as doctor, professor, socialite, and even lover, both faithful and unfaithful. He is the personification of correctness. In all aspects of his life he seems perfect: socially, aesthetically, economically, religiously, and (almost) morally. He is the scion of a distinguished family. He completed advanced studies in medicine and surgery in Paris. He is knowledgeable in his field, in literature, in music, and in fashion; he is captivating and seducing; he is a good dancer and pianist; he possesses all the graces to make him, at the age of twenty-eight, "the most desirable of bachelors" (128). He favors classical music and prefers French literature to Spanish authors. For this purpose, he has a bookseller who periodically sends him the latest publications from Paris. Among other authors, he reads Anatole France, Pierre Loti, Remy de Gourmont, Paul Bourget, Oscar Wilde, and Victor Hugo (195–97). Although he is a practicing and extremely pious Catholic, who invokes the Holy Spirit and punctually attends all religious functions, he is unfaithful to his wife. He betrays her with Bárbara Lynch, a beautiful mulatta with whom he enjoys the pleasures of a passionate affair (291–304). Consistent with his religious and moral principles, however, he repents. He confesses to his wife, asks her to forgive him, and remains faithful until he dies. However, behind all this correctness, his real self is somehow camouflaged.

Indeed, he is conscious that he is not in love with his wife. He loves her exterior, but they are not compatible in temperament.

Florentino Ariza, in very many ways, is the antithesis of Dr. Juvenal Urbino. He is everything Juvenal Urbino is not. He is homely and sickly looking, has no sense of fashion, comes from a poor and broken family, holds no university degrees (in fact, he may not have finished high school), is not a practicing Catholic, prefers to read minor Spanish authors, is not a socialite, and seems to have no direction in life. However, of all the characters, he is the one who feels love the most; he loves passionately and with tremendous abandonment.

As with Fermina, Florentino's character can be seen in three stages of development. The first stage presents Florentino as a phantom-like character. He lives a quiet life, passing unnoticed in the crowd. His only reason for existence is to watch Fermina walk through the park on her way to school and back. Other than the time he spends as a clerk at the post office, he passes most of his time reading and writing love letters to Fermina. This platonic love, which is more spiritual than physical, ends after three years with a vitrious rejection by Fermina. However, the flame of his passion for her does not fade. He waits—for fifty-one years, nine months, and four days—to reiterate his love for her.

The second developmental stage, which covers the near half-century between their meetings, turns Florentino into a man of business and of great social and economic success. His phantom-like appearance is now only the disguise for a life of indiscriminate sex. He had wanted to keep himself a virgin, to honor Fermina, but fails. From writing letters to Fermina in the first stage, he turns to writing a diary of his love affairs, and in twenty-five booklets he records 622 entries. Despite these many affairs, however, he remains single, hoping one day to marry Fermina. However, he may never have imagined how long he would have to wait.

The third stage finds Florentino an old man, bald and wearing dentures. His love for Fermina has not changed, but neither has her stubbornness, for she rejects him again at her husband's funeral. This time, however, the rejection lasts only two weeks. Over the course of the following year, in the same way he did when they were young, Florentino writes Fermina 132 letters, and this time he wins her love. Florentino Ariza is given a second chance, and this time he is ready. He has undergone a complete metamorphosis, including his dress code (the only thing he would not change before). Florentino, from the start, is a kind of Eros (the god of love in Greek mythology), and it is his character that sustains the narrative.

It is interesting to see how García Márquez plays with the symbolism of names, as if he wanted to challenge the reader's response regarding the moral values of Florentino. Florentino Ariza is a son of the streets, a bastard, by the mere fact that his father would not recognize him; *son of the streets* in Spanish is *hijo de la calle*. This is very close to the name that Dr. Juvenal Urbino holds proudly as part of his noble name: The doctor's full name is Juvenal Urbino de la Calle, with a capital C.

There are also many secondary characters whose presences contribute to the changes the main characters go through. Aunt Escolástica is a loving, illiterate spinster who raises Fermina as if she were her own until the day her brother realizes that she is responsible for letting Florentino come close to his daughter. Then he sends her, penniless, back to San Juan de la Ciénaga.

Lorenzo Daza, Fermina's father, is an upstart who leaves Spain looking for a better future. In the Colombian mountain region, in San Juan de la Ciénaga, the illiterate Spaniard's good fortune begins when he marries Fermina Sánchez, a rich farm girl whose parents are against her love for Lorenzo Daza. Lorenzo Daza's wife gives birth to a girl called Fermina, like her mother. After his wife's death, Lorenzo, his daughter, and his sister, Escolástica, move to the coastal city of Cartagena de Indias. Although lacking social skills, Lorenzo Daza buys and remodels an old colonial house in the Park of the Evangelists. A strong disciplinarian, he rules his house with an iron fist. He lacks the company of friends, enjoys drinking, and gets involved in illegal business.

Among the long list of 622 lovers are several worth mentioning, including Leona Cassiani, Sara Noriega, Olimpia Zuleta, Prudencia Pitre, Angeles Alfaro, and Ausencia Santander. Leona Cassiani represents, by far, the longest of the 622 affairs. (In the section on a feminist reading of this chapter, the reader can find more information regarding this character.) Sara Noriega, who is overweight but happy, can be best described as a "Fat Venus." She is particularly important as a lover because she is Florentino's projection as a poet. He stays with her for several years, and records in his diary that he loved her. She is forty years old, ten years older than Florentino, yet she cannot climax unless she sucks on an infant's pacifier (238). Olimpia Zuleta is among the shortest-lived affairs. She is a married woman whom it took Florentino six months to seduce. Olimpia finally gives in to desire and goes to bed with him, on a beautiful afternoon in one of his riverboats. However, an obscenity written by Florentino on her belly causes the story to end in tragedy. That same night, when Olimpia goes to bed, "having forgotten what was scrawled there," she undresses in front of her husband, who, with a single slash of his razor, cuts her throat (263).

Prudencia Pitre is a widow like many of the women whom Florentino recorded in his diary. However, Prudencia Pitre is known as the Widow of Two because she has outlived two husbands. Like all his lovers, Angeles Alfaro, a music teacher whom Florentino describes in his diary as "the ephemeral one," teaches Florentino something about love. He records that with her (although he had already experienced this before), "one can be in love with several people at the same time, feel the same sorrow with each, and not betray any of them" (328). Ausencia Santander, like many of the female characters in *Love in the Time of Cholera*, displays a total independence regarding her sexuality. It is unclear, says the narrator, whether her husband left her or she left him. Hers was a conventional marriage. They had three children, the children got married, and she began to see men at her own desire. Besides teaching him about love, all his lovers, argues Florentino Ariza, contributed to his need for being loved, for understanding love itself.

Florentino's long list of lovers seems to contribute more to *Love in the Time of Cholera* than the character development of Fermina's son and daughter; Marco Aurelio Urbino Daza and Ofelia Urbino Daza.

THEMATIC ISSUES

It may seem obvious that love is the central theme in *Love in the Time of Cholera*. However, the theme of love in this novel is multifaceted; it can be looked at from different perspectives. Among other thematic possibilities are the evils of a socially divided city and the implicit acts of reading and writing. All these themes, however, are intertwined and, as a result, it is difficult to separate one from the other. The theme of love, however, is the only one that encompasses them all, and it is therefore examined in the most detail.

The impetuous, idealistic, strong, and youthful love between Florentino and Fermina is totally platonic. It starts with a look, which soon turns into a gaze. Theirs is certainly the "look of love." Florentino, at that time an apprentice at the Postal Agency, takes a telegram to Lorenzo Daza's home address and sees the young girl reading. Fermina raises her eyes to see who is coming "and that casual glance was the beginning of a cataclysm of love that had not ended half a century later" (68). Florentino's love is awakened first. When it starts, he is content to sit in the park by her house, to see her walk by four times a day, always in the company of her aunt, Escolástica. As Florentino feels his love grow stronger, he moves from the passive mode of seeing to a more active mode, that of writing. To declare his love to her, he writes a sixty-page letter using both sides of each page. Thus starts an epistolary love affair of immeasurable frequency and intensity. It is precisely the letter writing, and not the physical encounters, that makes their love possible. In fact, over a three-year period they only have the opportunity to talk three times. The first time is an afternoon at the end of January when Florentino wants to give Fermina a letter but she rejects it, arguing that she does not have her father's permission. The second time is a week later, when she accepts the letter and they exchange only a few words. The third time is to receive an answer to his letter; since she has none, he insists, saying that it is a lack of courtesy to accept a letter and not to answer it. That is the last time they talk for over fifty years. Their epistolary is all they have and is what causes her expulsion from her school. Fermina's father tries to convince her that love at her age is an illusion; he wants her to beg for forgiveness to get back into the Academy and offers her help finding happiness with a worthy suitor (99). However, Fermina, as her name implies, remains firm in her love for Florentino and does not give up. In despair, after talking with Florentino, who has also decided not to give up, Lorenzo Daza decides to take his daughter away to make her forget. They go back to the small town where they came from, San Juan de la Ciénaga. Paradoxically, although their postal contact does not stop while she is away, a love that seemed eternal crumbles when she, once again, sees him. After coming back from her trip, Fermina writes Florentino a two-line letter asking him to please "forget it" (126).

Another facet of love, no less interesting than the first, is that of love between the married couple, Fermina Daza and Dr. Juvenal Urbino. Although the omniscient narrator suggests that Fermina married for convenience, there are ample suggestions that this sentiment changes over time. She enjoys her wedding trip, lovemaking, and living in Paris. After sixteen months, upon returning to Cartagena de Indias pregnant with her first child, she feels like "the happiest woman on earth" (194).

After some years, the couple goes back to Europe to renew a love that was beginning to decay because of the drudgeries and sameness of the daily routine. As a result of this second honeymoon, Fermina comes back pregnant once again. The instances of love that she shows for her husband are many, particularly the gestures of love in their old age. In the last few minutes before his death, the omniscient narrator discloses that between them there was indeed a true love, a love that Dr. Juvenal Urbino seemed to realize he had failed to communicate to her, when he speaks his last words, "only God knows how much I loved you" (56).

Dr. Urbino is more a spiritual man than a physical one. He loves Fermina conceptually, for being his wife and the mother of his children, rather than for being the woman she is. He is rather incapable of looking at sex without pondering the scientific insight regarding how the human body functions. His moral and religious values do not allow him to be a good lover, at home or elsewhere. With the sensuous and sexual, young, beautiful Miss Lynch, the sex act becomes comical but sad. He spends the exact amount of time needed to give an injection during a routine visit (298). However, for Fermina, being conceptually happy is not enough. After returning from the honeymoon happy and remaining so for six years (until they move to their own house), she feels like a prisoner in a strange house and, even worse, that she is with a man who was not her dream (249). During that time, Fermina comes to believe that behind the professional authority and worldly charm of her husband there is a hopeless weakling (250). When they move into their own house, things are not much different. While she is loved, catered to, and even feared in public, at home she feels like a deluxe servant, not a loved wife (268). While discussing this second facet of love—the love between Fermina and Dr. Urbino—it is worth noting what Fermina feels for Florentino. Although she represses any feeling toward him, the narrator reveals that she often thinks of him. During the fifty-one years while she is married to Juvenal Urbino, she thinks of Florentino with compassion and nostalgia; she even feels tormented by guilt (247).

The third facet of love is described in the last chapter of the novel. Fermina is now seventy-two years old and Florentino is seventy-seven. He feels he has the right to make up for lost time and on the very day of her husband's burial, he expresses once again his vow of everlasting love, but again she rejects him.

Although Florentino and Fermina are now an elderly couple, their ability to deal with love seems unchanged. Once again, the means of bringing them together is letter writing, which is how they express their feelings. This time it is Fermina who writes first, sending a three-page letter full of insults. Over the following year, Florentino writes her 132 letters. He starts writing once a week, then twice a week, and then every day. While Fermina does not answer any of the letters, she keeps them to find solace and to reflect upon Florentino's writing. On the first anniversary of her husband's death, Florentino attends the memorial mass, without being invited. This is his chance to talk to Fermina again. She greets him and thanks him for coming.

Two weeks later Florentino comes to visit her. Although he is uninvited and unannounced, she receives him, nevertheless. Hereafter, their

Tuesday visits are as frequent and consoling as the letters, and they become great friends. Fermina's son approves of their relationship, but her daughter does not. Ofelia tenaciously opposes, arguing that love at their age "is revolting" (392). Neither Ofelia, the rumor of Florentino's homosexuality, nor anything else convinces Fermina to stop seeing him. Instead, she accepts Florentino's invitation to go on a riverboat cruise along the Magdalena River. Playfully, García Márquez gives the boat the name *New Fidelity*. The couple's unstoppable drive to be together is finally realized.

A different facet of love that the novel brings to the reader's attention is unfaithfulness. Violating the marriage vows, Dr. Juvenal Urbino embarks on an extramarital affair. Contrary to his impeccable correctness at home, in public, and in his profession, Dr. Urbino breaks social and racial codes and, after thirty years of marriage, falls in love with Bárbara Lynch. Thirty years younger, the beautiful twenty-eight-year old mulatta causes the marriage to crumble. Dr. Urbino's desire for Bárbara Lynch is out of control. He thinks of her all day and, incapable of stopping his passion, he feels the torment of guilt. After six months he ends the affair, but Fermina leaves him and stays away for two years.

Florentino Ariza enjoys yet another kind of love, if, indeed, promiscuous affairs with over 600 women can be described as a form of love. As a kind of hunter, Florentino engages in casual love. Florentino responds to raw desire. His sex partners are simply outlets to appease his desire and ward off his desperate solitude. Regardless, however, he feels they all teach him something.

The second theme in *Love in the Time of Cholera* is the division of classes in society. The difference between rich and poor in the novel is remarkable. Although the novel does not suggest the existence of any turmoil or open conflict between the different social classes, the disparities are obvious to the reader. The social, economic, and racial scenery of the novel brings to the forefront a small group of rich, white people, among which the Urbino de la Calle family is one of the most prestigious. This group constitutes the ruling class: it includes civil authorities, the high ranks of the military, and a few impoverished aristocratic families. Different racial groups make up the balance of the classes and represent the majority: Chinese immigrants, blacks, mulattos, and Indians, many of whom live in abject poverty. A good number of these people work as slave-like servants in the households of the wealthy.

The novel repeatedly takes notice of the differences between the rich and the poor. While the rich live in the ancestral homes in the district of the Viceroys and the residential district of La Manga, the aspiring middle classes live elsewhere. The poor live in a section of the city where the landscape includes pestilence, unnumbered houses, loud music, and children running around nude—a part of the city not surprisingly known as the old slave quarter—which is a death trap for the poor (23).

The rich in the novel attend lavish parties. They accompany their celebrations and dances with string quartets, bands, and orchestras playing music by Mozart and Schubert. Although the poor are seen everywhere, the rich do not mingle with them. Upward mobility can be achieved through economic success, but entrance to social clubs of the elite is reserved for legitimate descendants, born into families with an ancestral name. The marked stratification of class is observed everywhere. At the cathedral, for example, the first few pews are reserved for their lifetime owners, whose names are engraved on copper nameplates on the back of the seats (360). The rest of the congregation can sit elsewhere; however, the poorest, being mostly mulattos and blacks, must sit in the back.

The novel also suggests that the boundary between rich and poor is not insurmountable. It is interesting to note that Lorenzo Daza, although a plebeian by birth, changes his fortune in life, as well as that of his daughter. Fermina, who because of her manners seems to define a new type of societal class, is the product of a well-thought-out, well-executed plan. First, Lorenzo Daza moves from the countryside to the coastal city to provide his daughter Fermina with the formal instruction she would need. He registers her in a religious school for rich girls. Then he manages to marry her to Dr. Juvenal Urbino. With this marriage, Fermina enters a social and economic world totally different from her own—a world she is not prepared to move into. Upon her return from her honeymoon and for six consecutive, painful, and hateful years, Fermina undergoes the "training" that her mother-in-law puts her through. While she learns and adapts to her new social class, she never fully abandons her roots, and she maintains her spontaneity, her love for nature, and a touch of crudeness in her speech.

Florentino Ariza is another example of someone who successfully changes his lot in life. Unlike Fermina's change of fate, his is the result of a decision of his own, made, not for upward mobility, but to make him worthy of Fermina's love. For thirty years, he works at all types of jobs within the River Company of the Caribbean, ending up as president of the Board of Directors, general manager, and, eventually, owner. He restores his house to reflect his new social economic status but also to be prepared to be worthy of Fermina Daza when his next opportunity comes along.

Another salient aspect on the theme of class division is the incorporation of mulattoes into different subplots within the novel. Jeremiah Saint-Love, the mulatto who kills himself at the outset of *Love in the Time of Cholera*, is Dr. Juvenal Urbino's friend. Two mulattas presented in the novel are alternately treated both as object and subject. Bárbara Lynch, some may argue, is the object of an elderly, powerful man who wants her for sexual favors. However, Dr. Urbino also expresses love for her. Leona Cassiani, also a mulatta, goes to all public functions with Florentino Ariza. She gains the respect of those with whom she works at the River Company of the Caribbean and moves into the highest ranks of the company. Florentino falls in love with her but she rejects him. In spite of this, however, they remain good friends.

An interesting aspect of the theme of a socially divided society is that it appears to be deteriorating. Fermina Daza, Florentino Ariza, and Leona Cassiani seem to signal a change in the social order, and to offer the availability of upward mobility. The old, rich, aristocratic, and insulated world of the elite, the highest social level (represented by families like the Urbinos de la Calle), is disappearing. Although the instances are many, the reader notices that the actions of Dr. Juvenal Urbino de la Calle seem to make the loudest statement of this change. First, he marries a woman outside his social class. Second, he moves from his former palace of the Marquis de Casalduero to a new house in a neighborhood of the *nouveaux riches* (the new rich). Third, and probably most significant, his family name will no doubt die with his children. His children, says the narrator, were two undistinguished ends of a line. His son, Marco Aurelio, continues the narrative, has done nothing worthy of note—he has not even produced a child. His daughter, Ofelia, has three daughters but no sons. Thus, the name, the tradition, and the old social order symbolically die with Dr. Urbino's children.

SOCIAL AND HISTORICAL CONTEXT

The reader may have the feeling that this is just a strange love story, but it is far more: the civil unrest, superstition, civil wars, disappearance of a colonial power, and birth of a new middle class that surround the love story are of significance in themselves. García Márquez goes to considerable efforts to document the historical setting of this novel. He uses actual historical figures such as the president of Colombia at the time of the tale, Rafael Núñez, a statesman and writer born in Cartagena de Indias (a favored physical setting of García Márquez's work), and several liberal generals in the Colombian armed forces, including Ricardo Gaitán Obeso, who, in fact, fought against the government of President Rafael Núñez. President Rafael Núñez and General Gaitán Obeso represent the two great opposing political forces in Colombia's government and in García Márquez's writing. The president was a member of the Conservative Party and the general was in the Liberal Party. The setting of *Love in the Time of Cholera* also includes, although as mere references, actual historical events such as the War of a Thousand Days and the massacre of striking banana workers in 1928.

Love in the Time of Cholera, on a much smaller scale than *One Hundred Years of Solitude*, is concerned with the Colombian civil wars of the last part of the nineteenth century and the violence of the first two decades of the twentieth century. These historical and political concerns, however, may pass unnoticed by the reader because that indeed is the intent. If *One Hundred Years of Solitude* disguises these concerns through the uses of myth, fantasy, hyperbole, and magic realism, *Love in the Time of Cholera* disguises them through its depiction of a long, sometimes exasperating, love affair. However, the cholera that appears like a sign in the title of the novel is, in fact, a bad omen and can be seen as a symbol of the historical violence that Colombia continues to undergo.

The superabundance of information in *Love in the Time of Cholera* will go unnoticed unless the reader is inquisitive and meticulous. For example, when García Márquez describes Fermina's bird, he says that it was bought right before the last civil war based on a rumor of an upcoming visit by the Pope. The government spread the rumor to scare the liberals. The reader, on the one hand, has to understand that the concept of a civil war is used to describe the ongoing political wars of liberals against conservatives that lasted through the 1960s; and, on the other hand, that the papal visit is indeed fictional, for no Pope ever visited Colombia until 1973. If the reader pays attention to references like this, then the novel can be seen to denounce what the government wanted to hide: the killings of people who appeared floating in the Magdalena River. There are allusions of discontent against the conservative government throughout the novel. Even the parrot, the indirect cause of Dr. Juvenal Urbino's death, shouts, "long live the Liberal Party damn it, a reckless cry that had cost many a carefree drunk his life" (33).

The time frame of the narrative pays close attention to a bygone era, some readers may say, and pays no attention to the violence that Colombia was undergoing in the mid-1980s, when *Love in the Time of Cholera* was published. There are readers, though, who may see the many references to violence, political turmoil, corruption, and the devastation of nature, along with the cholera in the title, as a way of pointing out that violence is a constant element of both social and political life in Colombia. If *Love in the Time of Cholera* were to be seen as irresponsible for not dealing with the oppression, violence, and the social and economic disparities that García Márquez is known to denounce, then the reader would still have to consider the treatment that García Márquez gives to love in this novel. Love in the novel is not carefree, easy flowing, spontaneous, and idealized. Although Florentino idealizes Fermina and the love he feels for her, everything around him is hostile. The narrative does not make life easy for an illegitimate child, Florentino, just because he is in love. As literary critic José Luis Méndez wrote, the social conventions, the economic ambitions, the ideological and political prejudices, and even the twisted understanding of patriotism, interfere with everyday life and the way the characters love and make love (Méndez 196). While it is true that love triumphs in the novel, García Márquez is not providing a model where love escapes social and biological laws, but rather the opposite. *Love in the Time of Cholera* refuses to accept the conventional time frame for falling in love and ignores the limitations thought to be imposed by aging; it rejects the fact that prestige and social rank must, in the end, destroy love, but furnishes the narration with the social and economic components that interfere with the love between Florentino and Fermina and between Dr. Juvenal Urbino and Fermina. Florentino has to undergo the transitional changes both socially and economically that make him deserving of Fermina's love, and Fermina has to learn the manners of the social group that she marries into when she marries Dr. Juvenal Urbino.

The comparison between *One Hundred Years of Solitude* and *Love in the Time of Cholera* mentioned in this chapter and observed by many readers and critics is perhaps inevitable. Almost everything García Márquez has written since the publication of *One Hundred Years of Solitude* in 1967 is compared to it. One of the best comparisons is that of sociologist and literary critic José Luis Méndez who points out that in *One Hundred Years of Solitude* there is no hope for starting anew, but in *Love in the Time of Cholera* there is hope for salvation through the power of love. The universe described by the narrative voice in *One Hundred Years of Solitude* is, in the end, completely destroyed "because races condemned to one hundred years of solitude did not have a second chance on earth," as the narrator explains in the closing paragraph of the novel (448). In *Love in the Time of Cholera*, however, in the end, the characters that inhabit the novel do not perish. The novel does not end with the total destruction of the universe it has created. A second chance on earth, which was denied to the characters of *One Hundred Years of Solitude*, is given to those who love in *Love in the Time of Cholera*.

Love is seen as the redeeming force that saves both humanity and its history. Love, then, appears as a driving force that defies everything. As if in biblical terms, the narrator seems to state that it is not yet too late to stop the end of humanity and to reach out for justice and happiness. However, there is no naive idealism in the narrative voice of the novel. Nothing is taken for granted, and the narrator is ready to remind us that the world around the characters of *Love in the Time of Cholera* is too oppressive to ignore. That is why the riverboat in which Fermina and Florentino travel, although utopian in its intent, sports a flag signaling cholera and cannot find a secure port to dock. The novel ends with the reader wondering if Fermina and Florentino will ever be able to come ashore and exercise their second chance.

Love, to García Márquez, is a kind of philosophical tool, a way of looking at the world. As the sociologist and literary critic José Luis Méndez pointed out, García Márquez expressed this philosophy "on love" three years before the publication of *Love in the Time of Cholera* when he addressed the Nobel Academy in Stockholm. On the occasion of accepting the Nobel Prize, García Márquez delivered a speech that argued against the scientific possibility of a nuclear disaster. In closing, Gabriel García Márquez spoke of a new utopia:

> Where no one will be able to decide for others how they die, where love will prove true and happiness possible, and where the races condemned to one hundred years of solitude will have, at last and forever, a second opportunity on earth. (García Márquez 1988, 91)

If the reader fails to see the political turmoil behind the story it is understandable, for once again, as in all of Gabriel García Márquez's writings, *Love in the Time of Cholera* is multilayered and can be read from multiple perspectives, depending on the reader. The art of storytelling is in the foreground, and this time readers of García Márquez will come away feeling they understand the book: it is a love story where reality is all around. It is a novel that is both romantic and realist.

ALTERNATIVE READING: FEMINIST THEORY

When a reader first hears the term *feminist*, he or she may immediately think in terms of the status of women. Feminism can be studied from different viewpoints: linguistic, political, economic, sociological, psychological, biological, or other. For some critics from developed nations of the Western world, it is nearly canonical that feminist literary criticism began with the women's movement that followed World War II. For such critics, the two most commonly referenced authors are Simone de Beauvoir and Kate Millett. However, dating the origin of feminism to these two authors seems rather simplistic if the reader realizes that the two books selected by such critics were not published until 1949, for *Le Deuxième Sexe* (*The Second Sex*) by Beauvoir; and 1970, for *Sexual Politics* by Millett. In *The Second Sex*, Beauvoir examines how male authors have developed female characters in literary texts.

The fight for equal rights for women, in whatever manner, however, goes back much further than 1949. By the turn of the twentieth century there was already a movement for women's suffrage (the right to vote). In fact, the struggle for women's rights may have started as early as the eighteenth century. Indeed, Mary Wollstonecraft published *A Vindication of the Rights of Woman* in 1792.

Nowadays, and as early as the late 1960s, those interested in feminist theory approached it as a subject of study in colleges and universities around the world. In a general way, feminist theory aims to accomplish the following:

- To review, expose, and critique those standards where the orientation is patriarchal, whether in literature, politics, civil rights, power, sexuality, race, and other aspects of life;
- To recover texts written by women that have been either forgotten, lost, or neglected;
- To understand the cultural parameters involved in the construction of gender and identity.

Many feminist critics, to some degree, continue to be misunderstood in the belief that the issues investigated by feminist theory not only have to be women centered, but also have to be seen from a woman's point of view. This not only excludes women who may look at a text from a viewpoint that disregards gender issues, but also prevents men from doing a feminist reading of any given text.

From a pedagogical point of view, feminist theory can be accepted as a method or technique to study a text. As such, the critic questions longstanding, dominant, male ideologies and patriarchal attitudes and interpretations of literature. Is such an approach more or less feminist because a male rather than a female critic carries it out? There is debate among feminists themselves on this question. According to American feminist writer and celebrity of the women's movement in the early and mid-1990s, Naomi Wolf, feminism "should be broadly understood as a humanistic movement for social justice" (139). Feminists in Latin America, possibly to gain support, sponsor the values of maternity and wifehood. They believe that these two roles bring reforms, first within the family, and thereafter within society as a whole. In literature, the Mexican writer Sara Sefchovich observes this in her novel *La señora de los sueños* (1993).

A feminist reading of *Love in the Time of Cholera* would show how the female characters are portrayed in the space and time where they live in the novel. Clearly, not all the female characters in the novel are alike, nor are the central female characters treated alike. A feminist reading might consider whether they reacted and responded in a manner often described as feminine (not feminist), regardless of social class, race, and education. The rich and educated women of the novel are not necessarily the ones with the strongest character or the women whom the male characters desire sexually, but they do exercise their own sexuality. The female characters in *Love in the Time of Cholera* are in control of their sexuality. They are developed as free, strong, and independent. They do not correspond to a stereotype, a ready-made model repeated by both male and female writers, where Latin American women are voiceless and submissive.

While *Love in the Time of Cholera* depicts such disparate female roles as those of mother and prostitute, neither one of the two characterizations lacks voice or will. The world of the novel is a matriarchal one. Without his mother, Fermina Daza, and all the women that come in and out of Florentino's life, the novel could not develop in the manner it does. Florentino Ariza and Juvenal Urbino are not sexist; they do not see women as inferior beings. Although, in itself, this is not a novel that shows the battle of the sexes, the roles played by women are the strongest. Even though written by a male, the novel points out significant signs of a matriarchal universe. To this extent, Gabriel García Márquez has expressed, in an interview with Ana Cristina Navarro, that women are the strong being, and thanks to them history is able to continue its normal course. My women, says the Colombian author, are more in touch with reality. They have their feet firmly planted on the ground. They are solid, patient, true. And García Márquez adds, men are creatures of dreams, capable of the most crazy and magnificent actions, but unable to be patient or trustworthy. They are weaklings in the face of adversity. They search for support in women, who are as firm as rocks. This, he concludes, is how the world is in Macondo and elsewhere.

Fermina Daza is certainly Florentino's sweetheart, and at the time of their youth, around the mid-1800s, she believes in romance and the power of the written word. To Fermina Daza, Florentino's letters carry more meaning than her own studies, her father, or even the Church. Her world, at the age of seventeen, is interrupted by her interfering father but never completely dominated by him. García Márquez provides her with a voice of her own. It is hard to imagine a young woman of the nineteenth century more independent than Fermina Daza. It is she who ends the relationship between herself and Florentino. She was fully aware when it started, and she calls it off without a tear or a fight, remaining in complete control. To neither of the two loves of her life—Florentino Ariza or Juvenal Urbino—is she an object. At all times she projects herself as a subject. She is a woman who is aware of her roles as mother, wife, friend, and public person. Fermina is stable, strong, confident, and poised. She knows exactly where she has been and where the winds of life are taking her. She fights for what she wants, and against a social world she does not embrace, old and decaying traditions of the noble families, hypocrisy and gossip, Ofelia, her own daughter (to defend Florentino), and her right to love and be loved.

Whereas the strength of Fermina is observed throughout the length of the book, the novel opens with the weakness of a male character who kills himself because he cannot endure the prospect of getting old. Jeremiah Saint-Amour, a photographer of children, commits suicide because he is turning sixty years old. Saint-Amour (the name translates into English as *Saint of Love*) is, without a doubt, the opposite of Fermina.

Love in the Time of Cholera contorts the roles of male and female characters that we are used to observing, but it does so without being biased or judgmental. Whereas the reader makes the association of a "Saint of Love" with Jeremiah's last name, García Márquez describes the black Haitian character as a saint but, he adds ironically, "An atheistic saint" (10). Another instance of contorting roles comes with the violence and sexual abuse inflicted on women during rape. Feminism looks at rape as a form of cultural oppression. In rape, women are treated as sex objects. The psychological scars of rape are so deep that most women have difficulty ever seeing themselves as subjects of love again. In *Love in the Time of Cholera*, this situation is inverted. The sexual assault is on a man, Florentino Ariza, whose rape is the result of a plan elaborated by the perpetrator in its smallest detail. As is expected in any rape, Florentino is desperate to know the identity of the violating mistress. It is interesting to note that the object of the rape, a male, feels gratitude. This version of rape, which inverts the structure of oppression in which the victim hates the perpetrator, is also observed in a female character. Leona Cassiani, like Florentino Ariza, is also raped in the novel. The circumstances for them both are similar. The victim is taken by surprise, the clothes are ripped off, and, in a forceful, frenetic fashion, he or she is raped. Florentino Ariza never sees the face of his perpetrator, nor does Leona Cassiani. However, both Florentino and Leona long to see that person again. Leona Cassiani goes on to say that she could recognize him in a crowd of a thousand men because of his shape and size and his way of making love (313). Leona spends years looking for him, not to turn him in to the authorities but to love him.

García Márquez not only inverts, but also subverts, the traditional way of looking at rape. The inversion comes from having women rape men, and the subversion by changing the feeling of hate into one of love. Neither Leona Cassiani nor Florentino Ariza develops a form of hatred of the opposite sex, as is expected to occur with rape. In fact, the two of them triumph in their own right and fall in love with each other. Leona, however, is the stronger of the two. While it is true, according to feminist author Simone de Beauvoir, that "all oppression creates a state of war" (717), the war that these two fight is one of self-growth, self-love, and self-respect.

In *Love in the Time of Cholera* the female characters are active beings in control of their own lives. There is no need to change from oppressed to oppressor, as some feminists would want, because there is no feeling of inferiority among the women characters. As the tone of the novel is ruled by love, the women do not have to dominate the men in order to defend themselves. There is no room for what Naomi Wolf calls "victim feminism" because there is no hatred within the female characters. In victim feminism, women look at themselves as weak beings, subjugated by men, and therefore must deny and attack the values and truths of what might be considered patriarchal. The women characters of *Love in the Time of Cholera* do not show such a reaction. In achieving economic independence (a basic feminist principle), none of the female characters resorts to victim feminism. Victim feminism, states Naomi Wolf, "depends on influence or persuasion rather than on seeking clout in a straightforward way" (Wolf 136). Tránsito Ariza, a single parent and Florentino's mother, manages to single-handedly buy and restore a colonial house, run a small private business, and even lend money to the rich. In addition, she spends time with Florentino, sharing with him her love for reading. The best example of a triumphant woman and the antithesis of victim feminism is Leona Cassiani. She is, without a doubt, a self-made woman. Black, young, and pretty, she is first taken for a prostitute. However, what she wants is employment. The head of personnel at the River Company of the Caribbean, where Florentino works, gives her the lowest-level job, and Leona Cassiani performs that job with seriousness, modesty, and dedication for three years (222). Meanwhile, driven by self-pride and obvious self-assurance, she studies English at home and takes an evening class in typing. This ambition comes from a woman whose only formal education is elementary school and the School of Millinery (where one learns to make hats). Her determination pays off; Leona Cassiani eventually becomes economically independent, a homeowner, socially active, and the personal assistant to Leo XII, president-owner of the River Company of the Caribbean. Florentino Ariza falls in love with her, but the night he declares his love, she answered "it was too late" (207). From that night on, "Florentino Ariza understood at last that it is possible to be a woman's friend and not go to bed with her" (227). This exemplifies the right of exercising complete control of one's sexuality and the right to be heard, two valued aspects of feminist theory. The female characters of *Love in the Time of Cholera* (some more than others) all have a voice of their own and control over their bodies, and they all look at themselves as subjects. Women like Fermina Daza, Leona Cassiani, and the Widow Nazaret are all capable of breaking away from the state of affairs they are in—the social order in which they are born. They manage to overcome inner conflict and even trauma in order to live a life of fulfillment and, better yet, a life where the love they feel rules.

Love in the Time of Cholera fares well under a feminist reading because it vindicates the possibilities of women triumphing over the prejudices of age, race, and social class. There are instances of violence against women and women who are voiceless and weak, common traits of patriarchal writing, but those instances are not the focus of the novel; they are peripheral. They confirm the fact that, although both males and females have the possibility to overcome everything and anything before them, there are obstacles that not all can surpass. Just as Jeremiah Saint-Amour committed suicide to keep his promise of never getting old, so does América Vicuña, who is young and beautiful and leaves no note. However, their deaths seem to reaffirm the thirst for love of Fermina and Florentino.

Bibliography

WORKS BY GABRIEL GARCÍA MÁRQUEZ (IN ENGLISH TRANSLATION)

Nonfiction

Clandestine in Chile: The Adventures of Miguel Littín. Trans. Asa Zatz. New York: Henry Holt, 1987.

News of a Kidnapping. Trans. Edith Grossman. New York: Knopf, 1997; New York: Penguin Books, 1998.

Novels

The Autumn of the Patriarch. Trans. Gregory Rabassa. New York: Harper and Row, 1976; New York: HarperPerennial, 1991.

Chronicle of a Death Foretold. Trans. Gregory Rabassa. New York: Knopf, 1983.

Collected Novellas: Leaf Storm, No One Writes to the Colonel, Chronicle of a Death Foretold. Trans. Gregory Rabassa and J. S. Bernstein. New York: HarperCollins, 1990; New York: Perennial Classics, 1999.

The General in His Labyrinth. Trans. Edith Grossman. London: Jonathan Cape, 1991.

In Evil Hour. Trans. Gregory Rabassa. New York: Harper and Row, 1979; New York: HarperPerennial, 1991.

Leaf Storm and Other Stories. Trans. Gregory Rabassa. New York: Harper and Row, 1972; New York: Harper Colophon Books, 1979.

Love in the Time of Cholera. Trans. Edith Grossman. New York: Knopf, 1988; New
    York: Knopf, 1997.
No One Writes to the Colonel and Other Stories. Trans. J. S. Bernstein. New York:
    Harper and Row, 1968.
Of Love and Other Demons. Trans. Edith Grossman. New York: Knopf, 1995; New
    York: Penguin Books, 1996.
One Hundred Years of Solitude. Trans. Gregory Rabassa. New York: Harper and
    Row, 1970; New York: Perennial Classics, 1998.

Short Stories

Collected Stories (an anthology containing the books *Eyes of a Blue Dog, Big Mama's
    Funeral,* and *The Incredible and Sad Tale of Inocent Eréndira and Her Heartless
    Grandmother*). Trans. Gregory Rabassa and J. S. Bernstein. New York: Har-
    per and Row, 1984; New York: HarperPerennial, 1991.
Innocent Eréndira and Other Stories. Trans. Gregory Rabassa. New York: Harper
    and Row, 1978.
*The Story of a Shipwrecked Sailor: Who Drifted on a Life Raft for Ten Days without
    Water, Was Proclaimed a National Hero, Kissed by Beauty Queens, Made Rich
    through Publicity, and Then Spurned by the Government and Forgotten for All
    Time.* Trans. Randolph Hogan. New York: Knopf, 1986.
Strange Pilgrims. Trans. Edith Grossman. New York: Knopf, 1993; New York:
    Penguin Books, 1994.

BIOGRAPHICAL INFORMATION AND INTERVIEWS

Apuleyo Mendoza, Plinio. *In Conversation with Gabriel García Márquez: The Fra-
    grance of Guava.* Trans. Ann Wright. London: Verso, 1983.
Gabriel García Márquez: Magic and Reality. Dir. Ana Cristina Navarro. Prod. Harold
    Mantell. Videocassette. Princeton, NJ: Films for the Humanities, Inc., 1981.
García Márquez, Gabriel. "The Solitude of Latin America (Nobel Lecture, 1982)."
    Trans. Marina Castañeda. In *Gabriel García Márquez and the Power of Fiction.*
    Ed. Julio Ortega. The Texas Pan American Series. Austin: University of
    Texas, 1988. 87–91.
———. "Sonata Inocente" in *Revista Cambio* (Cambio magazine). December 2000.
    18–25. <http://www.revistacambio.com>.
Guibert, Rita. Excerpts from "Seven Voices: Seven Latin American Writers Talk
    to Rita Guibert." In *Gabriel García Márquez: A Study of the Short Fiction.* Ed.
    Harley D. Oberhelman. Boston: Twayne Publishers, 1991. 75–77.
Simons, Marlise. "The Best Years of His Life: An Interview with Gabriel García
    Márquez." *New York Times Book Review,* April 11, 1988, p. 48.
———. "A Talk with Gabriel García Márquez." In *Gabriel García Márquez: A Study
    of the Short Fiction.* Ed. Harley D. Oberhelman. Boston: Twayne Publishers,
    1991. 78–79.

Vargas Llosa, Mario. *García Márquez: Historia de un deicidio*. Barcelona: Barral
    Editores, 1971.

REVIEWS AND CRITICISM

Leaf Storm

Choice, September 1970: 19.

Christian Science Monitor, February 24, 1972: 8.

Duffy, Martha. "Back to Macondo." In *Critical Essays on Gabriel García Márquez*.
    Ed. George R. McMurray. Critical Essays on World Literature. Boston:
    G. K. Hall, 1987. 25–26.

New York Review of Books, April 6, 1972: 18.

New York Times Book Review, January, 20, 1972: 1.

Sims, Robert Lewis. *The Evolution of Myth in Gabriel García Márquez: From "La
    hojarasca" to "Cien años de soledad."* Miami, FL: Universal, 1981.

Time, March 13, 1972: 99.

No One Writes to the Colonel

Carlos, Alberto J. "Review of *No One Writes to the Colonel and Other Stories*." In
    Critical Essays on Gabriel García Márquez. Ed. George R. McMurray. Critical
    Essays on World Literature. Boston: G. K. Hall, 1987. 31–33.

Gutiérrez Mouat, Ricardo. "The Economy of the Narrative Sign in *No One Writes
    to the Colonel* and *In Evil Hour*." In *Gabriel García Márquez and the Power of
    Fiction*. Ed. Julio Ortega. The Texas Pan American Series. Austin: Univer-
    sity of Texas Press, 1988. 17–33.

Library Journal, May 15, 1968: 93.

The Nation, December 2, 1968: 207.

New York Times Book Review, September 19, 1968: 56.

Saturday Review, December 21, 1968: 51.

Woods, Richard D. "Time and Futility in the Novel *El coronel no tiene quien le
    escriba*." In *Critical Essays on Gabriel García Márquez*. Ed. George R. Mc-
    Murray. Critical Essays on World Literature. Boston: G. K. Hall, 1987. 86–
    93.

The Short Stories (*Collected Stories*)

Choice Journal, March 1985: 22.

Foster, David William. "The Double Inscription of the *Narrataire* in 'Los funerales
    de la Mamá Grande.' " In *Critical Essays on Gabriel García Márquez*. Ed.
    George R. McMurray. Critical Essays on World Literature. Boston: G. K.
    Hall, 1987. 102–13.

Fraser, Howard. "Review of *La increíble y triste historia de la cándida Eréndira y de
    su abuela desalmada*." In *Critical Essays on Gabriel García Márquez*. Ed. George

R. McMurray. Critical Essays on World Literature. Boston: G. K. Hall, 1987. 47–49.

Kaplan, Martin. "Review of *Innocent Eréndira and Other Short Stories.*" In *Critical Essays on Gabriel García Márquez.* Ed. George R. McMurray. Critical Essays on World Literature. Boston: G. K. Hall, 1987. 49–52.

The New Republic, February 4, 1985: 192.

The New Yorker, May 20, 1985: 61.

Quill Quire, January 1985: 51.

Time, December 31, 1984: 124.

One Hundred Years of Solitude

Book World, February 22, 1970: 4.

Choice Journal, September 1970: 7.

Christian Science Monitor, April 16, 1970: 11.

Ciplijauskaité, Biruté. "Foreshadowing as Technique and Theme in *One Hundred Years of Solitude.*" In *Critical Essays on Gabriel García Márquez.* Ed. George R. McMurray. Critical Essays on World Literature. Boston: G. K. Hall, 1987. 140–46.

Echevarría, Roberto González. "*Cien años de soledad*: The Novel as Myth and Archive." In *Gabriel García Márquez.* Ed. Harold Bloom. Modern Critical Views. New York: Chelsea House Publishers, 1989. 107–23.

González, Aníbal. "Translation and the Novel: *One Hundred Years of Solitude.*" In *Gabriel García Márquez.* Ed. Harold Bloom. Modern Critical Views. New York: Chelsea House Publishers, 1989. 271–82.

Janes, Regina. "Liberals, Conservatives, and Bananas: Colombian Politics in the Fictions of Gabriel García Márquez. In *Gabriel García Márquez.* Ed. Harold Bloom. Modern Critical Views. New York: Chelsea House Publishers, 1989. 125–46.

———. *One Hundred Years of Solitude: Modes of Reading.* Boston: Twayne Publishers, 1991.

Joset, Jacques, ed. *Cien años de soledad.* Gabriel García Márquez. Madrid: Ediciones Cátedra, 1997.

Kiely, Robert. "Review of *One Hundred Years of Solitude.*" In *Critical Essays on Gabriel García Márquez.* Ed. George R. McMurray. Critical Essays on World Literature. Boston: G. K. Hall, 1987. 42–45.

Library Journal, February 15, 1970: 95.

Marco, Joaquín. Introducción. *Cien años de soledad.* Gabriel García Márquez. Madrid: Espasa Calpe, 1993. 9–54.

New York Review of Books, March 26, 1970: 14.

New York Times Book Review, March 8, 1970: 5.

Newsweek, March 2, 1970: 75.

Ortega, Julio. "Exchange System in *One Hundred Years of Solitude.*" In *Gabriel García Márquez and the Power of Fiction.* Ed. Julio Ortega. The Texas Pan American Series. Austin: University of Texas Press, 1988. 1–16.

Review: Latin American Literature and Arts. Supplement on Gabriel García Már-
    quez's *One Hundred Years of Solitude.* Ed. Ronald Christ. New York: Center
    for Inter-American Relations, 1976. 101–91.

Rodríguez-Monegal, Emir. "*One Hundred Years of Solitude*: The Last Three Pages."
    In *Critical Essays on Gabriel García Márquez.* Ed. George R. McMurray. Crit-
    ical Essays on World Literature. Boston: G. K. Hall, 1987. 147–52.

Saturday Review, March 7, 1970: 53.

Time, March 16, 1970: 95.

Valdés, María Elena de, and Mario J. Valdés, eds. *Approaches to Teaching García
    Márquez's "One Hundred Years of Solitude."* New York: Modern Language
    Association, 1990.

Woods, Michael. "Review of *One Hundred Years of Solitude.*" In *Critical Essays on
    Gabriel García Márquez.* Ed. George R. McMurray. Critical Essays on World
    Literature. Boston: G. K. Hall, 1987. 36–40.

Yale Review, October 1970: 60.

Zamora, Lois Parkinson. "The Myth of Apocalypse and Human Temporality in
    García Márquez's *Cien años de soledad* and *El otoño del patriarca.*" In *Gabriel
    García Márquez.* Ed. Harold Bloom. Modern Critical Views. New York:
    Chelsea House Publishers, 1989. 49–63.

Chronicle of a Death Foretold

Alonso, Carlos J. "Writing and Ritual in *Chronicle of a Death Foretold.*" In *Gabriel
    García Márquez.* Ed. Harold Bloom. Modern Critical Views. New York:
    Chelsea House Publishers, 1989. 257–69.

Alvarez-Borland, Isabel. "From Mystery to Parody: (Re) Readings of García Már-
    quez's *Crónica de una muerte anunciada.*" In *Gabriel García Márquez.* Ed.
    Harold Bloom. Modern Critical Views. New York: Chelsea House Pub-
    lishers, 1989. 219–26.

The Christian Science Monitor, January 1983: 9.

Díaz-Migoyo, Gonzalo. "Truth Disguised: *Chronicle of a Death* (Ambiguously)
    Foretold." In *Gabriel García Márquez and the Power of Fiction.* Ed. Julio Or-
    tega. The Texas Pan American Series. Austin: University of Texas Press,
    1988. 74–86.

González, Aníbal. "The Ends of the Text: Journalism in the Fiction of Gabriel
    García Márquez." In *Gabriel García Márquez and the Power of Fiction.* Ed.
    Julio Ortega. The Texas Pan American Series. Austin: University of Texas
    Press, 1988. 61–73.

The New Republic, May 2, 1983: 188.

New York Review of Books, April 14, 1983: 30.

Penuel, Arnold M. "The Sleep of Vital Reasons in García Márquez's *Crónica de
    una muerte anunciada.*" In *Critical Essays on Gabriel García Márquez.* Ed.
    George R. McMurray. Critical Essays on World Literature. Boston: G. K.
    Hall, 1987. 188–209.

Shaw, Donald L. "*Chronicle of a Death Foretold*: Narrative Function and Interpretation." In *Critical Perspectives on Gabriel García Márquez*. Ed. Bradley A. Shaw and Nora Goodwin. Lincoln, NE: Society of Spanish and Spanish-American Studies, 1986. 91–104.

Times Literary Supplement, September 10, 1982: 963.

Love in the Time of Cholera

America, September 3, 1988: 159.

Bell, Michael. "Not Flaubert's Parrot: *Love in the Time of Cholera*." In *Gabriel García Márquez: Solitude and Solidarity*. Ed. Michael Bell. Modern Novelists. New York: St. Martin's Press, 1993. 106–26.

Bell-Villada, Gene H. "The Novelist of Love." In *García Márquez: The Man and His Work*. Chapel Hill: University of North Carolina Press, 1990. 86.

Choice Journal, September 1988: 26.

The Christian Science Monitor, May 12, 1988: 20.

Economist, January 1988: 308.

Library Journal, March 15, 1988: 113.

Méndez, José Luis. *Cómo leer a García Márquez: Una interpretación sociológica*. 2nd ed. Puerto Rico: Editorial de la Universidad de Puerto Rico, 1992.

New York Review of Books, April 28, 1988: 35.

New York Times Book Review, April 10, 1988: 1.

Newsweek, April 25, 1988: 111.

Rodríguez, Carlos R. "El amor y el cólera en tiempos de García Márquez." In *Repertorio crítico sobre Gabriel García Márquez*. Ed. Juan Gustavo Cobo Borda. Vol. 2. Bogotá: Instituto Caro y Cuervo, 1995. 239–44.

Simons, Marlise. "García Márquez on Love, Plagues, and Politics." *New York Times Book Review*, February 21, 1988: 1, 23–25.

Time, March 28, 1988: 131.

Tratos y Retrators: Relations and Portraits. Dir. Silvia Lemus. Trans. Carla V. Smallwood. Films for the Humanities and Sciences, 1998.

General Reviews and Criticism

Acker, Bertie. "Religion in Colombia as Seen in the Works of García Márquez." In *Religion in Latin American Life and Literature*. Ed. Lyce C. Brown and William F. Cooper, Waco, TX: Baylor University Press, 1980. 339–50.

Anderson, Jon Lee. "The Power of García Márquez." *The New Yorker*, September 27, 1999: 56–71.

Bell, Michael. *Gabriel García Márquez: Solitude and Solidarity*. Modern Novelists. New York: St. Martin's Press, 1993.

Bell-Villada, Gene H. ed. *García Márquez: The Man and His Work*. Chapel Hill: University of North Carolina Press, 1990.

Bloom, Harold, ed. *Gabriel García Márquez*. Modern Critical Views. New York: Chelsea House Publishers, 1989.

Cobo Borda, Juan Gustavo. *Para llegar a García Márquez*. Bogotá: Ediciones Temas de Hoy, 1997.

Fau, Margaret Eustella. *Gabriel García Márquez: An Annotated Bibliography, 1947–1979*. Westport, CT: Greenwood Press, 1980.

Fau, Margaret Eustella, and Nelly Sfeir de Gonzalez. *Bibliographic Guide to Gabriel García Márquez, 1979–1985*. Westport, CT: Greenwood Press, 1986.

Hahn, Hannelore. *The Influence of Franz Kafka on Three Novels by Gabriel García Márquez*. New York: Peter Lang Publishing, 1993.

Janes, Regina. *Gabriel García Márquez: Revolutions in Wonderland*. Columbia: University of Missouri Press, 1981.

Latin American Literary Review 13 (January–June 1985). *Special Issue: Gabriel García Márquez*. Ed. Yvette E. Miller and Charles Rossman.

Lemus, Silvia. "América Latina y Europa son culturas irreconciliables." In *Repertorio crítico sobre Gabriel García Márquez*. Ed. Juan Gustavo Cobo Borda. Vol. 2. Bogotá: Instituto Caro y Cuervo, 1995. 263–77.

McMurray, George R., ed. *Critical Essays on Gabriel García Márquez*. Critical Essays on World Literature. Boston: G. K. Hall, 1987.

———. *Gabriel García Márquez*. New York: Frederick Ungar, 1977.

McNerney, Kathleen. *Understanding Gabriel García Márquez*. Columbia: University of South Carolina Press, 1989.

Minta, Stephen. *Gabriel García Márquez: Writer of Colombia*. London: Jonathan Cape, 1987.

Oberhelman, Harley D., ed. *Gabriel García Márquez: A Study of the Short Fiction*. Boston: Twayne Publishers, 1991.

———. *The Presence of Faulkner in the Writings of García Márquez*. Lubbock: Texas Tech Press, 1980.

Ortega, Julio, ed. *Gabriel García Márquez and the Power of Fiction*. The Texas Pan American Series. Austin: University of Texas Press, 1988.

Palencia-Roth, Michael. "Prisms of Consciousness: The 'New Worlds' of Columbus and García Márquez." In *Gabriel García Márquez*. Ed. Harold Bloom. Modern Critical Views. New York: Chelsea House Publishers, 1989. 125–46.

Penuel, Arnold M. *Intertextuality in García Márquez*. York, SC: Spanish Literature Publications, 1994.

Plummer, William. "The Faulkner Relation." In *Gabriel García Márquez*. Ed. Harold Bloom. Modern Critical Views. New York: Chelsea House Publishers, 1989. 33–47.

Pombo, Roberto. "García Márquez habla de su nuevo libro." In *Repertorio crítico sobre Gabriel García Márquez*. Ed. Juan Gustavo Cobo Borda. Vol. 2. Bogotá: Instituto Caro y Cuervo, 1995. 453–60.

Rodríguez-Monegal, Emir. "García Márquez: The Long Road to the Nobel Prize."

In *Contemporary Latin American Culture: Unity and Diversity*. Ed. C. Gail Guntermann. Tempe: Arizona State University Press, 1984. 95–110.

Vargas Llosa, Mario. *García Márquez: Historia de un deicidio*. Barcelona: Barral, 1971.

Volkening, Ernesto. *Gabriel García Márquez: Isabel viendo llover en Macondo*. Argentina: Estuario, 1967.

Williams, Raymond. "The Autumn of the Patriarch." In *Gabriel García Márquez*. Ed. Harold Bloom. Modern Critical Views. New York: Chelsea House Publishers, 1989. 147–68.

———. *Gabriel García Márquez*. Boston: Twayne Publishers, 1984.

RELATED WORKS

Barthes, Roland. *Criticism and Truth*. Ed. and trans. Katrine Pilcher Keuneman Minneapolis: University of Minnesota Press, 1987.

Beauvoir, de Simone. *The Second Sex*. Ed. and trans. H. M. Parshley. New York: Vintage Books, 1989.

Brushwood, John S. *The Spanish American Novel: A Twentieth Century Survey*. Austin: University of Texas Press, 1975.

Columbus, Christopher. *Four Voyages to the New World: Letters and Documents*. Trans. and ed. R. H. Major. New York: Corinth, 1961.

Cuddon, J. A. Comp. *A Dictionary of Literary Terms and Literary Theory*. 3rd ed. Cambridge: Basil Blackwell, 1991.

De las Casa, Bartolomé. *The Diary of Christopher Columbus's First Voyage to America, 1492–1493*. Trans. Oliver Dunn and James E. Kelley, Jr. Norman: University of Oklahoma, 1989.

Donoso, José. *The Bloom in Spanish American Literature*. Trans. Gregory Kolovakos. New York: Columbia University Press, 1977.

Eagleton, Terry. *Literary Theory: An Introduction*. 2nd ed. Minneapolis: University of Minnesota Press, 1996.

Echevarría, Roberto González, ed. *Latin American Short Stories*. New York: Oxford University Press, 1997.

Faulkner, William. *Absalom! Absalom!* New York: Random House, 1966.

———. *As I Lay Dying*. New York: Random House, 1964.

———. *Sartoris*. 1929: New York: New American Library, 1953.

Foster, David William. *Studies in the Contemporary Spanish-American Short Story*. Columbia: University of Missouri Press, 1979.

Frakes, James R., and Isadore Traschen, eds. *Short Fiction: A Critical Collection*. 2nd ed. Englewood Cliffs, NJ: Prentice-Hall, 1969.

Fry, Northrop. *Anatomy of Criticism: Four Essays*. Princeton, NJ: Princeton University Press, 1957.

Fuentes, Carlos. *The Buried Mirror: Reflections on Spain and the New World*. Boston: Houghton Mifflin, 1999.

Genette, Gérard. *Narrative Discourse: An Essay in Method*. Trans. Jane E. Lewin. 1980: Ithaca, NY: Cornell University Press, 1995.

Goldmann, Lucien. *Towards a Sociology of the Novel*. Trans. Alan Sheridan. London: Tavistock Publications, 1975.

Gracia, Jorge J. E., and Mireya Camurati, eds. *Philosophy and Literature in Latin America: A Critical Assessment of the Current Situation*. Albany: State University of New York Press, 1989.

Hemingway, Ernest. *The Short Stories of Ernest Hemingway*. New York: Macmillan, 1987.

Henao, Jesús María, and Gerardo Arrubla. *History of Colombia*. Trans. and ed. J. Fred Rippy. Chapel Hill: University of North Carolina Press, 1938.

Henderson, James D. *When Colombia Bled: A History of Violence in Tolima*. University: University of Alabama Press, 1985.

The Holy Bible. Ed. Philip Caraman and John J. Dougherty. 2nd ed. New York: Hawthorn Books, 1966.

Hooks, bell. *Feminist Theory: From Margin to Center*. Boston: South End Press, 1994.

Iser, Wolfgang. *The Act of Reading: A Theory of Aesthetic Response*. 1978; Baltimore: Johns Hopkins University Press, 1987.

Joyce, James. *Ulysses*. New York: Random House, 1967.

Kafka, Franz. *Selected Short Stories*. Trans. Willa and Edwin Muir. New York: Random House, 1952.

Kristeva, Julia. *Desire in Language: A Semiotic Approach to Literature and Art*. Ed. Leon S. Roudiez; Trans. Thomas Gora, Alice Jardine, and Leon S. Roudiez. New York: Columbia University Press, 1980.

"Kristeva, Julia." In *Merriam Webster's Encyclopedia of Literature*. Springfield, MA: Merriam-Webster, 1995. 647.

Kuiper, Kathleen, ed. *Merriam-Webster's Encyclopedia of Literature*. Springfield, MA: Merriam-Webster, 1995.

Kurzweil, Edith. *The Age of Structuralism: Lévi-Strauss to Foucault*. New York: Columbia University Press, 1980.

Lindstrom, Naomi. *Twentieth-Century Spanish American Fiction*. Austin: University of Texas Press, 1994.

Lukács, Georg. *The Theory of the Novel: A Historico-philosophical Essay on the Forms of Great Epic Literature*. Trans. Anna Bostock. 9th ed. Cambridge, MA: MIT Press, 1989.

Millett, Kate. *Sexual Politics*. New York: Garden City, 1970.

Peden, Margaret Sayers, ed. *The Latin American Short Story: A Critical History*. Boston: Twayne Publishers, 1983.

Rabelais, François. *The Histories of Gargantua and Pantagruel*. Trans. J. M. Cohen. Baltimore: Penguin, 1955.

Robbe-Grillet, Alain. *For a New Novel: Essays on Fiction*. Trans. Richard Howard. New York: Grove Press, 1966.

Sarup, Madan. *An Introductory Guide to Post-structuralism and Postmodernism*. 2nd ed. Athens: University of Georgia Press, 1993.

Schwartz, Kessel. "Sexism in the Spanish American Novel, 1965–1975." In *Studies on Twentieth-Century Spanish and Spanish American Literature*. Lanham, MD: University Press of America, 1983. 341–52.

Sefchovich, Sara. *La señora de los sueños*. México: Planeta, 1993.

Sophocles. *Antigone*. Trans. Elizabeth Wyckoff. In *Sophocles I*. Ed. David Grene. Chicago: University of Chicago Press, 1960.

Thrall, William Flint, and Addison Hibbard. *A Handbook to Literature*. Revised and enlarged by C. Hugh Holman. New York: Odyssey Press, 1960.

Wallace, Susan Helen, ed. *Saints for Young Readers for Every Day*. Vol. 2. Boston: Pauline Books & Media, 1995.

White, Hayden. *Tropics of Discourse: Essays in Cultural Criticism*. 3rd ed. Baltimore: Johns Hopkins University Press, 1987.

Williams, Raymond L. *The Colombian Novel, 1847–1987*. Austin: University of Texas Press, 1991.

Wolf, Naomi. Fire with Fire. New York: Random House, 1993.

Woolf, Virginia. *"Jacob's Room" and "The Waves": Two Complete Novels*. New York: Harcourt Brace, 1950.

———. *Mrs. Dalloway*. New York: Harcourt Brace, 1964.

———. *Orlando*. New York: Harcourt Brace, 1973.

Index

Note: Characters from the works of Gabriel García Márquez are listed in alphabetical order by first name.

About the Author

RUBÉN PELAYO COUTIÑO is Associate Professor of Spanish at Southern Connecticut State University, where he teaches courses in Language and Literature. His work has appeared in *Texto Critico, Revista de Literatura Mexicana Contemporanea, Connecticut Review,* and *Monoculo.*

Critical Companions to Popular Contemporary Writers
First Series—*also available on CD-ROM*

V. C. Andrews
  by E. D. Huntley

Tom Clancy
  by Helen S. Garson

Mary Higgins Clark
  by Linda C. Pelzer

Arthur C. Clarke
  by Robin Anne Reid

James Clavell
  by Gina Macdonald

Pat Conroy
  by Landon C. Burns

Robin Cook
  by Lorena Laura Stookey

Michael Crichton
  by Elizabeth A. Trembley

Howard Fast
  by Andrew Macdonald

Ken Follett
  by Richard C. Turner

John Grisham
  by Mary Beth Pringle

James Herriot
  by Michael J. Rossi

Tony Hillerman
  by John M. Reilly

John Jakes
  by Mary Ellen Jones

Stephen King
  by Sharon A. Russell

Dean Koontz
  by Joan G. Kotker

Robert Ludlum
  by Gina Macdonald

Anne McCaffrey
  by Robin Roberts

Colleen McCullough
  by Mary Jean DeMarr

James A. Michener
  by Marilyn S. Severson

Anne Rice
  by Jennifer Smith

Tom Robbins
  *by Catherine E. Hoyser and Lorena Laura
  Stookey*

John Saul
  by Paul Bail

Erich Segal
  by Linda C. Pelzer

Gore Vidal *by*
  Susan Baker and Curtis S. Gibson